French Tutor
Grammar and Vocabulary Workbook

French Tutor

Grammar and Vocabulary Workbook

Mary C. Christensen and Julie Cracco

CONTENTS

SCOPE AND SEQUENCE OF UNITS

UNIT	CEFR	TOPIC	LEARNING OUTCOME
UNIT 1 **Rencontre des familles** pages 1–11	A2	*Family*	• Understand and describe family and events • Use nouns and articles
UNIT 2 **Sous l'océan** pages 12–21	A2	*Leisure and hobbies*	• Use personal pronouns • Talk about hobbies
UNIT 3 **Toi, ton signe** pages 22–31	B1	*Horoscopes*	• Use adjectives to give information about self, family and friends
UNIT 4 **En plein air** pages 32–41	B1	*Nature*	• Use adverbs • Make comparisons • Discuss likes and dislikes related to the outdoors
UNIT 5 **Tout le monde est connecté** pages 42–53	A2	*Technology and communication*	• Ask and answer questions • Discuss technology and modes of communication
UNIT 6 **On y va!** pages 54–63	B1	*Travel*	• Use prepositions • Discuss travel
UNIT 7 **Qu'est-ce qu'on mange?** pages 64–71	B1	*Food*	• Use relative pronouns • Talk about food
UNIT 8 **Métro, boulot, dodo** pages 72–82	B1	*Work*	• Use regular and irregular present tense verbs • Discuss the workplace and work habits

LANGUAGE		SKILLS	
GRAMMAR	**VOCABULARY**	**READING**	**WRITING**
Nouns and articles	Family, relatives, life events	A wedding in Bordeaux; read the description of an upcoming wedding	Write an e-mail to invite a friend to an upcoming important event
Pronouns	Activities, hobbies	Read a description of scuba diving	Write about your favourite pastimes
Adjective formation, agreement, placement, usage	Describing self, family, friends; astrology	Read a description of the 12 signs of the horoscope	Write a blog post about your astrological sign and what you think about astrology
Adverbs	Outdoor activities	Read a website with information about a camp site in Eastern Québec	Write an e-mail to the camp site director to reserve your space and describe the activities that interest you
Asking questions, answering questions	Work, social media, technology	Read an online article about social media and the workplace	Write a comment in response to the article describing your use of social media at work
Prepositions of time, place, function and cause	Travelling, geographical locations	Read an e-mail from a friend about her trip to Morocco	Write a message about the last trip you took
Relative pronouns	Eating and drinking, meals, restaurants	Read a description of the French tradition of a drink before meals	Write to a friend who is coming to dinner and ask about dietary restrictions and preferences
Regular and irregular present tense verbs, negation	Working, studying, applying for jobs	Read the description of Sylvie's work life	Write about your current job

LANGUAGE		SKILLS	
GRAMMAR	**VOCABULARY**	**READING**	**WRITING**
Impersonal verbs, modal verbs, idiomatic expressions	Weather	Read a weather report	Write a blog post about the weather in the town where you live and describe your favourite season
Future tense	Shopping, buying things in stores and online	Read the newspaper article describing how shopping will be different in the future	Write a message to the editor of the newspaper reacting to the article and describing your own attitudes and habits when shopping
Imperatives	Household tasks	Read the user manual for an electrical appliance	What household task are you good at doing? Write an email to a friend explaining how to do it properly
Infinitives	Talking about feelings and opinions	Read an article about what it takes to be happy	Write a diary entry about your degree of happiness with your life
Imperfect	Childhood, describing how things used to be	Read the story of Jérôme's childhood	Write a message to a friend describing your childhood
Passé composé	House and home, renting a property, moving	Read Marie-Ange's story about moving to northern France	Write a blog post telling the story about a place where you have lived, how you found it and why you lived there
Conditional	The environment and personal habits	Read a blog post from an environmentally friendly website	Write a comment in response to the blog post regarding your attitudes and actions regarding the environment

LANGUAGE		SKILLS	
GRAMMAR	**VOCABULARY**	**READING**	**WRITING**
Pronominal verbs (reflexive, reciprocal and idiomatic)	Daily routine, common activities, relationships with others	Read Martin's description of his life now and how it used to be	Write a note to a friend describing your daily routine and how it differs from when you were younger
Present subjunctive	Health and wellness	Read the interview of a doctor who works at a seaside spa	Write to the doctor about what you must do to improve your health, ask her advice
Passive voice and indirect speech	Transport, urban planning, driving, commuting	Read the article about road rage and what to do to avoid it	Respond to the article by stating what your friends and family think of the issue and whether or not you agree with them
Pluperfect, past conditional, future perfect	Journalism, media, radio, TV, cinema	Read an article about publicly funded media in France	Write a blog post about your use of media and how media affects events in your country
Passé simple, past anterior	Architecture and cities	Read about urban planning in Paris beginning in the 17th century	Write a blog post giving a brief history of the town where you live

For me, learning languages was a natural extension of my early passions for grammar and reading, which I explored with the support and encouragement of my parents. They facilitated the three extended experiences I've had in a French-speaking environment: a summer French immersion programme studying and living with a family in Québec, a year in a French lycée studying alongside French high school students, and serving as an English teaching assistant in a Paris high school after finishing my undergraduate degree in French. These and other trips abroad for work and pleasure sparked my desire to share my love of the French language and francophone literature and culture. After receiving my doctorate in French at the University of Michigan, I earned tenure at the State University of New York at New Paltz where I teach all levels of French language, literature and culture, from beginners to graduate students. I encourage everyone to use language as a tool, to learn how it works, how to read, write, understand and speak in context-driven, communicative situations where making oneself understood and understanding others is the primary goal of learning and using a language. I continue to be fascinated by how language works and how we need to constantly strive for mutual understanding and work to bridge cross-cultural divides.

Mary C. Christensen

Bonjour à tous!

I have been teaching high school French in New York State for the past twelve years. Since the day I started teaching I have continued to educate myself in various and fun ways. I obtained my Masters Degree in Instructional Technology from New York Institute of Technology. I taught introductory French at the university level, I also worked on several projects as a copy editor and development editor for various language books. Such experiences have only broadened my exposure and appreciation of language teaching and learning.

In addition, in the meantime, I have continued to travel, often, to discover new people, languages and cultures, as well as return home to France. When busy teaching, I still take the time to often sit in on my colleagues' classes to continue being exposed to other languages and teaching methods.

Having left France as an adolescent, and moving to the United States, after a three-year stop in England, not knowing a word of English, I can only appreciate the work and dedication of people like you; people striving to continue their language studies. I know first hand that this is not an easy process but the rewards are worth all the struggles. As the flower said in *The Little Prince* 'il faut bien que je supporte deux ou trois chenilles si je veux connaître les papillons.' (*I have to endure two or three caterpillars if I want to see the butterflies.*) So, no doubt you will face some hurdles along the way, or chenilles, but the pay-off will be worth every effort and we hope that this book will help you on your journey.

Alors, bon voyage et bon courage!!

Julie Cracco

If you have studied French before, but would like to brush up on or improve your grammar, vocabulary, reading and writing skills, this is the book for you. The *French Tutor* is a grammar workbook that contains a comprehensive grammar syllabus from advanced beginner to upper intermediate level and combines grammar and vocabulary presentations with over 200 practice exercises.

The language you will learn is presented through concise explanations, engaging exercises, simple infographics, and personal tutor tips. The infographics present complex grammar points in an accessible format while the personal tutor tips offer advice on correct usage, colloquial alternatives, exceptions to rules, etc. Each unit contains reading comprehension activities incorporating the grammar and vocabulary taught as well as a freer writing practice and real-life tasks. The focus is on building up your skills while reinforcing the target language. The reading stimuli include emails, blogs, social media posts and business letters using real language so you can be sure you're learning vocabulary and grammar that will be useful for you.

You can work through the workbook by itself or you can use it alongside our *Complete French* course or any other language course. This workbook has been written to reflect and expand upon the content of *Complete French* and is a good place to go if you would like to practise your reading and writing skills on similar topics.

Icons

 Discovery

 Vocabulary

 Writing

 Reading

 Personal tutor

THE DISCOVERY METHOD

There are lots of philosophies and approaches to language learning, some practical, some quite unconventional, and far too many to list here. Perhaps you know of a few, or even have some techniques of your own. In this book we have incorporated the Discovery Method of learning, a sort of awareness-raising approach to language learning. What this means is that you will be encouraged throughout to engage your mind and figure out the language for yourself, through identifying patterns, understanding grammar concepts, noticing words that are similar to English, and more. This method promotes language awareness, a critical skill in acquiring a new language. As a result of your own efforts, you will be able to better retain what you have learned, use it with confidence, and, even better, apply those same skills to continuing to learn the language (or, indeed, another one) on your own after you've finished this course.

Everyone can succeed in learning a language – the key is to know how to learn it. Learning is more than just reading or memorizing grammar and vocabulary. It's about being an active learner, learning in real contexts, and, most importantly, using what you've learned in different situations. Simply put, if you figure something out for yourself, you're more likely to understand it. And when you use what you've learned, you're more likely to remember it.

As many of the essential but (let's admit it!) challenging details, such as grammar rules, are introduced through the Discovery Method, you'll have more fun while learning. Soon, the language will start to make sense and you'll be relying on your own intuition to construct original sentences independently, not just reading and copying.

Enjoy yourself!

1 **Make a habit out of learning**
   ▶ Study a little every day, between 20 and 30 minutes is ideal.
   ▶ Give yourself **short-term goals**, e.g. work out how long you'll spend on a particular unit and work within this time limit, and create a study habit.
   ▶ Try to create **an environment conducive to learning** which is calm and quiet and free from distractions. As you study, do not worry about your mistakes or the things you can't remember or understand. Languages settle gradually in the brain. Just give yourself enough time and you will succeed.

2 **Maximize your exposure to the language**
   ▶ As well as using this book, you can listen to radio, watch television or read online articles and blogs.
   ▶ Do you have a personal passion or hobby? Does a news story interest you? Try to access French information about them. It's entertaining and you'll become used to a range of writing styles.

3 **Vocabulary**
   ▶ The *French Tutor* introduces a lot of new and very helpful vocabulary. Look up what you do not yet know. The vocabulary list at the end only covers vocabulary items or idioms that might be harder to find. Looking up words – either in an online or paper-based dictionary – is part of the learning!
   ▶ Group new words under **generic categories**, e.g. *food, furniture*, **situations** in which they occur, e.g. under restaurant you can write *waiter, table, menu, bill*, and **functions**, e.g. *greetings, parting, thanks, apologizing*.
   ▶ Write the words over and over again. Keep lists on your smartphone or tablet, but remember to switch the keyboard language so you can include all accents and special characters.
   ▶ Cover up the English side of the vocabulary list and see if you remember the meaning of the word. Do the same for the French.
   ▶ Create flash cards, drawings and mind maps.
   ▶ Write French words on sticky notes and stick them to objects around your house.
   ▶ **Experiment with words**. Look for patterns in words or word families.
   ▶ Try using a French **thesaurus-style dictionary** every now and then as it will help you broaden your vocabulary and improve your style.

4 **Grammar**
   ▶ **Experiment with grammar rules**. Sit back and reflect on how the rules of French compare with your own language or other languages you may already speak.
   ▶ Use known vocabulary to practise new grammar structures.
   ▶ When you learn a new verb form, write the conjugation of several different verbs you know that follow the same form.

5 **Reading**

The passages in this course include questions to help guide you in your understanding. But you can do more:

▶ **Imagine the situation**. Think about what is happening in the extract/passage and make educated guesses, e.g. a postcard is likely to be about things someone has been doing on holiday.

▶ **Guess the meaning of key words before you look them up**. When there are key words you don't understand, try to guess what they mean from the context. If you're reading a French text and cannot get the gist of a whole passage because of one word or phrase, try to look at the words around that word and see if you can work out the meaning from context.

6 **Writing**

▶ Practice makes perfect. The most successful language learners know how to overcome their inhibitions and keep going.

▶ When you write an email to a friend or colleague, or you post something on social media, pretend that you have to do it in French.

▶ When completing writing exercises see how many different ways you can write it, imagine yourself in different situations and try answering as if you were someone else.

▶ Try writing longer passages such as articles, reviews or essays in French, it will help you to formulate arguments and convey your opinion as well as helping you to think about how the language works.

▶ Try writing a diary in French every day, this will give context to your learning and help you progress in areas which are relevant to you.

7 **Visual learning**

▶ Have a look at the infographics in this book. Do they help you to visualize a useful grammar point? You can keep a copy of those you find particularly useful to hand to help you in your studies, or put it on your wall until you remember it. You can also look up infographics on the Internet for topics you are finding particularly tricky to grasp, or even create your own.

8 **Learn from your errors**

▶ Making errors is part of any learning process, so don't be so worried about making mistakes that you won't write anything unless you are sure it is correct. This leads to a vicious circle: the less you write, the less practice you get and the more mistakes you make.

▶ Note the seriousness of errors. Many errors are not serious as you will still get the meaning across.

9 **Learn to cope with uncertainty**

▶ Don't over-use your dictionary.
Resist the temptation to look up every word you don't know. Read the same passage several times, concentrating on trying to get the gist of it. If after the third time some words still prevent you from making sense of the passage, look them up in the dictionary.

1 Rencontre des familles

Meeting of families

In this unit, you will learn how to:

- Use correct noun forms with proper gender and number.
- Use definite, indefinite and partitive articles with nouns.

CEFR: Can understand short, simple texts about families (A2); Can write a short simple text describing family (A2).

Meaning and usage

Nouns and their forms

1 Nouns are words that name things (**ville**, *city*), people (**frère**, *brother*), animals (**giraffe**, *giraffe*), places (**marché**, *market*) and abstractions (**bonheur**, *happiness*).

2 In French, nouns can be masculine or feminine. This is called their gender. They can also be singular, naming just one thing, or plural, referring to more than one thing. The words that go with nouns, such as articles and adjectives, also need to show gender and number to agree with the noun they modify. Definite articles, **le, la, l', les** *(the)* will be used in the sections on gender and number that follow.

Gender

A Look at the sentences and underline the definite article le (masculine) or la (feminine). What is the gender of the noun that follows it? What do you notice about the spelling of these nouns?

    1 C'est la femme de Jacques.

    2 Il a le tableau.

    3 La famille de Claire est très grande.

    4 Est-ce que le chien est méchant?

1 In order to guess the gender of a noun that is unfamiliar to you, you can look at the ending.

2 Most nouns that end in a consonant are masculine.

    le chat *(the cat)*   **le chien** *(the dog)*

    Nouns with these endings are masculine:

    -age, -ment, -é, -eau, -eu, -isme, -ème, -ège

3 Most nouns that end in -**e** are feminine.

la famille *(the family)* **la femme** *(the woman)*

Most nouns with these endings are feminine:

-**tion**, -**sion**, -**son**

4 Nouns that are derived from verbs and end in -**eur** are masculine:

le coiffeur *(the hairdresser)*, **le vendeur** *(the salesman)*

Nouns that are derived from adjectives and end in -**eur** are feminine:

la largeur *(the width)*, **la douceur** *(softness)*

 *Not all nouns that end in -**e** are feminine. For example, **un arbre généalogique** (a family tree) and **un oncle** (an uncle) are masculine. While there is no foolproof way to know the gender of a noun besides memorizing it, the rules provided here can help determine the gender of a noun with 80% accuracy.*

B Identify the gender of each noun by giving the definite article le (masculine) or la (feminine).

1	_____ fils	7	_____ père
2	_____ fille	8	_____ parent
3	_____ mariage	9	_____ mère
4	_____ famille	10	_____ paternité
5	_____ tante	11	_____ bébé
6	_____ nom de famille	12	_____ chat

5 Some nouns change meaning depending on which gender is used.

Masculine		Feminine	
le critique	*the critic*	la critique	*the criticism/review*
le livre	*the book*	la livre	*the pound*
le manche	*the handle*	la manche*	*the sleeve*
le poste	*the set [TV/radio], the job*	la poste	*the post office*
le somme	*the nap*	la somme	*the sum*
le tour	*the tour, walk around*	la tour	*the tower*
le voile	*the veil/headscarf/hijab*	la voile	*the sail*

*You may also see the proper noun **la Manche** which refers to *the English Channel*.

Some professions have both a feminine and masculine form, which is not necessarily the case in English.

serveur, serveuse *(waiter, waitress),* **boulanger, boulangère** *(baker)*

Some professions have been traditionally masculine and there is resistance to feminizing them.

un médecin *(doctor, masculine only),* **un écrivain** *(a writer, masculine only)*

To refer to women in these professions, the term **femme** *can be added, but it is not necessary.*

une femme médecin *(a female doctor),* **une femme écrivain** *(a female writer)*

Number

1   To form the plural of most nouns in French, as in English, an **-s** can be added to the noun, though it is not usually pronounced.

	Singular	Plural
Masculine	le cousin (*the cousin*)	les cousins (*the cousins*)
Feminine	la cousine (*the cousin*)	les cousines (*the cousins*)

When talking about a group of people that includes both males and females, use the masculine form.

J'ai vu les cousins de Caroline: Amandine, Monique, André et Paul. *(I saw Caroline's cousins: Amandine, Monique, André and Paul.)*

C   **Read the text and identify the plural nouns that have the definite article les. Then give their singular form using the definite article. The first one is done for you.**

La France championne les familles nombreuses

Depuis 1921, avec la création de la carte famille nombreuse, les bénéfices d'avoir trois enfants ou plus en France sont considérables. Avec des réductions de prix pour les transports, pour la cantine ou encore pour les musées, l'état vient en aide. Bien qu'il y ait actuellement de moins en moins de familles nombreuses, les traditions régionales et le niveau d'éducation des parents continuent de jouer un rôle important dans les habitudes des français. Effectivement, les habitants du Nord de la France ont souvent un taux de natalité plus important que dans le Sud. Les diplômés ont moins de chance d'avoir une famille nombreuse en comparaison avec les non-diplômés. Les immigrés vivent plus souvent avec plus de trois enfants, mais les descendants de ceux-ci, nés donc en France, ont tendance à se comporter comme le reste de la population. Par ailleurs, la politique française permet aux familles de concilier vie professionnelle et vie familiale et offre les congés maternité et paternité ainsi que les allocations familiales croissantes selon le nombre d'enfants.

Plural	Singular
les bénéfices	le bénéfice

2 The following tables show how to make nouns plural based on their endings. Take note of some of the exceptions.

Nouns ending in -ail will take an -s to form the plural.		
Singular	Plural	Exceptions take an -aux
le chandail (*the sweater*)	les chandails (*the sweaters*)	le travail – les travaux
le portail (*the portal*)	les portails (*the portals*)	(*the work – the works*)
		corail, vitrail

Nouns ending in -ou will take an -s to form the plural.		
Singular	Plural	Exceptions take an -x
le clou (*the nail*)	les clous (*the nails*)	le bijou – les bijoux
le trou (*the hole*)	les trous (*the holes*)	(*the jewel – the jewellery/jewels*)
		caillou, chou, genou, hibou, joujou, pou

Nouns ending in -al will change to an -aux ending in the plural.		
Singular	Plural	Exceptions take an -s
le journal (*the newspaper*)	les journaux (*the newspapers*)	festival – les festivals
l'animal (*the animal*)	les animaux (*the animals*)	(*the festival – the festivals*)
		bal, carnaval, chacal, récital, régal

Nouns ending in -au, -eau, -eu or -oeu will take an -x to form the plural.		
Singular	Plural	Exceptions take an -s
le bateau (*the boat*)	les bateaux (*the boats*)	le pneu – les pneus
le jeu (*the game*)	les jeux (*the games*)	(*the tyre – the tyres*)
le noyau (*the pit*)	le noyau (*the pits*)	landau, bleu
le voeu (*the wish*)	les voeux (*the wishes*)	

Nouns ending in -s, -x or -z do not change in the plural.		
Singular	Plural	No exceptions
le bras (*the arm*)	les bras (*the arms*)	
le nez (*the nose*)	les nez (*the noses*)	
le prix (*the price*)	les prix (*the prices*)	

D Form the plural of these nouns.

1 la tante _____
2 la fille _____
3 le mari _____
4 le foyer _____

5 le cheval _____
6 la sœur _____
7 l'enfant _____
8 le détail _____

9 le pneu _____
10 la famille _____
11 le bijou _____
12 le couple _____

Articles

1 Articles, also called determiners, are placed before the noun in French and reflect the number and gender of the noun.

E Read the email from your friend Julia and indicate the gender and number of the underlined articles.

De:	Julia
Date:	le 18 juin
Sujet:	Les quatre-vingts printemps de l'arrière-grand-mère

Bonjour! Il faut que je te raconte mon week-end. Pour l'anniversaire de mon arrière-grand-mère, Anne, toute **(1)** _la_ famille s'est réunie. Nous avions loué **(2)** _une_ salle dans **(3)** _le_ village qui l'avait vue naître. Ce jour-là, j'ai fait connaissance d' **(4)** _un_ homme que je n'avais jamais rencontré avant; c'était un de mes oncles. Pendant **(5)** _la_ fête, nous avons parlé, de plus, nous avons bu du vin et nous avons mangé **(6)** _des_ plats régionaux qui m'ont rappelé mon enfance. J'ai pris **(7)** _du_ coq au vin et ensuite **(8)** _de la_ tarte aux pommes comme dessert. Que c'était bon! Nous avons beaucoup dansé, nous nous sommes vraiment bien amusés. Quelle journée incroyable!

Comment vas-tu? Bien, j'espère.

Bises,

Julia

1 _____
2 _____
3 _____
4 _____

5 _____
6 _____
7 _____
8 _____

Since 1993, France has allowed parents to freely decide the name of their child, though the state may intervene if the name they choose is not in the best interest of the child. For instance, the courts decided in 2015 that a couple could not name their daughter Nutella, the trademarked name for a chocolate and hazelnut spread and instead decreed that her name would be Ella. Before the 1993 law, acceptable first names were dictated by the French government and these choices relied heavily on the Catholic tradition of biblical names and names of saints.

2 There are three basic types of articles.

	Definite articles	Indefinite articles	Partitive articles
Masculine (sing.)	le	un	du
Feminine (sing.)	la	une	de la
Before a vowel (singular)	l'		de l'
Plural	les	des	des

Definite articles

1 Definite articles, **le, la, l', les** *(the)*, are used when talking about something or someone specific or previously mentioned. In E, the narrator is talking about her family, *the* specific village where the great grandmother was born and *the* party for her birthday. This is why definite articles are used.

L'homme en bleu que vous voyez là-bas. *(The man in blue that you see over there.)*

Le jour de l'arrivée de son enfant. *(The day her child arrived.)*

2 Definite articles can also be used when expressing likes and dislikes.

J'aime le café. *(I like coffee.)*

In this example, the speaker is talking about coffee in general rather than talking about some specific coffee.

3 **Le** is also used before a date whereas in English we use the preposition *on*.

Son anniversaire, c'est _le_ 22 juin. *(His birthday is <u>on</u> 22nd June.)*

4 Definite articles are used in French when speaking of general concepts whereas this is not the case in English.

L'argent ne rend pas les gens heureux. *(Money doesn't make people happy.)*

L'amour est aveugle. *(Love is blind.)*

F   Complete the sentences with the appropriate definite article.

1   Tu ne connais pas _____ femme de Serge?

2   Ce n'est pas _____ mari de Sophie.

3   Les enfants regardent toujours _____ télévision.

4   la famille adore _____ chocolat.

5   Vous aimez _____ enfants?

6   J'ai _____ sœur de Sophie au téléphone.

Indefinite articles

1   Indefinite articles, **un**, **une**, *(a, an)*, **des** *(some* or *a few)* are used with unspecified nouns that can be counted.

   Tu as un ami. *(You have a friend.)*

   Elles veulent une fille. *(They want a girl.)*

   Nous avons des frères et des sœurs. *(We have brothers and sisters.)*

2   **Un/une** can be used to indicate that there is just *one* of something.

   Elle a seulement un frère. *(She has only one brother.)*

   Tu veux une glace? *(Do you want an ice cream?)*

Unlike in English, you don't use the indefinite article to designate what someone's profession is in French. In French, you leave the article out.

Son frère est professeur. *(Her brother is a teacher.)*

Elle est médecin. *(She is a doctor.)*

G   Complete the sentences with *un, une* or *des*.

1   Ma mère et moi, nous regardons _____ film.

2   Vous avez _____ oncles?

3   Tu sors avec _____ garçon?

4   La copine de Pierre a _____ appartement assez petit.

5   Son cousin a _____ chat.

6   Elle a _____ cousins en Australie.

Partitive articles

Partitive articles are used to talk about quantities that cannot be counted. **Du** (masc. sing.), **de la** (fem. sing.), **de l'** (before a vowel, sing.) can be translated as *some* in English. They designate a part of something or an unknown quantity of something: **du café** (*some coffee*), **de la pizza** (*some pizza*).

De (*or* **d'** *before a vowel) is used instead of an article with expressions of quantity:* **beaucoup** (*a lot*), **trop** (*too much*), *etc., even if followed by a plural noun.*

J'ai mangé trop de glace. (*I ate too much ice cream.*)

Ils ont beaucoup d'enfants. (*They have a lot of children.*)

Other expressions, or adverbs, of quantity include:

plus (*more*), **moins** (*less*), **autant** (*as many/much*), **tant** (*so many/much*), **un tas** (*a lot of/a pile*), **assez** (*enough*), **la majorité** (*the majority*), **la minorité** (*the minority*), **pas mal** (*quite a few*).

H Complete the sentences with the appropriate partitive article or **de**.

1 Ma grand-mère a _____ patience. Elle ne rouspète jamais.

2 Ma famille a beaucoup _____ chats.

3 Mon oncle voudrait bien reprendre _____ jambon.

4 Sa cousine boit _____ eau car c'est bon pour la santé.

5 Le mari de Sandrine boit _____ café toute la journée.

6 Elle a _____ enfants formidables!

I Articles can change the meaning of a sentence. Match the sentence with the correct article and explanation.

		Article used	Reason
1	Le petit garçon mange <u>du</u> gâteau.	**a** indefinite	**i** This is a specific cake. For example, one that was bought that morning.
2	Le petit garçon mange <u>un</u> gâteau.	**b** partitive	**ii** The little boy is eating an entire cake.
3	Le petit garçon mange <u>le</u> gâteau.	**c** definite	**iii** The little boy is eating part (some) of a cake.

J Complete the paragraph with the appropriate definite, indefinite or partitive articles.

(1) _____ tante de Pierre est (2) _____ vieille dame plutôt traditionnelle.
(3) _____ dimanche, elle invite toute (4) _____ famille à prendre
(5) _____ grand repas chez elle. Il y a toujours (6) _____ entrée,
(7) _____ plat principal, (8) _____ fromage, (9) _____ salade et
(10) _____ gâteau ou (11) _____ tarte comme dessert. Après
(12) _____ dessert, il y a (13) _____ café et parfois (14) _____ cognac.
Pierre ne manque pas d'y aller parce que (15) _____ repas est toujours très bon et il
peut passer du temps avec (16) _____ autres membres de sa famille.

Vocabulary

K Match the French with the English.

1	se trouver	a	the arrival
2	un invité	b	well known
3	l'arrivée	c	to get together
4	se réunir	d	to rent
5	louer	e	several
6	de nos jours	f	the in-laws
7	rencontrer	g	to meet, to meet up
8	la veille	h	to be expensive/to not be cheap
9	rappeler	i	the night before/the eve
10	déguster	j	to be located
11	plusieurs	k	to remind, to recall
12	la belle-famille	l	a guest
13	ne pas être donné	m	nowadays
14	bien connu	n	to savour, to taste

Reading

L Read the first part of an e-mail from your friend Katherine describing a family gathering and answer the questions.

1 Pourquoi les familles se réunissent-elles? _____

2 Quand et où les familles vont-elles se voir? _____

De:	Katherine
Date:	Le 11 avril
Sujet:	Le mariage de Claire et Marc

Bonjour!

Claire et Marc, mes deux amis français qui vivent à New York, se marient au mois de mai. Les deux familles vont se réunir à Bordeaux, dans le sud de la France pour plusieurs jours. Il y a des invités qui vont venir de loin; certains de New York et d'autres du Sénégal. C'est pour cette raison que les futurs mariés ont décidé de s'occuper de réserver des chambres d'hôtel; parce que de nos jours, les billets d'avion ne sont pas donnés.

M Now read the rest of the email and answer the questions.

> Les festivités vont commencer la veille, une fois que tout le monde sera arrivé. Pour la cérémonie, ils vont aller à la mairie, mais ils ont décidé de ne pas aller à l'église comme c'est le cas de beaucoup de jeunes couples français. Le soir, tout le monde mangera dans un restaurant bien connu. Le jeune couple a commandé beaucoup de très bonnes bouteilles de vin. Après tout, comment peut-on se marier à Bordeaux sans déguster du bon vin français? Pour la lune de miel, Marc et Claire vont aller en Islande en rentrant à New York.
>
> Je suis invitée et on m'a prise une chambre double. Tu veux venir avec moi?
>
> Bises,
>
> Katherine

1 Les invités, viennent-ils tous de la France? _____

2 Pourquoi Marc et Claire ont-ils décidé de payer les chambres d'hôtel des invités?

   _____

3 Quand est-ce que tout le monde va arriver? _____

4 Est-ce qu'ils vont se marier à l'église? _____

Writing

N What is your family like? Is it large or small? Describe your family and give as many details as possible. (80–100 words)

_____

_____

_____

_____

_____

_____

_____

Self-check

Tick the box that matches your level of confidence.

    1 = very confident   2 = need more practice   3 = not confident

Cochez la case qui correspond à votre niveau d'aisance.

    1 = très sûr(e) de vous   2 = j'ai besoin de plus de pratique   3 = pas sûr(e) du tout

	1	2	3
Can use correct noun forms in terms of gender and number.			
Can use definite, indefinite and partitive articles with nouns.			
Can understand short, simple texts about families (CEFR A2).			
Can write a short, simple text describing family (CEFR A2).			

2 Sous l'océan

Under the sea

In this unit, you will learn how to:

✔ Understand vocabulary related to hobbies and leisure activities.

✔ Use personal pronouns (subject, direct and indirect object, tonic, y and en)

CEFR: Can understand short narratives about leisure activities (A2); Can write about aspects of everyday life such as leisure activities and hobbies (A2).

Meaning and usage

Personal pronouns

Pronouns are words that replace people, places, things and even whole phrases. They are used to avoid repetition. As with French nouns, they have gender and number.

Les filles adorent voyager. _Elles_ veulent découvrir le monde. *(The girls love to travel. _They_ want to discover the world.)*

Arnaud et sa meilleure amie sont très proches. Il _la_ voit toutes les semaines. *(Arnaud and his best friend are very close. He sees _her_ every week.)*

Tu écris à ta mère souvent? _Elle te_ répond? *(Do you write to your mother often? Does _she_ answer _you_?)*

Subject pronouns

1   When the noun you are replacing is the subject of a sentence, whether it is a person or a thing, use subject pronouns.

 A   **Read the text and identify the pronouns. Which nouns do they replace?**

Anne-Sophie et ses amies aiment sortir ensemble pour manger ou prendre un pot. Elles vont toujours au même café. Elles retrouvent leur serveur préféré, Gaston. Il est bavard et aimable. Elles commandent à boire et Gaston les sert avec un sourire.

2   Subject pronouns agree in gender and number with the nouns they replace:

Singular	Plural
je *I*	nous *we*
tu *you*	vous *you*
il/elle/on *he/she/one*	ils/elles *they*

Je *drops the* -e *and takes an apostrophe when followed by a vowel or an unaspirated (silent)* h.

J'aime faire du vélo. *(I like cycling.)* **J'habite en ville.** *(I live in town.)*

Unlike I *in English,* **je** *is only capitalized at the beginning of a sentence.*

3   **On** is used with the same verb form as **il** and **elle**. It can be translated as *one, people, you, we* or *they* depending on context.

B   How do these two sentences show the different ways on can be translated?

1   Si on parle le français, on peut communiquer avec d'autres Francophones.

2   Qu'est-ce qu'on fait ce soir?

4   When a pronoun refers to a group of both men and women, use the masculine pronoun.
Philippe et Marie font de la randonnée. *(Philippe and Marie go hiking.)*
Ils vont souvent à la montagne. *(They often go to the mountain.)*

C   Select the subject pronouns you would use to replace these nouns.

1   les clients (m.)   **a** elle
2   une robe   **b** ils
3   les commerçantes   **c** elles
4   Patrick et Francine   **d** il
5   le magasin

Remember that **tu** *is used informally for close friends, children and animals. It is often shortened to* **t'** *in spoken informal French:* **T'es là?** *(Are you there?)* **Vous** *is the plural you, and it is also typically used as a singular pronoun when addressing someone you want to show respect to, someone you don't know or someone you don't know well.*

Direct object pronouns

1   A direct object is the person, people, thing or things receiving the action of the verb. Just as with subject pronouns, direct object pronouns are used to replace a direct object already mentioned, to avoid repetition and redundancy. Usually a direct object can be found by asking *who?/what?* after the verb. Note that not all verbs can take a direct object.

2   Direct object pronouns also align in gender and number with the word they replace:

Direct object pronouns	
me *me*	nous *us*
te *you*	vous *you (plural/formal)*
le *him/it (m.)*, la *her/it (f.)*	les *them (m. and f.)*

Me, te, le *and* **la** *drop the* -e *and become* **m', t'** *and* **l'** *when followed by a vowel or unaspirated* **h.**

3 Direct object pronouns are usually placed in front of the verb. In the negative, they come after **ne**. In the past, they are placed in front of the auxiliary verb and the past participle must agree in gender and number with the pronoun. With infinitives, they go in front of the infinitive.

Nous le faisons. *(We are doing it.)*   **Nous ne le faisons pas.** *(We are not doing it.)*

Nous l'avons fait. *(We did it [the housework].)*   **Nous l'avons faite.** *(We did it [the laundry].)*

Nous allons le faire. *(We are going to do it.)*

D Look at the translation. Then add the appropriate *direct object pronoun* to the sentence.

1 Mon père _____ appelle tous les soirs. *(My father calls me every night.)*

2 Je _____ emmènerai à la soirée de Monique. *(I will take you to Monique's party.)*

3 Elle _____ apprend à faire du jardinage. *(She teaches us to do the gardening.)*

4 Nous _____ verrons au cinéma. *(We will see you all at the cinema.)*

5 Nous _____ regarderons ce week-end. *(We will watch it this weekend.)*

6 J'admire les athlètes. Je _____ admire. *(I admire the athletes. I admire them.)*

E Rewrite the sentences replacing the underlined elements with a direct object pronoun.

1 Nous regardons *les matchs à la télé*.

_____

2 Micheline adore *faire du ski*.

_____

3 Ils ont fait *les courses*.

_____

4 Elle aime faire *la cuisine*.

_____

5 Vous avez fait *le tour du monde*?

_____

6 J'adore *cette nouvelle de Jules Renard*.

_____

Le and **l'** *can replace more than a noun – they can also replace an adjective, a verb or an idea.*

– **Crois-tu qu'il fera le marathon?** *(Do you think he will do the marathon?)*

– **Oui, je le crois, il adore courir.** *(Yes, I believe so, he loves to run.)*

Je suis française et il l'est aussi. *(I am French and he is [it – as in French] too.)*

Indirect object pronouns

1 An indirect object is always a living thing and it receives the action of the verb indirectly. In French, the indirect object is always preceded by the preposition **à**; in English it is the same, *to*.

La fille donne un cadeau à son père. *(The girl gives a gift to her father.)*

2 An indirect object pronoun replaces **à** and the person or other living thing that follows it. As with direct object pronouns in the negative, **ne** comes before the indirect object pronoun.

La fille lui donne un cadeau. *(The girl gives him a gift.)*

La fille ne lui donne pas un cadeau. *(The girl doesn't give him a gift.)*

3 Indirect object pronouns also change according to number, but gender is not differentiated:

Indirect object pronouns	
me *to/for me*	nous *to/for us*
te *to/for you*	vous *to/for you (plural/formal)*
lui *to/for him/her*	leur *to/for them (m./f.)*

4 Indirect object pronouns follow the same placement rules as direct object pronouns, except they don't agree in the past tense.

Je lui téléphone. *(I'm calling her.)*   **Je lui ai téléphoné hier.** *(I called her yesterday.)*

F What pronoun would you use in the following situations?

1 to talk to two of your friends   **a** lui

2 to give a box of chocolate to someone   **b** vous

3 to tell someone you talked to your friends   **c** leur

4 to tell a friend you will speak to him   **d** te

G Fill in the gaps with the correct indirect object pronoun.

1 Je lis le conte de fée aux enfants. Je _____ lis le conte.

2 Il offre des fleurs à sa petite amie. Il _____ offre des fleurs.

3 Nous envoyons un colis à vous. Nous _____ envoyons un colis.

4 Ils vont acheter des tickets à moi. Ils vont _____ acheter des tickets.

5 Je passe un coup de fil à toi ce soir. Je _____ passe un coup de fil ce soir.

6 Vous demandez à votre mère de vous aider. Vous _____ demandez de vous aider.

H Review the previous sections and complete the table.

Subject pronouns	Direct object pronouns	Indirect object pronouns
je/j' (1) _____	me/m' (5) _____	me/m' *to me*
tu *you*	te/t' *you*	te/t' *to you*
il *he* elle *she* on (2) _____	(6) _____ *him/it* (m.) la (7) _____	(10) _____ *to him/to her*
nous *we*	nous (8) _____	nous *to us*
vous (3) _____ (plural/formal)	vous *you* (plural/formal)	vous (11) _____ (plural/formal)
ils/elles (4) _____ *they*	les (9) _____	leur *to them*

*It's useful to remember that the subject pronoun does the action; the direct object receives the action. The indirect object is to whom the action is done. In French, indirect objects are introduced by the preposition **à**.*

Tonic pronouns

1   Tonic pronouns, also known as disjunctive or stressed pronouns, refer only to people. They are used in short answers, for emphasis and with some specific expressions.

2   Tonic pronouns also align in gender and number with the person they are replacing:

Tonic pronouns	
moi *me*	nous *us*
toi *you*	vous *you*
lui *him*	eux *they/them (m.)*
elle *her*	elles *they/them (f.)*
soi *one*	

3   Tonic pronouns are used mainly:
- after other than **à**
  Tu veux venir chez moi?   *(Do you want to come to my house?)*
- when you have a double subject
  Pierre et moi allons faire du ski.   *(Paul and I are going to go skiing.)*
- alone in an answer to a question or for emphasis
  Moi? Je ne sais pas.   *(Me? I don't know.)*
- with **même**
  moi-même *(myself)*, **elle-même** *(herself)*
- after **c'est** and **ce sont**
  C'est moi qui l'ai fait!   *(I made it!)*
- sometimes after the preposition **à** such as when indicating possession or with verbs like **penser (à)**, *(to think (about))*.
  Cette planche de surf est à moi.   *(This surfboard is mine.)*
  Tu penses à elle tout le temps.   *(You think about her all the time.)*

I   **Translate the following sentences. Look up any words you don't know.**

   1   I am buying ice skates for you. _____
   2   This helmet is mine. _____
   3   Her? I think she did it. _____
   4   He is going himself. _____
   5   Watch out! There's a car in front of you! _____
   6   We are watching a movie at her place tonight. _____

The pronoun Y

1   The pronoun **y** can have different meanings based on context. It can be used to replace phrases introduced by a preposition other than **de**.
   La grand-mère répond *à la carte postale de ses petits enfants*.
   (The grandmother replies <u>to her grandchildren's postcard</u>.)
   La grand-mère *y* répond. *(She replies <u>to it</u>.)*

2   Note the difference in the following examples:

Ils donneront une présentation _au travail_. (They will give a presentation _at work_.)

Ils _y_ **donneront une présentation.** (They will give a presentation _there_.)

Elle a rendu sa chemise _à Jean-Marc_. (She gave _Jean-Marc_ his shirt back.)

Elle _lui_ **a rendu sa chemise.** (She gave his shirt back _to him_.)

 When **à** is followed by a person, do not use **y** – remember to use an indirect object pronoun.

3   When **y** replaces a preposition and a location, it is translated as _there_. Notice how **y** goes after the subject and before the conjugated verb, but goes before an infinitive. Like other pronouns, it goes after **ne**, shortened to **n'**.

Tu voyages _en Europe_? (Do you travel _to Europe_?)

Oui, j'_y_ **vais tous les ans.** (Yes, I go _there_ every year.)

Je vais _y_ **aller cette année aussi et toi?** (I am going to go _there_ this year too, and you?)

Moi non, je n'_y_ **vais pas.** (Me? No. I'm not going (_there_).)

J   **Rewrite the sentences and replace the underlined words with y.**

1   Nous allons <u>à l'aéroport</u> demain matin. <u>Nous y allons demain matin.</u>

2   Je mets les fleurs <u>sur la table</u>. _____

3   Ils assisteront <u>au match de foot</u>. _____

4   Nous pensons souvent <u>à nos prochains voyages</u>. _____

5   Tu réponds <u>aux lettres de ta grand-mère</u>. _____

6   Elle va <u>au tabac</u> pour acheter le journal. _____

7   Vous n'allez pas souvent <u>à la piscine</u>? _____

En

1   The pronoun **en** can also have different meanings based on context. It is used to replace a phrase introduced by **de**. It follows the same placement rules as direct and indirect objects and it also goes after **ne** in the negative.

Elle sort <u>de la gym</u>. **Elle** **en** **sort.** (She is leaving _the gym_. She is leaving _it_.)

Elle n'en **sort pas.** (She isn't leaving _it_.)

2   When **en** is used with numbers, you keep the number in the sentence.

Ils ont <u>cinq télévisions</u>? **Ils** **en** **ont** <u>cinq</u>? (They have _five televisions?_ They have _five of them?_)

K   **Rewrite the sentences and replace what is underlined with en.**

1   Je reviens <u>de France</u>. _____

2   Ils ont trop <u>de livres</u>. _____

3   Tu as besoin <u>de voyager</u>. _____

4   En France, on mange beaucoup <u>de pain</u>. _____

5   Tu te souviens <u>de la soirée</u>? _____

6   Nous n'avons pas deux <u>voitures</u>. _____

L   Choose the appropriate pronoun to complete the sentences.

1   Tous les jours, _____ allons à la pêche.

    a   nous   **b**   vous   **c**   je

2   La famille reviendra de vacances bientôt. Ils _____ reviendront en TGV.

    a   les   **b**   en   **c**   nous

3   Tu adores ses films, tu _____ as tous vus.

    a   il   **b**   leur   **c**   les

4   Je vais en boîte demain soir. J' _____ serai toute la soirée.

    a   y   **b**   vous   **c**   en

5   Il va voir Cynthia et il va _____ parler.

    a   la   **b**   te   **c**   lui

6   Tu connais Isabelle? Oui, je _____ connais.

    a   la   **b**   lui   **c**   me

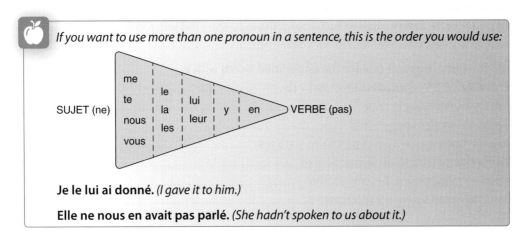

If you want to use more than one pronoun in a sentence, this is the order you would use:

Je le lui ai donné. *(I gave it to him.)*

Elle ne nous en avait pas parlé. *(She hadn't spoken to us about it.)*

Vocabulary

M   Match the French term with the English.

1	écrire à	**a**	to exercise
2	répondre à	**b**	to garden
3	faire de l'exercice	**c**	to reply to / to answer
4	pratiquer	**d**	to make a phone call
5	passer le temps à	**e**	to stay in shape
6	rester en forme	**f**	to write to
7	faire du jardinage	**g**	to buy tickets
8	offrir des fleurs	**h**	to spend time
9	acheter des billets	**i**	to give flowers
10	passer un coup de fil	**j**	to practise

N Find the odd one out.

1 faire du bricolage | faire du jardinage | passer un coup de fil | cuisiner
2 lire | danser | sortir entre ami(e)s | sortir en boîte
3 jouer aux cartes | jouer à des jeux de société | sortir au restaurant | jouer du piano
4 faire du karaté | jouer au tennis | jouer sur l'ordinateur | faire de la natation

Reading

O Read the first two paragraphs of a blog post about a sporting activity. Indicate if the following statements are V (**vrai**/true) or F (**faux**/false). Correct the false statements.

1 Elle fait de la plongée sous-marine.   V/F
2 Elle n'est pas certifiée.   V/F
3 Elle va souvent à la Guadeloupe.   V/F

V	
entourer	*to surround*
faire de la plongée sous-marine	*to scuba-dive*
plonger	*to dive*
nuire	*to damage*
le moniteur de plongée	*the diving instructor*

Blog quotidien

J'aime la tranquillité qui m'entoure lorsque je plonge en mer. Je suis certifiée et je fais de la plongée sous-marine chaque été avec ma famille. Nous plongeons tous les jours pendant nos vacances, souvent plusieurs fois par jours. J'ai obtenu ma licence de plongée au Mexique et j'y retourne souvent.

Même certifiée, il faut quand même continuer à être prudente pendant les sorties. Quand on fait beaucoup de plongée, il faut tout d'abord boire beaucoup d'eau et manger beaucoup de bananes pour éviter les crampes. Typiquement, on en boit et on en mange avant et après les plongées.

P **Now read the rest of the blog post and answer the questions.**

Je vous conseille d'être bien reposé juste au cas où il y a beaucoup de courant. Nager contre le courant peut fatiguer et rendre les sorties un peu moins agréables. Il est important de rester calme et de respirer profondément sans trop s'exercer pour ne pas consommer trop d'oxygène trop vite. Il faut bien écouter les moniteurs de plongée et suivre leurs consignes et conseils. Une fois dans l'eau, s'il y a le moindre problème, il est important d'attirer l'attention des moniteurs et de leur indiquer ce qui ne va pas. Ils peuvent vous assister le plus vite possible, si nécessaire.

Une fois dans l'eau, il faut être attentif à ce qui se passe autour de vous, pour ne pas donner des coups de palmes dans le corail et ne pas détruire ou nuire à la vie marine. Il est important d'observer mais de ne pas toucher toutes les merveilles qu'on peut voir sous l'océan, afin de les préserver pour ceux qui plongeront après vous.

1   Pourquoi est-il important de boire beaucoup d'eau? Que faut-il faire d'autre?

_____

2   Qu'est-ce qui peut rendre les sorties moins plaisantes et pourquoi?

_____

3   Quels sont les conseils offerts pour conserver l'environnement?

_____

Q **Find the French equivalent in the text for the following expressions. Identify the pronouns and say why they are used.**

1   I like the tranquility that surrounds me _____

2   I return (there) often. _____

3   Typically, you drink and eat some before … _____

4   I advise you to be well-rested _____

5   … it's important to get the instructors' attention, and to indicate to them what's wrong …

_____

6   It's important to observe but not to touch the wonders that we can see in the sea, in order to preserve them … _____

Writing

R Write an e-mail to a friend describing your preferred hobby or leisure activity. Use a variety of pronouns. (80–100 words)

_____

_____

_____

_____

_____

_____

Self-check

Tick the box that matches your level of confidence.

  1 = very confident   2 = need more practice   3 = not confident

Cochez la case qui correspond à votre niveau d'aisance.

  1 = très sûr(e) de vous   2 = j'ai besoin de plus de pratique   3 = pas sûr(e) du tout

	1	2	3
Understand vocabulary related to hobbies and leisure activities.			
Use personal pronouns (subject, direct and indirect object, tonic, y and en).			
Can understand short narratives about leisure activities (CEFR A2).			
Can write about aspects of everyday life such as leisure activities and hobbies (CEFR A2).			

3 Toi, ton signe
You, your sign

In this unit, you will learn how to:

✓ Use adjectives and place them in the correct position.

✓ Use proper gender and number agreement with nouns/pronouns and adjectives.

✓ Use adjectives to describe self, family and friends.

CEFR: Can identify important information in a simple magazine article about horoscopes (A2); Can produce a simple connected text on familiar topics such as personality traits (B1).

	Masculine		Feminine	
Singular	un livre vert	*a green book*	une voiture verte	*a green car*
	un garçon paresseux	*a lazy boy*	une fille paresseuse	*a lazy girl*
	un blouson orange	*an orange jacket*	une robe orange	*an orange dress*
Plural	des livres verts	*green books*	des voitures vertes	*green cars*
	des garçons paresseux	*lazy boys*	des filles paresseuses	*lazy girls*
	des blousons orange	*orange jackets*	des robes orange	*orange dresses*

Meaning and usage

Adjectives

1 Adjectives are words like **intéressant** *(interesting)* or **beau** *(beautiful, handsome)*, which provide more information about a noun or a pronoun.
C'était une conversation intéressante. *(That was an interesting conversation.)*
Il est très beau. *(He is very handsome.)*

A **Look at the table. How are French and English adjectives different in terms of their position with respect to the noun they qualify?**

B **Explain the different endings for intelligent in une fille intelligente, des garçons intelligents, des réponses intelligentes.**

2 In French, adjectives agree in gender (masculine or feminine) and number (singular or plural) with the noun they qualify: **un cheval blanc** *(a white horse)*, **une chemise blanche** *(a white shirt)*, **des livres blancs** *(white books)*, **des maisons blanches** *(white houses)*.

3 If the adjective refers to more than one noun or pronoun, one masculine and the other feminine, use the masculine plural form of the adjective:

Il portait une chemise et un pantalon blancs. *(He was wearing a white shirt and trousers.)*

Jean et Marie sont très gentils. *(Jean and Marie are very nice.)*

4 When used as adjectives, nationalities are not capitalized like they are in English:

Il est anglais. *(He is English.)*

Ce sont des voitures italiennes. *(Those are Italian cars.)*

C **Jacques and Jérôme are twins, but they are nothing alike. Read how they describe themselves. Use adjectives to say how they are *opposite*.**

> Je m'appelle Jacques. Je suis petit, brun et travailleur.

> Je m'appelle Jérôme. Je suis gentil, intelligent, beau et honnête.

1 Jérôme est grand, _____ et _____.

2 Jacques est _____, _____, _____ et _____.

Forms of adjectives

Masculine forms

1 The following masculine adjectives change form when they are placed before a noun that begins with a vowel or vowel sound:

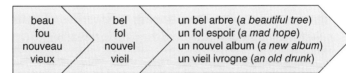

beau	bel	un bel arbre (*a beautiful tree*)
fou	fol	un fol espoir (*a mad hope*)
nouveau	nouvel	un nouvel album (*a new album*)
vieux	vieil	un vieil ivrogne (*an old drunk*)

 In the plural in front of a noun that begins with a vowel or vowel sound, all of these adjectives have their regular form: **de beaux immeubles** *(beautiful buildings),* **de nouveaux habits** *(new clothes),* **de vieux amis** *(old friends). In spoken French, you make a 'z' sound for the 'x' when it comes before a vowel.*

D   Rewrite the sentences using the adjective in brackets with the underlined noun.

1   Ils ont *un appartement* qui donne sur la rue. (beau)

_____

2   Pierre a mis longtemps avant de s'acheter *un téléphone portable*. (nouveau)

_____

3   Elle m'a beaucoup parlé de *son amour*, mais je n'ai jamais fait la connaissance de son petit ami. (fou)

_____

4   Nous avons *un ami* que nous connaissons depuis vingt ans. (vieux)

_____

5   Stéphanie aurait envie de trouver *un emploi* plus intéressant que celui qu'elle a maintenant. (nouveau)

_____

6   Elle aime beaucoup *son ordinateur portable*, mais il ne fonctionne plus. (vieux)

_____

Feminine forms

1   To form the feminine of many adjectives in French add an **-e**: **anglais/anglaise** *(English)*, **amusant/amusante** *(funny)*, **brun/brune** *(brunette)*, **blond/blonde** *(blond)*, **content/contente** *(content, glad)*, **élégant/élégante** *(elegant)*, **fort/forte** *(strong)*, **joli/jolie** *(pretty)*, **laid/laide** *(ugly)*, **ouvert/ouverte** *(open)*, **parfait/parfaite** *(perfect)*, **petit/petite** *(little, small)*, **poli/polie** *(polite)*, **prochain/prochaine** *(next)*, **vrai/vraie** *(true)*, etc.

2   If an adjective ends in **-e**, then the feminine and masculine forms are the same: **aimable** *(nice, kind)*, **célèbre** *(famous)*, **comique** *(comical)*, **confortable** *(comfortable)*, **drôle** *(funny)*, **facile** *(easy)*, **faible** *(weak)*, **honnête** *(honest)*, **malade** *(sick)*, **mince** *(thin)*, **sale** *(dirty)*, etc.

3   Adjectives that end in **-eur** have three possible endings in the feminine: **travailleur/travailleuse** *(hardworking)*, **protecteur/protectrice** *(protective)*, **supérieur/supérieure** *(superior)*.

 *Adjectives like **travailleur/travailleuse** (hardworking) that change from **-eur** to **-euse** in the feminine are always derived from verbs: **travailler** (to work).*

4   Some adjectives have feminine forms that differ considerably from the masculine form and must be learned: **beau/belle** *(beautiful)*, **blanc/blanche** *(white)*, **cher/chère** *(dear, expensive)*, **cruel/cruelle** *(cruel)*, **doux/douce** *(soft)*, **faux/fausse** *(false)*, **fou/folle** *(mad, crazy)*, **frais/fraîche** *(fresh, cool)*, **gentil/gentille** *(nice)*, **grec/grecque** *(Greek)*, etc.

 *A change in spelling can change the way an adjective is pronounced. A word you don't recognize but that sounds familiar may be a form of a word you already know. For example, the masculine form **frais** sounds like 'fray' and the feminine form **fraîche** sounds like 'fresh,' they both mean fresh or cool.*

E   Complete the sentences using the feminine form of the adjective listed in brackets.

   1   Marie est une femme absolument _____. (charmant)
   2   Claire porte une robe _____. (blanc)
   3   Notre serveuse n'était pas très _____. (poli)
   4   Cette marionnette ne me fait pas rire, elle n'est pas _____. (drôle)
   5   La vendeuse ne sourit pas beaucoup, elle ne doit pas être _____. (heureux)
   6   J'ai un peu chaud, pouvez-vous me donner un verre d'eau _____? (frais)

F   Rewrite each sentence using the opposite gender.

   1   Il n'est pas très gentil. _____
   2   Son mari n'est pas très beau, mais il n'est pas laid non plus. _____
       _____
   3   La jolie fille n'est pas très intellectuelle, elle est plutôt rêveuse. _____
       _____
   4   Nous avons un chien blanc et noir. _____
   5   La femme avec qui vous avez parlé était agressive et n'a pas été très aimable. _____
       _____
   6   Elle était grande, brune, travailleuse et un peu folle. _____
       _____

Plural forms

1   Adjectives that describe plural nouns have plural forms. Most plural adjectives are formed by adding an **-s** to the feminine or masculine singular forms.
    un homme intelligent (an intelligent man)   **des hommes intelligents** (intelligent men)
    une femme intelligente (an intelligent woman) **des femmes intelligentes** (intelligent women)

2   Some adjectives that have the masculine singular ending **-al** have irregular forms in the masculine plural, but their feminine plural does not:

Masculine singular	Feminine singular	Masculine plural	Feminine plural
royal	royale	royaux	royales
final	finale	finals	finales

*The only words other than **final** that have the **-als** ending in the masculine plural are **bancal** (rickety), **banal** (banal), **fatal** (fatal), **glacial** (glacial), **natal** (native) and **naval** (naval).*

3   Like for nouns, the adjective takes the masculine plural form if the nouns it modifies are different genders.
    La rue et le quartier sont bruyants. (The street and the neighbourhood are noisy.)

4   Some adjectives don't change forms at all. These are called invariable, and they include adjectives that are colours derived from nouns: **argent** (silver), **citron** (lemon), **crème** (cream), **marron** (chestnut), **or** (gold) and **orange** (orange).
    These also include compound adjectives: **Elle s'est teint les cheveux en bleu clair.** (She dyed her hair light blue.)

G   Choose the correct form.

1   Mon frère s'occupe de ses poissons _____.
   a   rouge   b   rouges
2   Tes amies ne sont pas très _____.
   a   sérieux   b   sérieuse   c   sérieuses
3   Ma sœur a acheté des chaussures _____.
   a   vert pomme   b   verte pomme   c   vertes pommes

Position of adjectives

1   Most often in French, adjectives are found after the noun they qualify:
   C'est un fauteuil confortable. *(It's a comfortable armchair.)*
2   Word order can be flexible in French, and sometimes adjectives are placed before the noun for emphasis: **un horrible accident/un accident horrible** *(a terrible accident.)*
3   While most adjectives are placed just after the noun, there are some exceptions. The following categories of adjectives are normally placed before the noun:

   ● cardinal and ordinal numbers: **trois euros** (three euros),
      le deuxième enfant *(the second child)*
   ● possessives and demonstratives: **ses cheveux** *(his/her hair),*
      cette pièce de théâtre *(this play)*
   ● the most commonly used adjectives also go before the noun: **autre, beau/belle, bon/ bonne, grand/grande, gros/grosse, jeune, joli/jolie, mauvais/mauvaise, nouveau/ nouvelle, petit/petite, vieux/vieille**

 H   What are the different meanings of unique in these expressions?

1   L'unique tableau. C'est le seul. _____
2   Un tableau unique. Cet artiste a une perspective très différente. _____
3   Elle est fille unique. Elle n'a pas de frères ou de sœurs. _____

4   Some adjectives change meaning depending on if they are placed before or after the noun they qualify. Usually, the meaning of the adjective after the noun is more concrete, while before the noun is more abstract.

un ancien soldat *(a former soldier)*	**un soldat ancien** *(an old soldier)*
un cher ami *(a dear friend)*	**un repas cher** *(an expensive meal)*
la dernière année *(the last year)*	**l'année dernière** *(last year)*
une femme grande *(a tall woman)*	**une grande femme** *(a great woman)*
le même jour *(the same day)*	**le jour même** *(the very day)*
un pauvre homme *(a poor or pitiable man)*	**un homme pauvre** *(a poor man, a man without money)*
mes propres draps *(my own sheets)*	**des draps propres** *(clean sheets)*

5 For adjectives that precede the noun in the plural, the article **des** becomes **de**.
   Ils ont de beaux enfants. *(They have beautiful children.)*

6 When there are two adjectives, one of them may go before the noun and one may go after, or
   they may both go before or both after. In the case of two adjectives after the noun, separate
   them with the word **et** *(and)*.
   Ils ont vu deux petites femmes brunes. *(They saw two short brunette women.)*
   Elle a reçu une jolie petite carte de sa copine. *(She received a pretty little card from her friend.)*
   Leur maison est grande et moderne. *(Their house is big and modern.)*

7 In comparison with the term **nouveau** *(new)*, which is always placed before the noun, the term
   neuf/neuve/neufs/neuves is used in French after the noun to say something is brand new or
   has never been used: **une voiture neuve** *(a brand new car)*, **des souliers neufs** *(brand new shoes)*.

I **Rewrite the sentences using the adjectives given to describe the underlined nouns.**

1 C'est une *femme*. (grand, sympathique) *C'est une grande femme sympathique.*

2 Ils n'aiment pas beaucoup les *trains*. (lent, vieux) _____

3 Pourquoi ne veulent-ils pas aller à cette *fête*? (somptueux, élégant) _____

4 Elle cherche une *colocataire* (nouveau, propre) _____

5 Tu n'as pas vu une *femme* dans le coin? (blond, petit) _____

6 Cette ville a beaucoup *d'immeubles* (ancien, impressionnant) _____

7 Nous avons une *voiture*. (bleu, nouveau) _____

8 Est-ce que vous voulez acheter un *ordinateur*? (nouveau, portable) _____

 Like in English, some adjectives are derived from verbs (action words). For example, **aimé** *(beloved)
comes from the verb* **aimer** *(to like/love) and* **fascinant** *(fascinating) comes from the verb* **fasciner**
(to fascinate). These always follow the noun.

Vocabulary

J **Complete the sentences with the appropriate French form of the adjectives in English.**

1 Les fromages _____ peuvent être _____. (French, strong)

2 Au printemps, les feuilles sur les arbres sont _____. (light green)

3 Julien et Martine sont super _____, ils n'ont pas beaucoup de temps _____ .
   (busy, free)

4 Je ne vais pas m'acheter cette robe _____, elle est trop _____. (black, long)

5 Juliette et Karine sont assez _____. Elles sont tout le temps _____.
   (lazy, tired)

6 Nous ne savons pas encore si nous allons acheter une voiture _____, celles que
   nous avons vues sont trop _____. (new, expensive)

K   Sort the words to describe yourself and your friends. Don't forget to use the correct form.

curieux   responsable   travailleuse   malheureux   content   roux   grand   petit
généreuse   sympathique   chauve   barbu   mince   gros   fort   rond   franche
rouspéteur   débrouillarde   maladroit   décontractée   doux   bronzé

Je suis …	*Mes amis sont …*

L   Match the astrological signs with the English.

1	Bélier		a	Scorpio
2	Taureau		b	Cancer
3	Gémeaux		c	Pisces
4	Cancer		d	Taurus
5	Lion		e	Capricorn
6	Vierge		f	Aquarius
7	Balance		g	Virgo
8	Scorpion		h	Libra
9	Sagittaire		i	Leo
10	Capricorne		j	Sagittarius
11	Verseau		k	Aries
12	Poissons		l	Gemini

Reading

**M   Read the description of the Aries sign and underline the adjectives.
What is an Aries like?**

L'Horoscope

Bélier (21 mars au 20 avril)

Premier signe du zodiaque puisque c'est le début du printemps. C'est le signe du renouveau et du commencement. Les natifs de ce signe sont pleins d'énergie, impulsifs et fiers. Leur nature courageuse et indépendante les pousse à l'aventure.

Taureau (21 avril au 21 mai)

Signe de stabilité et de patience, les taureaux se caractérisent par leur nature réservée et timide. Calme et fidèle, le taureau est souvent conservateur et traditionnaliste.

Gémeaux (22 mai au 21 juin)

Les gémeaux possèdent une dualité de caractère s'alliant avec une présence volage et instable. Le gémeau a le goût du jeu et dans la vie et dans l'amour et passe une grande partie de son temps à rechercher l'amour parfait.

Cancer (22 juin au 22 juillet)

Signe lunaire, les cancers sont connus pour leur nature aimante, sensible et affable. Communicatif et sentimental, le cancer se concentre sur le foyer familial. Séduisant et attentionné, son amour et sa tendresse sont profonds et durables.

Lion (23 juillet au 22 août)

Gouverné par le soleil, les lions sont maîtres de leur royaume. Orgueilleux, ambitieux, dynamique … voilà quelques unes des qualités du lion. Plus agressif que le bélier, il se montre en même temps plus généreux et plus chaleureux.

Vierge (23 août au 22 septembre)

Ceux qui se trouvent sous ce signe sont raisonnables et prudents. Le natif de la Vierge est réfléchi, pragmatique et perfectionniste. Prudent et nerveux, il est incapable d'agir avec précipitation.

Balance (23 septembre au 22 octobre)

Les balances sont sociables, charmantes et agréables. Elles aiment avant tout maintenir l'équilibre. En effet, elles recherchent l'harmonie et fuient les conflits. En même temps, elles sont romantiques et évitent la solitude.

Scorpion (23 octobre au 22 novembre)

Un scorpion est remarquable pour ses sentiments passionnés et sensuels. C'est un signe d'eau qui aime le mystère et la séduction. De nature méfiante, le scorpion peut être jaloux ou agressif. Rebuté par la trahison, il est fidèle quand il sait que son partenaire l'est aussi.

Sagittaire (23 novembre au 21 décembre)

Signe de la sagesse, les natifs de ce signe sont impatients et audacieux mais optimistes.

Le sagittaire est aventurier de nature, il aime voyager et changer d'environnement. Aimant la liberté, il n'aime ni les contraintes ni les ennuis quotidiens.

Capricorne (22 décembre au 20 janvier)

D'un tempérament calme et responsable, il est à la fois ambitieux et conformiste. Il a un sens aigu du devoir et démontre un courage hors norme.

Verseau (21 janvier au 19 février)

Astucieux, le verseau est poussé vers la spiritualité plus que par la réalité. Il recherche surtout la liberté et les nouvelles expériences. D'une intelligence exceptionnelle, c'est un être sensible sous une apparence froide.

Poissons (20 février au 20 mars)

Versatile et affectueux, le natif de ce signe est aussi rêveur que poétique. Convivial, il se fait facilement des amis mais n'est jamais chef de la bande.

Quel signe est le suivant?

1 reserved and shy _____

2 wise but impatient _____

3 dreamy and poetic _____

4 avoids conflict and looks for harmony _____

5 flighty _____

O **Find examples of the following in the text.**

1 An ordinal number used as an adjective. _____

2 A feminine plural adjective. _____

3 An adjective that has the same form in the masculine singular and masculine plural.

_____

4 An adjective in the masculine plural used to denote one masculine noun and one feminine noun. _____

5 Two adjectives that can both be translated as proud. _____

6 Possessive adjectives. _____

P **For some extra practice, highlight all of the adjectives in the article and deduce their meaning from the context. If you need to look them up, remember to look in the dictionary for the masculine singular form.**

Writing

Q **What do you think of horoscopes? Do you recognize yourself in the description of your sign? Write a blog post on the topic of astrology and say if you and the members of your family have personalities that resemble your signs. [80–100 words]**

_____

_____

_____

_____

_____

_____

_____

_____

_____

_____

_____

Self-check

Tick the box that matches your level of confidence.

    1 = very confident   2 = need more practice   3 = not confident

Cochez la case qui correspond à votre niveau d'aisance.

    1 = très sûr(e)   2 = j'ai besoin de plus de pratique   3 = pas sûr(e) du tout

	1	2	3
Use adjectives and place them in the correct position.			
Use proper gender agreement with nouns/pronouns and adjectives.			
Use adjectives to describe self, family and your friends.			
Can identify important information in simple magazine article about horoscopes (CEFR A2).			
Can produce a simple connected text on familiar topics such as personality traits (CEFR B1).			

4 En plein air

Outdoors

In this unit, you will learn how to:

✅ Use adverbs.

✅ Use comparatives and superlatives.

CEFR: Can understand an informational website about a tourist attraction (A2); Can write an e-mail to enquire about accommodation and activities (B1).

Meaning and usage

Adverbs

1 Adverbs are invariable words normally used to say how or when an action is performed. They function in French much as they do in English.

Nous allons _souvent_ à la montagne. (_We go often to the mountains._)

Elle part _demain_ pour la mer. (_She is leaving tomorrow for the seaside._)

2 Adverbs may also be used to qualify an adjective.

Il fait une randonnée _très_ longue. (_He is taking a very long hike._)

La description de la plage est _totalement_ fausse. (_The description of the beach is totally false._)

3 Adverbs may also qualify other adverbs.

Vous jouez _très bien_ au tennis. (_You play tennis very well._)

Le parc est _assez loin_. (_The park is quite far._)

 A **Match each sentence with its usage. The adverbs are underlined.**

1 Il voyage _fréquemment_. (_He travels frequently._)

2 Ce vin est _vraiment_ délicieux.
   (_This wine is truly delicious._)

3 Vous parlez _très_ bien le français.
   (_You speak French very well._)

a The adverb is used to modify an adverb.

b The adverb is used to modify an adjective.

c The adverb is used to modify a verb.

4 Adverbs may also qualify a complete sentence.

Heureusement, il a fait beau jusqu'au dernier jour de notre séjour. (_Fortunately, there was nice weather until the last day of our stay._)

 Some speakers of English use adjectives in the place of adverbs. This does not happen in French, so be careful to use the appropriate adverb in sentences like these.

French	Incorrect in English	Correct in English
J'ai **bien** réussi à l'examen.	_I did good on the test._	_I did well on the test._
Vous l'avez fait **facilement**.	_You did that easy._	_You did that easily._
Mangez **sainement**.	_Eat healthy._	_Eat healthily._

5   Exclamatory adverbs are used to express a strong emotion. They are placed at the beginning of a sentence.

Comme il fait beau! *(How nice the weather is!)*

Que c'est bon! *(It's so good!)*

6   Most adverbs fall into six main categories according to the type of information they provide such as time, frequency, sequence, place, manner and quantity. Here are some examples:

Types of adverbs	
Adverbs of time (when something takes place)	actuellement *(now)*, autrefois *(in the past)*, bientôt *(soon)*, pendant *(during)*, déjà *(already)*, depuis *(since)*, dernièrement *(lately/recently)*, désormais *(from now on)*, immédiatement *(immediately)*, tard *(late)*, tôt *(early)*
Adverbs of frequency (how often something takes place)	encore *(again)*, de temps en temps *(from time to time)*, une fois *(once)*, jamais *(never)*, parfois *(sometimes)*, rarement *(rarely)*, toujours *(always)*, souvent *(often)*, tous les jours/mois/ans, etc. *(every day, month, year, etc.)*, quelquefois *(sometimes)*
Adverbs of sequence (when things happen in relation to others)	alors *(then)*, après *(after)*, d'abord *(first [of all])*, donc *(therefore)*, en conclusion *(in conclusion)*, ensuite *(then)*, enfin *(lastly)*, finalement *(finally)*, premièrement *(firstly)*, puis *(then)*
Adverbs of place (where something takes place)	ailleurs *(elsewhere)*, autour *(around)*, dedans *(inside)*, dehors *(outside)*, devant *(in front)*, ici *(here)*, loin *(far)*, n'importe où *(anywhwere)*, nulle part *(nowhere)*, partout *(everywhere)*
Adverbs of manner (how an action is done)	ainsi *(so)*, amicalement *(amicably)*, aveuglément *(blindly)*, bien *(well)*, gentiment *(kindly)*, mal *(badly/wrongly)*, méchamment *(spitefully/badly)*, normalement *(normally/typically)*, patiemment *(patiently)*, rapidement *(quickly)*, volontiers *(gladly/willingly)*
Adverbs of quantity or degree (how many, how much or how often)	beaucoup *(a lot)*, combien *(how many/much)*, la plupart *(most/the majority)*, pas mal *(a fair amount/quite a bit)*, plus *(more)*, moins *(less)*, trop *(too much)*, sans *(without)*, tant *(so much/so many)*, tellement *(so much)*

Many adverbs of quantity are followed by **de/d'**. *When this is the case, there is no article between* **de** *and the noun, even when it is plural.*

Il a beaucoup de temps libre. *(He has a lot of free time.)*

Nous n'avons pas assez de vacances. *(We don't have enough holiday.)*

B   Choose the appropriate adverbs from the box to complete the paragraph.

après	normalement	enfin	dehors	parfois	dans	sous	bien

Mes amis font (1) _____ du ski en février, mais (2) _____ ils doivent partir plus tard, au mois de mars en fonction du temps. Ils aiment être à la montagne avec la neige (3) _____ les skis et le vent (4) _____ le dos. (5) _____ une longue journée à être (6) _____, ils retournent au chalet pour (7) _____ manger auprès du feu. (8) _____ ils n'oublient pas le vin chaud aux épices.

Some adjectives are used as adverbs in French. In these cases they are invariable.

Nous parlons bas. *(We speak quietly.)*

Elle s'habille jeune. *(She dresses young.)*

Claudine sent mauvais. *(Claudine smells bad.)*

Forms and placement

How to form adverbs

1   In French, as in English, many adverbs are derived from adjectives. Most of the time, the ending **-ment**, the French equivalent of *-ly*, is added to the feminine form of the adjective.

doux, douce *(soft)*	**doucement** *(softly)*
partiel, partielle *(partial)*	**partiellement** *(partiallly)*
lent, lente *(slow)*	**lentement** *(slowly)*

Note that **gentil** is an exception.

gentil *(nice)*	**gentiment** *(nicely)*

2   For adjectives that end in a vowel in the masculine, add **-ment**.

facile *(easy)*	**facilement** *(easily)*
poli *(polite)*	**poliment** *(politely)*
vrai *(true)*	**vraiment** *(truly)*

 C   **Look at the following adjectives and their corresponding adverbs and identify the rule for how they are formed.**

bruyant *(noisy)*	**bruyamment** *(noisily)*
intelligent *(intelligent)*	**intelligemment** *(intellingently)*
récent *(recent)*	**récemment** *(recently)*
suffisant *(sufficient)*	**suffisamment** *(sufficiently)*

3   Some adjectives that end in **-e** have an accent added to the adverb for pronunciation purposes.

aveugle *(blind)*	**aveuglément** *(blindly)*
énorme *(enormous)*	**énormément** *(enormously)*
précis *(precise)*	**précisément** *(precisely)*
profond *(profound)*	**profondément** *(profoundly)*

D   **Convert the following adjectives into adverbs. Look up new words in the dictionary for extra help if needed.**

1	sérieux _____	6	méchant _____
2	éventuel _____	7	aisé _____
3	apparent _____	8	sincère _____
4	patient _____	9	attentif _____
5	heureux _____	10	évident _____

*Some adverbs such as **souvent** (often), **très** (very) and **trop** (too much) do not follow any formation rule.*

Adverb placement

1   The position of adverbs in French is largely the same as in English. They usually follow a verb and precede adjectives and other adverbs.
    Il écoute _attentivement_ le guide. *(He listens _attentively_ to the guide.)*
    Je voyage _très_ souvent. *(I travel _very_ often.)*
    L'agent de voyage qui s'occupe de moi est _toujours_ serviable. *(The travel agent who takes care of me is _always_ helpful.)*

2   Like in English, adverbs in French usually come after an infinitive.
    Elle doit marcher lentement. *(She has to walk slowly.)*
    Nous préférons manger assez tard. *(We prefer to eat rather late.)*

3   With compound tenses in French, the adverb is usually placed after the auxiliary (**être** or **avoir**) unless the adverb has more than two syllables.
    Elle a _trop_ bronzé. *(She tanned _too much_.)*
    Ce voyage nous a plu _énormément_. *(This trip pleased us _enormously_.)*

4   Adverbs of place usually go after the direct object.
    Il a mis ses baskets _là-bas_. *(He put his trainers _over there_.)*
    Ils ont fait un pique-nique _ici_. *(They had a picnic _here_.)*

5   With long adverbs and adverbs referring to specific days or times, the adverb usually comes at the beginning or end of the sentence.
    Généralement, il fait du surf tout le week-end. *(_Generally_, he goes surfing all weekend.)*
    Nous allons faire de l'escalade _cet après-midi_. *(We are going to go mountain climbing _this afternoon_.)*

6   If an adverb is used in a negative construction, it usually goes after the negation.
    Vous ne courrez pas _vite_. *(You don't run _quickly_.)*
    Elle ne reste jamais _longtemps_ à la plage. *(She never stays _long_ at the beach.)*

E   **Rewrite the sentences about Philippe and Marie's hiking trip to make them more descriptive. Use the adverbs given in brackets.**

1   Philippe et Marie s'installent dans leur site de camping. (facilement)
    _____

2   Ils partent pour faire une randonnée. (hâtivement)
    _____

3   Ils regardent la carte. (attentivement)
    _____

4   Marie trouve la piste. (aisément)
    _____

5   Ils veulent monter au sommet pour profiter de la vue avant le coucher du soleil. (rapidement)
    _____

6   Tous les deux respirent l'air frais de la montagne. (profondément)
    _____

7   En descendant de la montagne, Philippe se tord la cheville. (malheureusement)

   _____

8   Philippe ne peut pas faire de la marche, il a trop mal. (le lendemain)

   _____

Meaning and usage

Comparatives and superlatives

Comparatives

1   Comparatives are used to make statements about the relative superiority, inferiority or equality of two or more people or things. They can be used with adjectives, adverbs, verbs and nouns.
2   For comparisons using adjectives, you can indicate superiority using **plus + adjectif + que** (*more + adjective + than*):
   Cet immeuble est _plus haut que_ l'autre. (*This building is _taller than_ the other.*)
   For comparisons of inferiority, use **moins + adjectif + que** (*less + adjective + than*):
   Sa voiture est _moins vieille que_ la mienne. (*His car is _less old than_ mine.*)
3   For comparisons of equality, use **aussi + adjectif + que** (*as + adjective + as*):
   Il est _aussi intelligent que_ lui. (*He is _as intelligent as_ him.*)
4   For comparisons using adverbs, use the same structure.
   Elle écrit _plus que_ sa sœur. (*She writes _more than_ her sister.*)
   Sa sœur écrit _moins qu'_elle. (*Her sister writes _less than_ her.*)
   Sa sœur écrit _aussi intelligemment qu'_elle. (*Her sister writes _as intelligently as_ her.*)

The adverbs **bien** *(well) and* **mal** *(poorly) have irregular comparative forms:* **mieux** *(better) and* **pire** *(worse).* **Pire** *may be replaced by* **plus mal** *(more poorly).*

Elle chante mieux que sa sœur. *(She sings better than her sister.)*

Oui, mais elle danse pire/plus mal. *(Yes, but she dances worse/more poorly.)*

5   To compare verbs, the same structure is used, but replace **aussi** with **autant**.
   Il va au parc _moins que_ sa femme. (*He goes to the park _less than_ his wife.*)
   Sa femme marche _plus que_ lui. (*His wife walks _more than_ him.*)
   Elle s'amuse _autant que_ lui. (*She has _as much_ fun _as_ him.*)

F   **Look at these comparisons using nouns. What is different from the sentences with comparisons using verbs?**

   1   Il a <u>plus de</u> cheveux <u>que</u> son père. (*He has <u>more</u> hair <u>than</u> his father.*)
   2   Son père a <u>moins de</u> soucis <u>que</u> sa mère. (*His father has <u>fewer</u> worries <u>than</u> his mother.*)
   3   Sa mère a <u>autant de</u> travail <u>que</u> son père. (*His mother has <u>as much</u> work <u>as</u> his father.*)

G   **Complete the sentences by using the French form of the English comparative in brackets.**

   1   Elle fait de l'escalade _____ lui. (*as much as*)
   2   Ahmed joue au tennis _____ sa femme. (*more often than*)
   3   Tu veux _____ amis que lui. (*more*)

4   Nous avons _____ idées que toi. (*fewer*)
5   Il ne chante pas _____ sa copine. (*as well as*)
6   Jean court _____ son frère Gaston. (*faster*)
7   Vous savez _____ votre frère au sujet de la pêche. (*less than*)
8   Louise ne travaille pas _____ Isabelle. (*as well as*)

 Sometimes with comparatives the thing being compared is only inferred.
Il voit tout <u>aussi bien</u>. (*He sees just as well.*)
Elle marche <u>plus vite</u>. (*She walks faster.*)

Superlatives

1   Superlatives are used to express the idea that something is the best or the worst.
2   Superlative adjectives are formed by placing the definite article before **plus** or **moins + adjectif**.
    L'homme <u>*le plus beau*</u> de tous. (<u>*The most handsome* man of all.</u>)
3   If the adjective follows the noun, put a definite article in front of both. Both the article and the adjective must agree in gender and number with the noun they modify.
    C'est la femme <u>la plus intelligente</u>. (*It's <u>the smartest</u> woman.*)

H   The adjective bon is irregular in French in the comparative and the superlative. Translate the following and indicate how the adjective changes and why.

un bon film (*a good film*)   **une bonne randonnée** (*a good hike*)
1   un meilleur film _____
2   de meilleurs films _____
3   le meilleur film _____
4   les meilleurs films _____
5   une meilleure randonnée _____
6   de meilleures randonnées _____
7   la meilleure randonnée _____
8   les meilleures randonnées _____

 *With a superlative, the preposition 'in' is used in English, but **de** is used in French.*
C'est le meilleur camping de la région. (*It's the best campsite in the area.*)

4   For superlatives with an adverb, use **le plus** and **le moins** after the verb. Adverbs don't have gender, so these are invariable.
    Elle parle le plus lentement. (*She speaks the most slowly.*)
    Bruno danse le moins bien. (*Bruno dances the least well.*)
5   The adverbs **bien** (*well*) and **mal** (*poorly*) are irregular in the superlative.
    Le mieux (*the best*) and **le pis** (*the worst*) are the traditional forms, but **le plus mal** (*the worst*) is used in modern French.
    Ils parlent le mieux. (*They speak the best.*)
    Elle chante le plus mal. (*She sings the worst.*)

> **Pis** *is still used in French in some fixed expressions.*
>
> **Tant pis!** *(Too bad!)*
>
> **au pis aller** *(at worst)*
>
> **aller de mal en pis** *(to go from bad to worse)*

6 With nouns, use **le plus de** *(the most)* and **le moins de** *(the least, the fewest).*

Tu a gagné le plus de matchs. *(You won the most games.)*

Paul lit le moins de livres. *(Paul reads the fewest books.)*

I **Use the elements provided to make complete sentences using the superlative indicated (+ or -). Add the definite article where needed. The first one is done for you.**

1 Pierre / être / fier / + *Pierre est le plus fier.*

2 Tu / appeler / tes parents / souvent / + _____

3 Pauline / être / beau / - _____

4 Marc et Simon / voir / arbres / vieux / + _____

5 Nous / regarder / paysage / magnifique / + _____

6 C'est Jean-Paul / qui / arriver / souvent / en retard / + _____

7 C'est Pascale / qui / aimer / faire du camping / - _____

8 Voici / l'endroit / apprécié / du monde / - _____

Vocabulary

J **Complete the sentences with the missing word. Use a dictionary if needed.**

1 Il n'a peur de rien ! La dernière fois, il a fait du _____.
   a lac   b coucher de soleil   c parapente   d vigne

2 Moi, j'adore faire du _____, dormir dans la nature et manger près du feu.
   a cheval   b camping   c vélo   d à pied

3 Il n'y a rien de comparable à une bonne randonnée pour _____ et se changer les idées.
   a agent de voyage   b le séjour   c se détendre   d le vignoble

4 Pour _____ des champs de lavande, il faut aller en Provence en juillet.
   a profiter   b à l'étranger   c le sommet   d respirer

5 _____ leur a pris trois heures. Ils ont pris de très belles photos.
   a Le lac   b Le séjour   c Le camping   d La balade

6 Comme il fait si chaud, les jeunes se baignent dans _____.
   a la montagne   b la rivière   c un tour   d le guide

K Match the French words with the English.

1	explorer	a	to go parasailing
2	la campagne	b	to take a walk
3	le camping	c	to relax
4	se détendre	d	outdoors
5	le paysage	e	to explore
6	la rivière	f	the summit
7	en plein air	g	to enjoy / take advantage of the nice weather
8	le sentier	h	the campsite
9	faire du parapente	i	to go hiking
10	profiter du beau temps	j	the trail
11	la balade	k	the country, countryside
12	se balader	l	the landscape, scenery
13	faire une randonnée	m	the river
14	le sommet	n	the walk

📖 Reading

L Read the first paragraph of the homepage of a website for a campsite in Northeastern Canada and answer the questions.

1 Où se trouve le Camping Auberge du Percé? _____

2 Qui aimerait venir ici? Pourquoi? _____

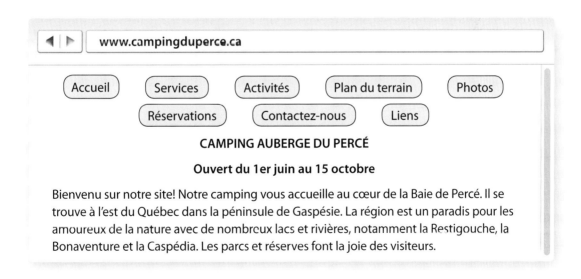

www.campingduperce.ca

Accueil Services Activités Plan du terrain Photos
Réservations Contactez-nous Liens

CAMPING AUBERGE DU PERCÉ

Ouvert du 1er juin au 15 octobre

Bienvenu sur notre site! Notre camping vous accueille au cœur de la Baie de Percé. Il se trouve à l'est du Québec dans la péninsule de Gaspésie. La région est un paradis pour les amoureux de la nature avec de nombreux lacs et rivières, notamment la Restigouche, la Bonaventure et la Caspédia. Les parcs et réserves font la joie des visiteurs.

M Now read the rest of the information from the website about the campsite and the area, then answer the questions.

www.campingduperce.ca

Le camping est situé au bord de la mer, vous n'avez qu'à faire deux pas pour avoir les pieds dans le sable. Que ce soit pour faire des randonnées, aller à la plage, faire de la plongée sous-marine, faire du parapente, magasiner, déguster la cuisine locale, aller à la pêche ou faire une excursion sur l'île Bonaventure, nous sommes à proximité de tout. Vous pouvez vous balader tranquillement sur de multiples sentiers aux alentours du site. On peut également profiter de la piste cyclable qui suit la route 132. La location de canoës et de kayaks se fait à proximité.

Notre grand terrain de 160 emplacements a été rénové récemment avec l'ajout d'une buanderie, d'un nouveau bloc sanitaire muni d'eau chaude, d'un gazébo et d'une salle de jeux pour enfants. Les emplacements à deux services (électricité et eau) se trouvent plus près du cœur du camping que ceux sans service qui sont plus près de l'eau. Nous vous assurons un service courtois et toujours à l'écoute.

Tarifs pour 2 adultes et 2 enfants: $27/nuit – $900/saison

Les tarifs sont sujets à changement et peuvent différer de ceux présentés ici.

Un site propre et reposant vous assure le meilleur séjour possible!

1 Quelles activités peut-on faire ici? _____
2 Qu'est-ce qu'on peut louer près du camping? _____
3 Quels services offre-t-on au camping? _____

N Find the adverbs in the text.

O Find one comparative and two superlatives in the text. _____

Accents, vocabulary and even syntax can change from one French-speaking country to another and even within a country. **Magasiner** *(to go shopping) is used in Canada, for example, but not in France. French-speaking Canadians also use the term,* **C'est fun!** *(It's fun!). Aside from words and expressions borrowed from English, some terms used in Canada are seen as archaic in France, such as* **un char** *(an automobile) used instead of* **une voiture.**

Writing

P   You are planning a trip to the Camping Auberge du Percé with your family. Write a
message in French to Monsieur Toubon, the director, to reserve your spot for an upcoming
holiday. Describe what accommodation you are seeking and the activities that interest you
and the members of your family. Use as many adverbs as possible. [60–80 words]

_____

_____

_____

_____

_____

_____

_____

_____

_____

Self-check

Tick the box that matches your level of confidence.

1 = very confident   2 = need more practice   3 = not confident

Cochez la case qui correspond à votre niveau d'aisance.

1 = très sûr(e) de vous   2 = j'ai besoin de plus de pratique   3 = pas sûr(e) du tout

	1	2	3
Use adverbs.			
Use comparatives and superlatives.			
Can understand an informational website about a tourist attraction (CEFR A2).			
Can write an email to reserve accommodation (CEFR B1).			

5 Tout le monde est connecté
Everyone is connected

In this unit, you will learn how to:

✓ Ask questions using interrogative adverbs, adjectives and pronouns.

✓ Provide answers using demonstrative pronouns and adjectives.

✓ Write about social media and the workplace.

CEFR: Can understand texts that consist mainly of high frequency everyday or job-related language (A2); Can write about everyday aspects of his or her environment regarding such things as people, places and jobs (A2).

Meaning and usage

Asking questions

In French, like in English, certain words or combinations of words are used to ask and answer questions. There are two types of questions: those that ask for a *yes* or *no* answer and those that ask for specific information.

Questions that ask for a *yes* or *no* answer

There are two ways to ask this type of question.

1   You can use **est-ce que** before the subject.
    Est-ce que tu regardes des films en ligne? *(Do you watch movies online?)*
2   You can invert the subject and verb. This is the most formal way to ask questions. It is more commonly used in writing than in speech. With inversion with proper nouns, keep the noun where it is and add the appropriate subject pronoun with a hyphen after the verb. Add **-t-** if the subject pronoun starts with a vowel.
    Regardes-tu des films en ligne? *(Do you watch movies online?)*
    Mary Laure, va-t-elle souvent au cinéma? *(Does Mary Laure go to the cinema often?)*

> *There are two other ways that people ask questions informally when speaking.*
>
> *You can add* **n'est-ce pas:**
>
> **Tu regardes des films en ligne, n'est-ce pas?** *(You watch movies online, don't you?)*
>
> *You can also use a rising intonation.*
>
> **Tu regardes des films en ligne?** *(You watch movies online?)*

Questions that ask for something more than a *yes* or *no* answer

These questions begin with an interrogative, or question word. This word can be an adverb, an adjective or a pronoun.

Interrogative adverbs: où *(where)*, quand *(when)*, combien *(how much)*, comment *(how)*, pourquoi *(why)*

With all of these words, except **pourquoi**, you can use either **est-ce que** or invert the subject and verb.

1 Place the question word at the beginning of the sentence, followed by either **est-ce que** or invert the subject and verb.
   Combien coûte cet ordinateur? Combien est-ce que cet ordinateur coûte? *(How much does this computer cost?)*
   Quand est-ce que vous aurez votre nouvelle tablette? Quand aurez-vous votre nouvelle tablette? *(When will you have your new tablet?)*
2 With **pourquoi**, the subject and verb do not move, but you add a hyphen and the corresponding subject pronoun to the end of the verb.
   Anne veut me parler. *(Anne wants to speak with me.)*
   Pourquoi **Anne veut-*elle* me parler?** *(Why does Anne want to speak with me?)*
3 To ask *How many*, use **combien** with the preposition **de**.
   Combien de fois dois-je répéter ma question? *(How many times must I repeat my question?)*

A Use **où, quand, combien (de), comment** or **pourquoi** to complete the sentences.

   1 _____ avez-vous payé votre nouveau téléphone? Je les trouve très chers, pas vous?
   2 _____ allez-vous ce soir? Au théâtre?
   3 _____ est-ce que vous me téléphonez si tard?
   4 _____ fait-il ça? Il le fait sur son ordinateur.
   5 _____ est-ce que vous allez commencer le nouveau boulot? Le 10 juin? C'est bientôt!
   6 _____ temps est-ce que ce téléchargement prendra?

Interrogative adjectives

As with adjectives in general, interrogative adjectives reflect the number and gender of the noun to which they refer.

   Quels réseaux sociaux utilisent-ils régulièrement?
   (Which social networks do they frequently use?)

In English, though grammatically incorrect, what *is commonly used to ask questions. For example, to many, the following English question seems correct:* <u>What</u> *social networks do they frequently use? The grammatically correct way to ask this question would be by using* which *in English. If starting out with a grammatically incorrect sentence in English, though commonly used, translating* what *might lead to an incorrect French translation of the question.*

1 **Quel** (*which*) is usually followed by the noun to which it refers.
   Quel type de travail cherchez-vous? (*What kind of work are you looking for?*)
   Quelle heure est-il? (*What time is it?*)
2 It can also go before the verb **être** and the noun.
   Quelles sont vos qualifications? (*What are your qualifications?*)
3 It can also follow a preposition.
   À quelle conférence vas-tu assister? (*Which conference are you going to attend?*)

Note the placement of the preposition. It is found before the interrogative adjective, not at the end of the question.

B Read the following conversation between two friends and answer the questions that follow.

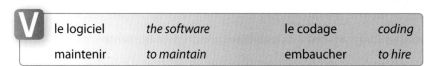

le logiciel	the software	le codage	coding
maintenir	to maintain	embaucher	to hire

Pierre: De quel logiciel te sers-tu pour maintenir les sites de tes clients?

Dominique: Aucun, je fais le codage moi-même.

Pierre: C'est impressionnant! C'est pour ça qu'ils ont un look si professionnel.

Dominique: Je fais de mon mieux.

Pierre: Et là, quelle compagnie vient de t'embaucher récemment?

Dominique: Une petite boîte qui s'appelle Soco. Je préfère travailler pour des clients comme eux.

Pierre: Quels en sont les avantages?

Dominique: Ils laissent plus de place à ma créativité, j'ai donc un peu plus de liberté.

Pierre: Quelle chance tu as d'avoir si bien réussi et de pouvoir choisir ta clientèle.

Dominique: Et toi, quelles ont été tes dernières aventures?

1 Quel est le logiciel que Dominique utilise pour maintenir les sites de ses clients?
2 Pourquoi Dominique préfère-t-elle son nouvel employeur?

C Based on the conversation, can you figure out the different forms of the interrogative adjective *which* in French?

	Masculine	Feminine
Singular	1 _____	2 _____
Plural	3 _____	4 _____

D Complete the questions with the appropriate interrogative adjective.

1 Sur _____ site as-tu vu ces photos?

2 De _____ réseaux sociaux parlez-vous?

3 Pour _____ raisons n'aimes-tu pas communiquer par SMS?

4 À _____ moment pourrions-nous nous parler sur Skype?

E Write four questions you could ask a friend about his or her use of technology and/or media. See Activity B for examples.

1 _____

2 _____

3 _____

4 _____

Interrogative pronouns

There are three different interrogative pronouns in English. As the name suggests, interrogative pronouns are used to ask about something.

1 **Qui** means *who* or *whom*, and it is used to refer to people. **Qui** as the subject means *who*, and it means *whom* when it is the object of the verb.
Subject: **Qui t'a envoyé ce courriel?** (*Who sent you this email?*)

Object: **Qui suis-tu sur les médias sociaux?** (*Whom do you follow on social media?*)

In both scenarios, the long question form can be used.

Qui est-ce qui is used before the subject:

Qui est-ce qui t'a envoyé ce courriel? (*Who sent you this e-mail?*)

Qui est-ce que/qu' is used before the object:

Qui est-ce que tu suis sur les réseaux sociaux? (*Whom do you follow on social networks?*)

*When **qui** is the subject, the verb is typically conjugated in the third person singular, even if the answer is plural.*

- **Qui parle?**   *Who is talking?*
- **Mes cousins.**   *My cousins.*

Qui *cannot be contracted when followed by a vowel, however **que** drops the -e and takes an apostrophe like in this sentence:* **Qu'est-ce qu'elle veut?** *(What does she want?).*

2 **Que** means *what* and is used to refer to things.

Subject: **Que se passe-t-il?** (*What is happening?*)

Object: **Que regardes-tu?** (*What are you watching?*)

In both scenarios, the long question form can be used. This will change depending on whether it is the subject or the object of the sentence.

Qu'est-ce qui is used for the subject:

Qu'est-ce qui se passe? (*What is happening?*)

Qu'est-ce que/qu' is used for the object:

Qu'est-ce que tu regardes? (*What are you watching?*)

In both cases the interrogative pronoun can be introduced by a preposition.

<u>Avec</u> **qui chattes-tu en ligne?** <u>Avec</u> **qui est-ce que tu chattes en ligne?** (<u>*With</u> whom do you chat online?*)

Note that **que** becomes **quoi** when preceded by a preposition.

<u>À quoi</u> **penses-tu?** <u>À quoi</u> **est-ce que tu penses?** (<u>*What</u> are you thinking <u>about?</u>*)

<u>De quoi</u> **parle-t-il?** <u>De quoi</u> **est-ce qu'il parle?** (<u>*What</u> is he speaking <u>about?</u>*)

3 **Lequel** means *which one*. This is the only interrogative pronoun that needs to reflect the number and gender of the noun it replaces. It can refer both to people or things.

- **Je lis le journal en ligne.** (*I read the newspaper online.*)

- **Lequel?** (*Which one?*) (The masculine singular form is used, as it is referring to **le journal.**)

	Masculine	Feminine
Singular	lequel	laquelle
Plural	lesquels	lesquelles

These may also be preceded by prepositions. However, when preceded by **à** or **de** some contractions occur.

	Masculine	Feminine		Masculine	Feminine
Singular	auquel	à laquelle	Singular	duquel	de laquelle
Plural	auxquels	auxquelles	Plural	desquels	desquelles

- **Nous parlons de ton ami.** (*We are talking about your friend.*)

- **Duquel parlez-vous?** (*Which one are you talking about?*)

F Complete the following questions with **qui**, **que** or **quoi**.

1. _____ téléchargez-vous?
2. À _____ envoies-tu des textos?
3. Qui est-ce _____ va acheter un nouvel ordinateur?
4. Qu'est-ce _____ tu préfères lire en ligne?
5. De _____ parles-tu sur ton blogue?
6. Qu'est-ce _____ tu utilises pour rédiger tes courriels?

G Complete the conversations with the correct form of **lequel**.

1. - J'aime bien ce nouveau portable.
   - _____, le Motorola™ ou le nouvel iPhone™?
2. - Il adore les films étrangers.
   - _____ préfère-t-il, les films français ou italiens?
3. - Vous aimez ces photos? D'après vous, _____ sont les plus belles?
4. - Nous avons écrit plusieurs posts sur ce blogue.
   - _____ avez-vous écrits?
5. - J'ai deux tablettes.
   - _____ est meilleur pour surfer le web?

H Translate the following questions.

1. What are you writing? _____
2. What are you going to give him? _____
3. Which social network do you prefer? _____
4. I've read all of his online articles, of which ones do you speak? _____
   _____

Demonstrative adjectives

Demonstrative adjectives are used to point people or things out using a form of **ce** (*this*).

1. As with other adjectives, there is a need for agreement in gender and number with the noun.

	Masculine	Feminine
Singular	ce	cette
Plural	ces	ces

2. These adjectives replace the article, so there is no need to use **le** (*the*) or **un** (*a*).
3. When there is a need to be specific, the suffixes **-ci** (*this*, used for something in closer proximity) or **-là** (*that*, used for something further away) can be added.

   Quel portable vous intéresse, ce portable-ci, ou ce portable-là? (*Which mobile phone interests you, this mobile phone (here), or that mobile phone (there)?*)

I   Complete the sentences with the appropriate demonstrative adjective.

1 _____ nouvelles me peinent.
2 Elle trouve _____ acteur tellement beau.
3 _____ téléchargement prend du temps.
4 _____ femmes-là ont toujours de belles photos sur leur blogue.
5 _____ portables ne marchent plus.
6 _____ logiciel ne marche pas très bien.
7 _____ tablette est toute neuve.
8 _____ messages datent d'il y a très longtemps.

The masculine singular demonstrative adjective **ce** *(this) does not contract by dropping the* **-e***, rather, it becomes* **cet** *in front of a noun starting with a vowel or mute* **-h***.*

Cet article est excellent.
(This article is excellent.)

Demonstrative pronouns

Like all pronouns, demonstrative pronouns typically refer to something or someone previously mentioned. They have to agree in number and gender with the noun that they replace. Unlike interrogative pronouns, these pronouns cannot stand alone.

1 Just as with the demonstrative adjectives, the suffixes **-ci** or **-là** can be used to specify proximity.
   - **Quelle montre préfères-tu?** (*Which watch do you prefer?*)
   - **Je préfère celle-ci.** (*I prefer this one.*)
2 Demonstrative pronouns can be followed by a preposition and a clause that offers more information.
   - **À qui appartiennent ces écouteurs?** (*Whose headphones are these?*)
   - **Ce sont ceux d'Émilie.** (*Those are Emily's.*)
3 They can also be followed by a relative pronoun.
   - **Quelle nouvelle?** (*Which short story?*)
   - **Celle que j'ai écrite l'année dernière.** (*The one (that) I wrote last year.*)

Forms of demonstrative pronouns

1 Demonstrative pronouns must agree in gender and number with the noun they are referring to:

	Masculine	Feminine
Singular	celui	celle
Plural	ceux	celles

J Complete the following sentences with the appropriate demonstrative pronoun.

1 La batterie de mon portable ne va pas durer, prenons _____ de François juste au cas où.

2 Elle a acheté une nouvelle tablette. _____ dont elle se servait était très vieille.

3 Les hommes les plus sympas sont _____ que j'ai rencontrés dans le Nord.

4 Des deux bouquins, j'aime mieux _____-ci.

5 _____ qui t'a appelé hier, c'est la femme en bleu.

6 D'habitude, je ne fais pas trop attention aux photos en ligne, mais _____ de mon frère sont drôles.

2 There are also indefinite or invariable demonstrative pronouns. These are used to talk about something abstract. There are four of them: **ce** (or **c'** before a vowel), **ceci**, **cela** and **ça**.

Ce/C' *this* or *it* is often used with the verb **être** *to be*.

C'est une bonne chose de se familiariser avec les nouvelles technologies.
(*It's a good thing to become familiar with new technologies.*)

Ceci *this* and **cela** *that*, can act as subject or object of the verb, but remain invariable.

Ceci vient d'arriver pour toi.
(*This has just arrived for you.*)

Je lui montrerai cela quand il rentrera.
(*I will show this to him when he comes home.*)

Ça can replace **cela**. It is more familiar and commonly used in spoken French.

Dis-lui ça la prochaine fois. (*Tell him this/that next time.*)

C'est/Ce sont *(It is/They are) are usually followed by a noun phrase. Use* **il/elle est** *(he or she is) or* **ils/elles sont** *(they are) with an adjective or with a profession, a nationality or a religion.*

C'est un nouvel ordinateur.
(It's a new computer.)

Ce sont de nouveaux ordinateurs. *(Those are new computers.)*

Il est anglais. *(He/It is English.)*

Ils sont anglais. *(They are English.)*

Elle est ingénieure. *(She is an engineer.)*

Elles sont ingénieures. *(They are engineers.)*

K   Translate the following sentences.

1   Ceci dit, je crois que je préfère écouter la radio sur l'Internet, c'est plus simple. _____
    _____

2   C'est très beau d'aimer son vieux téléphone, mais as-tu pensé à ça, les nouveaux
    téléphones portables sont meilleurs. _____
    _____

3   On a laissé ceci dans la boîte aux lettres, c'est sans doute pour vous. _____
    _____

4   Qu'est-ce que vous lui avez dit pour qu'il croit cela? _____
    _____

5   Je ne crois pas ça de lui, il n'en est pas capable. _____
    _____

6   Qui croit cela de nos jours? _____
    _____

Vocabulary

L   Match the expressions with the French.

1	un réseau social	a	a program/software
2	assister à	b	to surf (the web)
3	les nouvelles technologies	c	to attend
4	un logiciel	d	to hire
5	des écouteurs (m.)	e	a text
6	surfer	f	the new technologies
7	utiliser	g	online
8	un texto	h	to use
9	embaucher	i	a social network
10	en ligne	j	headphones

M   Complete the sentences using a word or phrase from the box in the correct position and form.

l'Internet   un texto   une souris   un clavier   le mot de passe   des écouteurs

1   J'ai _____ qwerty.
2   Quel est votre _____?
3   J'ai _____ sans fil.
4   Je suis accro à _____.
5   Souvent j'écoute de la musique
    avec _____.
6   Quand m'as-tu m'envoyé
    _____?

When discussing electronic messaging in French, people often use the English term, e-mail. You can use e-mail, mél or courriel. Depending on the country and even the age group, one of these terms might be preferred. You should check with French speakers you know or meet. Be aware that these terms and new technologies are in constant evolution.

 # Reading

N Read the first paragraph of the following online article and answer the questions.

   1 Quelles sont les différentes activités mentionnées que l'on fait sur les réseaux sociaux?

      _____

   2 De quoi les utilisateurs de réseaux sociaux doivent-ils se protéger?

      _____

 www.informatiqueactuelle.fr

TOUT LE MONDE EST CONNECTÉ

Depuis 2004, quand Facebook a vu le jour, la grande famille des réseaux sociaux ne cesse de se propager. Entre le fameux like, les amis faits, les photos à partager et les messages instantanés qui traversent le monde entier, de plus en plus de gens sont connectés et dans la vie privée et dans la vie professionnelle. Au travail, on passe des heures à répondre aux courriels, à se parler via Skype et à partager des documents sur le cloud (ce nuage qui n'en est pas un). Quels sont les avantages et les inconvénients de toutes ses connexions? A l'échelle de l'entreprise, on ne se demande plus si ce phénomène est positif ou négatif, on fait avec et on établit des règles d'usage. Toujours est-il qu'il faut penser aux utilisateurs, ces milliers de personnes qui utilisent leurs ordinateurs et qui doivent apprendre maintenant à se protéger et du piratage et parfois même de leur employeur.

O Now read the rest of the article and answer the questions.

 www.informatiqueactuelle.fr

De nos jours, une entreprise doit penser à mettre en place un système de communication entre employés et éventuellement entre ses employés et ses clients. Ceux-ci voient de plus en plus de travail après la fin de la journée officielle avec des courriels auxquels il faut répondre le soir et le week-end, tandis que ceux-là s'attendent avec impatience à avoir une réponse instantanée. Si la direction pense surtout à rendre le travail plus efficace, elle doit également assurer la protection des informations sensibles. Acheter et vendre en ligne exige des stratégies pour attirer, servir et garder ses clients et sécuriser les paiements. En même temps, l'entreprise doit soigner sa présence sur Internet et éviter la dégradation de l'image de l'entreprise.

Toutefois, il ne faut pas oublier l'employé, qui risquerait non seulement de ne plus arriver à faire la distinction entre la vie professionnelle et la vie privée, mais qui verrait aussi ses risques se multiplier. Si l'employeur peut limiter le temps passé sur les réseaux sociaux pour des raisons personnelles, il a pareillement accès à tous les mails envoyés depuis la messagerie électronique du bureau et peut facilement dépister les activités en ligne de ses employés. Effectivement, la cour d'appel à Orléans a validé le licenciement d'un salarié pour raison d'envoi de messages « grivois » dès 2008. De plus, trois salariés ont été licenciés en 2010 après avoir dénigré la hiérarchie dans un message privé. D'autres se verraient refuser un emploi à cause de leur profil sur un réseau social que ce soit en raison d'une photo compromettante ou une blague mal placée, on doit maintenant se méfier de ce que l'on poste en ligne.

Au bout du compte, il faut prendre en considération tous ces risques avec leurs bénéfices et se dire que si tout le monde est connecté, on doit se surveiller et surtout s'informer sur l'utilisation et la sécurité des réseaux sociaux. Après tout, qui n'est pas concerné?

1 A quelles fins une entreprise utilise-t-elle les réseaux sociaux? De quoi doit-elle se méfier?

_____

2 Quels sont les risques pour l'employé? _____

3 Quelle est la conclusion de l'article? _____

P **Highlight all the interrogative and demonstrative adjectives and pronouns in the article. Identify if they are adjectives or pronouns and if they are demonstrative or interrogative.**

Writing

Q **Write a response to the article in which you discuss your use of social media at work and outside of work (80–100 words). Include the following:**

- **ce que vous aimez/n'aimez pas sur les réseaux sociaux**
- **ce que vous faîtes tous les jours sur les réseaux sociaux**
- **ce que vous voudriez changer en ce qui concerne votre usage des réseaux sociaux**

_____

_____

_____

_____

_____

_____

_____

_____

_____

 Try looking up Francophone blogs of interest to you. Read them and see if you can post a reply. This would be great practice. Try to select blogs from credible sources. The downfall with online posts from individuals may be incorrect usage (grammar, spelling, etc.).

Self-check

Tick the box that matches your level of confidence.

1 = very confident　　　2 = need more practice　　　3 = not confident

Cochez la case qui correspond à votre niveau d'aisance.

1 = très sûr(e) de vous　　2 = j'ai besoin de plus
　　　　　　　　　　　　　　　de pratique　　　3 = pas sûr(e) du tout

	1	2	3
Ask questions using interrogative adverbs, adjectives and pronouns.			
Provide answers using demonstrative adjectives and pronouns.			
Write about social media and the workplace.			
Can understand texts that consist mainly of high frequency everyday or job-related language (CEFR A2).			
Can write about everyday aspects of his or her environment regarding such things as people, places and jobs (CEFR A2).			

6 On y va!

Let's go!

In this unit, you will learn how to:

- ✓ Use prepositions of time, place, function, cause and consequence.
- ✓ Use prepositional phrases.
- ✓ Use vocabulary related to travel.

CEFR: Can understand the description of events, feelings and wishes in a personal e-mail (B1); Can write personal e-mails describing experiences and impressions (B1).

Meaning and usage

Prepositions

1   A preposition is a word or group of words that links a noun, noun phrase or a pronoun to the rest of a sentence. **À**, **de**, **avec** and **sur** *(to, of, with* and *on)* are examples of prepositions.
    Je vais à Nice cet été. *(I am going to Nice this summer.)*
    Tu viens de Barcelone? *(You are from Barcelona?)*
    Nous partons au ski avec nos amis. *(We're going skiing with our friends.)*
    Elle a posé ses lunettes de soleil sur sa serviette de plage. *(She put her sunglasses on her beach towel.)*

2   Prepositions serve different purposes. They indicate such things as time, place, function, cause and consequence.

3   Some prepositions are single words, others are prepositional.
    Je vais travailler _à_ 8 heures. *(I am going to work _at_ 8 o'clock.)*
    Je vais travailler _jusqu'à_ 18 heures. *(I am going to work _until_ 6 o'clock.)*

4   Many prepositions in French have more than one meaning in English depending on their use, and there isn't always a one-to-one correlation. Sometimes a preposition is needed in French where there isn't one in English. Sometimes the preposition in English is one word, and the equivalent in French has more than one word, or vice versa.

A Underline the prepositions and translate them into English.

1 Elle avait tout préparé avant son départ, valises, passeport, billets d'avion, etc.

_____

2 Si elle y va sans son téléphone, je ne sais pas comment elle fera. _____

3 Ils ont pu changer leurs billets à la gare. _____

4 Tout le monde est exaspéré par les embouteillages. _____

5 Nous ne pourrons pas partir cet été à moins de pouvoir faire des économies. _____

6 Il a dû être hospitalisé à la suite d'un accident de voiture. _____

Single-word prepositions

À

1 À is sometimes translated as *at* or *to*. It is used with cities and islands, with time, with possession, with purpose and with price.
Nous arrivons à 15 heures. *(We arrive at 3 p.m.)*
Elle va à Paris. *(She is going to Paris.)*
Cette valise est à moi. *(This suitcase is mine.)*
Une cuillère à café, une brosse à dents. *(A teaspoon, a toothbrush.)*
Un billet d'avion à 200€. *(A €200 plane ticket.)*

Remember that **à** *is combined with definite articles as follows:*

masculine singular: **à + le = au**

masculine and feminine plural: **à + les = aux**

BUT not in the feminine singular or in the masculine singular before a vowel:

feminine singular: **à la**

masculine singular before a vowel: **à l'**

B Translate the sentences using a form of à.

1 Pierre leaves at ten tomorrow morning. _____

2 That red car is ours. _____

3 We are taking a cruise that starts in Barcelona. _____

4 They went to the theatre yesterday evening. _____

5 Did you go to the toilets in that bar? _____

6 Jean forgot his rucksack. _____

7 She is going to primary school this year. _____

8 He is looking for a car for €1000. _____

De

1   **De** generally means *from, of* or *about*. It is used to say where someone or something comes from, to express distance, to speak of contents or description, to indicate possession or belonging and means or manner. It is also necessary to use **de** after some verbs.

Ma mère vient de Nice. *(My mother comes from Nice.)*

La plage est à deux kilomètres d'ici. *(The beach is two kilometres from here.)*

Elle m'a servi une tasse de thé. *(She served me a cup of tea.)*

C'est la maison de Fakir. *(It's Fakir's house.)*

Qu'est-ce que tu penses de cette compagnie aérienne? *(What do you think of that airline?)*

2   Some impersonal expressions in French use **de**.

Il est bon d'étudier. *(It is good to study/Studying is good.)*

Il est facile de trouver l'aéroport. *(It's easy to find the airport.)*

*Remember that **de** is combined with definite articles as follows:*

masculine singular: **de** + **le** = **du**

masculine and feminine plural: **de** + **les** = **des**

BUT not in the feminine singular or in the masculine singular before a vowel:

feminine singular: **de la**

masculine singular before a vowel: **de l'**

*Also, make sure to differentiate between the two versions of **des** (**de** + **les**—a preposition plus a definite article, and the indefinite article **des**).*

Elles viennent des États-Unis. *(They come from the United States.)*

Il y a des taxis partout. *(There are taxis everywhere.)*

C   **Translate the sentences using a form of de.**

1   The train station is two kilometres from here. _____

2   It's Jennifer's suitcase. _____

3   The train from Paris arrived late. _____

4   They were all in the conference room when the boss arrived. _____

_____

5   There is a better way to go to Lyon. _____

6   You can recite that poem from memory? _____

7   They are the neighbour's friends. _____

8   That's the cat's water. _____

En and dans

1   **En** is used with lengths of time, with seasons or months, with means of transport, with places (without an article) and with some states, regions or countries. It can also be used to say what something is made from.

L'avion va entre Londres et Bruxelles en une heure et dix minutes.
(The plane goes from London to Brussels in one hour and ten minutes.)
Je vais y aller en avril. *(I will go there in April.)*
Claire et son mari feront le trajet en train. *(Claire and her husband will make the trip by train.)*
Tu vas en prison? *(You're going to prison?)*
J'ai envie d'aller en Égypte. *(I feel like going to Egypt.)*
Vous voyez cette chaise en bois? *(Do you see that wooden chair?)*

2 **Dans** is used with something that occurs within a decade, when something is going to happen, and to mean *in* with a location that is preceded by an article. It is also sometimes used with regions, especially with masculine American states.
Dans les années quatre-vingt-dix. *(In the 90s.)*
Elle partira dans deux heures. *(She'll leave in two hours.)*
Nous sommes dans la maison. *(We're in the house.)*
J'habite dans le Maine, aux États-Unis. *(I live in Maine, in the United States.)*

D Complete the sentences with **en or dans**.

1 Elles arriveront _____ cinq minutes.
2 Tu y vas _____ voiture?
3 Paul m'a appelé, il était déjà _____ l'avion.
4 Nous avons décidé de ne pas y aller _____ hiver, car il fait trop froid.
5 Cette chaise _____ plastique est de mauvaise qualité.
6 Il fait plus beau _____ le sud.

Sur and sous

1 **Sur** means *on* and **sous** means *under* or *beneath*.
Les billets sont sur la table. *(The tickets are on the table.)*
La valise est sous la chaise. *(The suitcase is under the chair.)*

2 Sometimes a different preposition from the French is used in the English translation.
Des nuages qui couraient <u>sur</u> un ciel très bleu. *(Clouds that were racing <u>across</u> a very blue sky.)*
Elle était <u>sous</u> la douche quand le téléphone a sonné. *(She was <u>in</u> the shower when the phone rang.)*

Sur and **dessus** *can both be translated as* on, *and* **sous** *and* **dessous** *can both be translated as* under *or* beneath. **Sur** *and* **sous** *are prepositions and must be followed by a noun.* **Dessus** *and* **dessous** *are adverbs and are used to modify verbs.*

E Complete the sentences using **sur or sous**.

1 Ne mettez pas les pieds _____ la chaise!
2 Je cherche ma montre. Je pensais l'avoir posée _____ la table de nuit à côté de la lampe.
3 Ils se sont embrassés _____ la pleine lune.
4 Vous avez perdu vos clés? Vous avez cherché _____ le canapé?
5 Le prix est marqué _____ ce tapis.
6 Nous nous sommes retrouvés _____ une pluie abondante.

*Use **pendant** to mean* for *when using the past tense.*

Il a voyagé en Chine pendant trois ans. *(He travelled in China for three years.)*

*Use **pour** to mean* for *in the future.*

Nous irons en vacances pour deux semaines. *(We'll go on holiday for two weeks.)*

Using prepositions with geographical names

Here is a useful table for knowing which preposition to use when referring to places:

Geographical location	to/in	from
a city or an island	à	de, d'
a feminine country, state, province or continent (usually ends in **-e**)	en	de, d'
a masculine country, state, province or continent	au	du
a masculine place that begins with a vowel	en	d'
a plural country or region	aux	des

*A small number of countries that end in **-e** are masculine. These are* **le Cambodge, le Mexique, le Mozambique, le Zaïre** *(now* **La République Démocratique du Congo***) and* **le Zimbabwe.**

F   Fill in the gaps with the appropriate preposition before the city or country.

1   Londres se trouve _____ Angleterre.
2   Vous êtes déjà allé _____ Mexique ? Moi, non.
3   La Tour Eiffel se trouve _____ Paris.
4   Vous êtes _____ Pays-Bas? J'aime beaucoup les Hollandais!
5   Elle va aller _____ États-Unis dans deux semaines.
6   Tu vas _____ Danemark? Tu as de la chance.
7   Nous passons des vacances _____ Irlande.
8   Sa copine est anglaise, elle vient _____ Londres.

Prepositional phrases

1   A preposition can consist of more than one word. In French this can be a combination of a preposition with an adverb or it can be a prepositional phrase.

G Match the preposition with the English.

1	à côté de	a	until, up until
2	en dessus de	b	thanks to
3	au dessous de	c	owing to / on account of
4	jusqu'à	d	before + verb + -ing
5	avant de + infinitive	e	for lack of
6	à cause de	f	around
7	grâce à	g	above, over
8	par suite de	h	underneath, beneath
9	faute de	i	next to
10	autour de	j	because of (when used before a noun)

Parce que and **à cause de** *both mean* because. **Parce que** *must be followed by a phrase including a subject and verb.* **A cause de** *is followed by a direct object and indicates a negative effect.* **Grâce à**, thanks to, *is also followed by a direct object, but with a positive effect.*

Nous voulons aller en France parce que nous étudions le français.
(We want to go to France because we are studying French.)

Il est parti à cause des enfants. *(He left because of the children.)*

Elle peut aller en Espagne grâce à une bourse. *(She can go to Spain thanks to a scholarship.)*

H Complete with the appropriate preposition.

1 _____ argent, ils n'ont pas pu partir en vacances cette année.
   a   En dessus d'   b   Par suite d'   c   Faute d'

2 Je dois me lever tôt ce matin _____ mon entretien à huit heures.
   a   faute de   b   à cause de   c   autour de

3 _____ aller en Chine, nous avons appris un peu la langue pour pouvoir nous exprimer une fois là-bas.
   a   Avant d'   b   Grâce à   c   À côté d'

4 Ils ont travaillé tard, _____ 21 heures!
   a   au dessous de   b   à cause de   c   jusqu'à

5 Nous avons mis notre petite valise dans le compartiment _____ nos têtes.
   a   autour de   b   par suite de   c   au dessus de

6 _____ un accident, ils ont dû faire un détour.
   a   Par suite d'   b   Autour d'   c   Avant d'

Vocabulary

I   **Use an expression from the box to complete the sentences.**

à l'aéroport	au guichet	la visite guidée	à la gare
le contrôleur	la place centrale	les congés payés	un visa

1   Pour prendre le train, on va _____.
2   Pour prendre l'avion, on va _____.
3   Pour acheter des billets de train, on va _____.
4   _____ passe dans le train et demande aux voyageurs de lui donner leur billets.
5   Pour mieux apprécier le musée, faites _____.
6   Il y a souvent une statue ou une fontaine au milieu de _____ de la ville.
7   En France, _____, ce sont cinq semaines de vacances accordées tous les ans.
8   Pour un séjour de plus de six mois en France, on a besoin d'_____.

J   **Match the French with the English.**

1	des chambres d'hôtel	a	a stay
2	un pays	b	to stay (somewhere)
3	un guide	c	a seaside resort
4	loger (quelque part)	d	body treatments/spa services
5	au bord de la mer	e	to reserve a room
6	une station balnéaire	f	swimming
7	des soins du corps	g	the welcome, the hospitality/to welcome
8	réserver une chambre	h	to clean
9	des baignades	i	by the sea/at the seaside
10	l'accueil/accueillir	j	hotel rooms
11	un séjour	k	a tour guide
12	nettoyer	l	a country

# Reading

K   Your friend Sophie has written you an email to let you know about a recent trip. Read the first paragraph and answer this question:

Est-ce que Sophie a trouvé que c'était un pays dangereux? Pourquoi ou pourquoi pas?

De:	Sophie
À:	Toi
Sujet:	Mon voyage

Bonjour! Après avoir passé deux semaines au Maroc, je peux dire que j'adore ce pays et j'ai envie d'y retourner aussi vite que possible. Pendant quatre jours, j'ai visité la ville de Marrakech au sud du pays. Le premier jour, j'avais un peu peur de sortir dans les rues. C'était tellement bruyant, il y avait du monde partout. Avant de partir, j'avais entendu dire que c'est une ville dangereuse, surtout pour les femmes. Il n'en était rien! J'ai évité les endroits sans trop de monde et j'ai pris un guide qui n'a pas coûté trop d'argent. Il m'a accompagnée partout et il était très charmant.

L   Now, read the rest of the message and answer the questions in French.

En plein milieu de la Médina, j'ai déjeuné dans un vieux restaurant. On m'a servi un tagine au poulet et aux olives vertes inoubliable, c'était tellement bon. Le restaurant s'appelle La Table du Palais et il se trouve dans un vieux palais qui a aussi des chambres d'hôtel. La prochaine fois que je passerai à Marrakech, je vais y loger. Toutefois, il fallait quitter la ville après un court séjour pour descendre plus au sud où j'avais réservé une chambre dans un spa au bord de la mer.

J'ai été bien accueillie à mon arrivée à la station balnéaire à Agadir. Très contente de me retrouver dans ce paradis loin de l'agitation de la ville, j'ai vite décompressé en m'offrant des massages, des soins du corps et des baignades. L'hôtel était élégant et surtout très propre. Le personnel était toujours à l'écoute des clients, je n'ai manqué de rien pendant tout mon séjour. La seule fausse note: on venait trop souvent nettoyer la chambre, presque cinq fois par jour et pas toujours à l'heure à laquelle on voulait être interrompue.

La douceur du climat, le soleil exceptionnel, l'accueil chaleureux des Marocains, tout a contribué à me ressourcer au fond de mon être. N'est-ce pas la raison pour laquelle on part en voyage?

Grosses bises !

Sophie

1 Où est-ce que Sophie est partie en vacances? _____
   _____

2 Qu'est-ce que Sophie a fait à Marrakech? _____
   _____

3 Où a-t-elle mangé ? Qu'est-ce qu'elle y a mangé ? _____
   _____

4 Où est-elle allée après Marrakech ? Qu'est-ce qu'elle y a fait? _____
   _____

5 A-t-elle aimé son hôtel à Agadir? _____
   _____

6 Retournera-t-elle au Maroc? Pourquoi ou pourquoi pas? _____
   _____

M **Find the prepositions in the email and explain their meaning from the context.**

Writing

N **Write an e-mail to a friend about the last trip you took. Put in as many details as possible about where you went, what you did and what you saw. (80–100 words)**

_____

_____

_____

_____

_____

_____

_____

_____

_____

_____

_____

_____

_____

_____

Self-check

Tick the box that matches your level of confidence.

1 = very confident   2 = need more practice   3 = not confident

Cochez la case qui correspond à votre niveau d'aisance.

1 = très sûr(e)   2 = j'ai besoin de plus   3 = pas sûr(e) du tout
     de vous   de pratique

	1	2	3
Use prepositions of time, place, function, cause and consequence.			
Use prepositional phrases.			
Use vocabulary related to travel.			
Can understand the description of events, feelings and wishes in a personal email (CEFR B1).			
Can write personal emails describing experiences and impressions (CEFR B1).			

7 Qu'est-ce qu'on mange?

What shall we eat?

In this unit, you will learn how to:

- ✅ Use relative pronouns.
- ✅ Use relative pronouns with prepositions.
- ✅ Form more complex sentences and avoid repetition.
- ✅ Understand and use vocabulary related to food, meals and restaurants.

CEFR: Can read and understand a cultural text about food and drink (A2); Can write about one's own culture and traditions (B1).

Meaning and usage

Relative pronouns

1 A relative pronoun is a word that introduces a relative clause, a part of a sentence that refers back to something already stated. It serves to avoid repetition and can elaborate on something or give more detail. It often translates as *who, which* or *that*.

Nous allons à un restaurant _que_ nous aimons beaucoup.
(We are going to a restaurant that we like a lot.)
C'est son ami Henri, _qui_ aime manger. *(It is her friend Henri who likes to eat.)*

2 In English, the relative pronoun can sometimes be omitted, but not in French.
Le repas _que_ j'ai mangé était excellent. *(The meal [that] I ate was excellent.)*

3 In the **passé composé**, when the direct object of a sentence comes before the past participle, it agrees in gender and number with the direct object.
La bouteille de vin _que_ j'ai achetée était bouchonnée.
(The bottle of wine [that] I bought was corked.)

 Que *is shortened to* **qu'** *before a vowel, but* **qui** *is never shortened.* **Qui** *and* **que** *do not automatically translate to* who *and* what. *Their use is dependent on the role they serve in the sentence, and these words are not always relative pronouns.*

 A Compare the two sentences. Can you say why one uses the relative pronoun que and the other uses qui?

La pomme que Charles a mangée était rouge. *(The apple that Charles ate was red.)*

Où est la pomme qui était sur la table? *(Where is the apple that was on the table?)*

Choosing between qui and que
qui + verb
que + subject + verb

B Which of the following examples of **qui** and **que** are relative pronouns?

1 Qui n'aime pas les pâtes? *(Who doesn't like pasta?)*
2 Les gens qui n'aiment pas les pâtes sont bizarres. *(People who don't like pasta are strange.)*
3 Il n'y a pas beaucoup de choses que je n'aime pas manger. *(There's not a lot that I don't like to eat.)*
4 Il n'aime que la pizza et le poulet. *(He doesn't like anything other than pizza and chicken.)*
5 Elle a mangé un steak qui avait l'air trop cuit à mon avis. *(She ate a steak that looked overcooked, in my opinion.)*
6 Le pot-au-feu qu'il a mangé était trop salé. *(The beef stew that he ate was too salty.)*

C Use **qui** or **que** to complete the sentences. Underline where there is agreement.

1 La réservation _____ nous avons faite pour ce restaurant italien était pour 20 heures.
2 C'est un restaurant _____ fait parler de lui dans la presse.
3 Le garçon _____ nous a servi au restaurant n'était pas trop aimable.
4 Les autres clients, _____ étaient nombreux hier soir, avaient l'air de bien aimer leur serveur.
5 Mes pâtes étaient trop cuites et la viande pas assez! Le chef _____ les avait préparées ne devait pas avoir fait attention.
6 Par contre, la salade et la pizza _____ tu as commandées avaient l'air bonnes!
7 Je sais _____ tu voudrais y retourner, mais moi, je ne suis pas sûr.

D Combine the two sentences using **qui** or **que** to form one sentence and avoid repetition. Underline to show agreement where necessary.

1 Mes amis vont à un restaurant. Ce restaurant coûte très cher.
   <u>Mes amis vont à un restaurant qui coûte très cher.</u>
2 C'est un gâteau en forme de bûche. Nous mangeons ce gâteau pour le réveillon de Noël.
   _____
3 J'ai commandé un café. J'ai bu le café.
   _____
4 J'ai parlé avec des amis. Mes amis avaient envie de sortir prendre un pot.
   _____
5 Elle a aimé ce vin. Ce vin date de l'année 2010.
   _____
6 Tu n'as pas aimé la quiche? Tu as commandé la quiche?
   _____

Relative pronouns with prepositions

1   When a verb takes a preposition, the preposition is placed before the relative pronoun.
    J'ai de l'admiration pour ce chef. *(I admire that chef.)*
    C'est un chef *pour qui* j'ai de l'admiration. *(That's a chef <u>that</u> I admire [lit.: <u>for</u> <u>whom</u> I have admiration].)*

2   If the object of the preposition is a thing, **que** becomes preposition + **lequel** (or one of its derivatives **laquelle, lesquels, lesquelles**).
    C'est le couteau <u>avec lequel</u> il aime couper la viande. *(It's the knife <u>with which</u> he likes to cut meat.)*
    La cuisine de ma tante est trop épicée. C'est la raison *pour laquelle* je ne l'aime pas. *(My aunt's cooking is too spicy. That's why [lit.: that's the reason <u>for which</u>] I don't like it.)*

3   If the preposition is **de** after a verb, use the relative pronoun **dont**.
    parler de:
    C'est le restaurant *dont* je t'*ai parlé*. *(That's the restaurant I told you about.)*
    avoir besoin de:
    C'est le supermarché *dont* nous *avons besoin*. *(That's the supermarket that we need.)*

4   If the preposition is **dans** or **au**, use **où**.
    C'est le café *où* elle prend le petit déjeuner presque tous les jours. *(That's the café <u>where</u> she has breakfast almost every day.)*
    Comment s'appelle la ville *où* se trouve ce restaurant? *(What's the name of the city <u>where</u> that restaurant is?)*

5   Remember that **lequel** and its forms, **laquelle, lesquels, lesquelles** agree in gender and number with the objects they replace.
    Remember also that when **lequel** is combined with the prepositions **à** or **de**, contractions may be necessary, as shown.

 *The relative pronoun **lequel** and its derivatives, **laquelle, lesquels** and **lesquelles**, do not usually refer to people. If the object of the preposition is human, use the relative pronoun **qui** along with the preposition.*

Le musée <u>auquel</u> nous sommes allés hier était excellent. (The museum we went to yesterday was excellent.)

BUT

L'homme <u>avec qui</u> j'ai parlé hier était très grand. (The man with whom I spoke yesterday was very tall.)

	With *à*	With *de*
Masculine singular	auquel	duquel
Feminine singular	à laquelle	de laquelle
Masculine plural	auxquels	desquels
Feminine plural	auxquelles	desquelles

La femme <u>à laquelle</u> j'ai parlé me semblait charmante. *(The woman <u>to whom</u> I spoke seemed charming.)*

Vous ne savez pas <u>desquels</u> il parle. *(You don't know <u>which ones</u> he is talking about.)*

Les restaurants <u>auxquels</u> j'ai téléphoné n'avaient pas de tables pour ce soir-là. *(The restaurants <u>that</u> I called didn't have any tables for that evening.)*

E   Read the text and underline the relative pronouns.

Quand j'étais petite, j'aimais beaucoup le homard. Mes parents, qui aimaient bien sortir au restaurant, n'avaient pas vraiment beaucoup d'argent. Cependant, à chaque fois qu'on sortait, je posais toujours la question, « Papa? S'il te plaît papa, je peux commander le homard? » Il me répondait toujours, « Ça dépend. Voyons voir le prix que le serveur va nous annoncer. » Et puis j'attendais le serveur à qui je demandais le prix du homard ce jour-là. S'il nous disait un prix pas trop élevé, je pouvais le commander, sinon, il fallait choisir autre chose, ce qui me faisait toujours attendre les sorties au restaurant avec impatience, mais non sans une certaine inquiétude. Mon frère, par contre, ne voulait que commander un hamburger et des frites sur lesquelles il déversait une montagne de ketchup.

F   Complete with an appropriate relative pronoun.

1   S'il y a une sorte de cuisine _____ je n'aime pas, c'est la cuisine chinoise.
   a   qui   **b**   que   **c**   dont   **d**   où

2   La personne _____ je mange le plus souvent, c'est mon copain.
   a   à qui   **b**   auquel   **c**   avec qui   **d**   de laquelle

3   Le restaurant _____ je trouve romantique, c'est celui où je vais souvent avec ma femme.
   a   qui   **b**   que   **c**   auquel   **d**   ce qui

4   Ce restaurant _____ on nous a parlé hier a une étoile Michelin.
   a   qui   **b**   auquel   **c**   dont   **d**   ce que

5   La personne _____ fait le plus souvent à manger chez moi, c'est mon mari.
   a   qui   **b**   que   **c**   auquel   **d**   où

6   Le chef _____ j'ai parlé après le repas était vraiment fantastique!

   a   qui   **b**   avec qui   **c**   où   **d**   auquel

Indefinite relative pronouns

1   When a phrase has no antecedent, meaning a complete idea or phrase before it, use **ce** before the relative pronoun: **ce qui**, **ce que**, **ce dont** (all of which mean *what* in English). When the object of the preposition is anything other than **de** or **lequel**, use **quoi**. **Quiconque** is used rarely, mostly in legal or formal French and serves as the subject of the relative clause it introduces. **Quiconque** translates as *whoever, whomever, whosoever* or *anyone who*.

   Ce que j'aime, ce sont les desserts au chocolat. *(What I like are chocolate desserts.)*

Nous ne savons pas <u>ce qui</u> se passe. *(We don't know what's going on.)*

<u>Ce dont</u> tu as besoin, c'est d'un bon repas, d'un bon bain et puis d'aller au lit de bonne heure. *(What you need is a good meal, a good bath and then to go to bed early.)*

Ils avaient parlé de plusieurs restaurants possibles. Je ne sais pas <u>lequel</u> ils ont choisi pour ce soir. *(They had spoken about several possible restaurants. I don't know which one they chose for tonight.)*

Voilà <u>à quoi</u> il s'intéresse. *(This/That is what interests him.)*

G Complete the text with the appropriate relative pronoun in the box. Make sure it agrees in gender and number.

ce qu'	ce que	ce dont	pour lesquels	avec qui	à qui

Nous n'avons pas beaucoup d'amis **(1)** _____ nous aimons prendre le dîner ou que nous invitons à manger chez nous. Les uns sont trop difficiles et n'aiment pas manger **(2)** _____ nous mangeons. Les autres, **(3)** _____ la cuisine n'est pas importante, ne font pas attention à **(4)** _____ on a préparé pour eux ou bien ils veulent tout le temps sortir dans de mauvais restaurants. **(5)** _____ j'aurais vraiment envie, ce serait des amis **(6)** _____ je pourrais téléphoner à l'improviste, qui seraient ravis que je les invite et qui mangeraient tout avec plaisir.

Vocabulary

H Here are some useful questions for ordering in a French restaurant. Translate them into English.

1 Je voudrais réserver une table pour quatre personnes pour samedi soir, à l'intérieur si possible. _____

2 Vous avez choisi? Qu'est-ce que vous voulez commander? _____

3 Qu'est-ce que vous recommandez? _____

4 Je peux vous servir quelque chose à boire? _____

5 Et pour commencer, qu'est-ce que vous voulez comme entrée? _____

6 Je voudrais le steak cuit à point, s'il vous plaît. _____

7 L'addition, s'il vous plaît. _____

8 Le service, est-il compris? _____

I   Look at the menu and then write a conversation between you and your server to order the meal of your choice.

Restaurant La Grenouillère

Les entrées

Potage de légumes

Carottes râpées vinaigrette

Céleri rémoulade

Poireaux vinaigrette

Salade de tomates

Salade frisée aux lardons

Salade verte mélangée

Bloc de foie gras de canard

Terrine de campagne

Six escargots

Les plats

Bar rôti au fenouil

Pavé de rumsteck grillé, frites

Tartare de bœuf assaisonné, frites

Poulet fermier rôti, frites

Andouillette grillée, moutarde

Côte d'agneau grillée, frites

Faux filet grillé maître d'hôtel

Tête de veau sauce gribiche

Choucroute alsacienne

Confit de canard, pommes de terre nouvelles

Les fromages

Bleu d'auvergne

Camembert

Fromage de chèvre

Pont-l'évêque

Les desserts

Baba au rhum, chantilly

Délice au chocolat, crème anglaise

Compote de pommes

Coupe Mont Blanc (crème de marron chantilly)

Pruneaux au vin, glace vanille

Pêche melba

Prix fixe: choix d'une entrée + un plat + un fromage ou un dessert 34€

_____

_____

_____

_____

_____

_____

_____

_____

_____

_____

_____

J Match the French with the English.

1	déjeuner	a	to savour or enjoy eating
2	dîner	b	a main course
3	grignoter	c	to have lunch
4	déguster	d	a drink
5	un hors d'œuvre ou un amuse-bouche	e	to munch (on something)
		f	appetite
6	une boisson	g	a dessert
7	une entrée	h	an appetizer or nibbles
8	un plat	i	to have dinner
9	un dessert	j	a first course
10	l'appétit		

Reading

K Read the first paragraph of this article on the French tradition of the apéritif. Indicate if the following statements are V (**vrai**/true) or F (**faux**/false).

1 L'apéritif se prend après le repas.   V/F

2 L'amuse-bouche est toujours quelque chose de compliqué.   V/F

L'APÉRO

En France, si l'on vous invite à déjeuner ou à diner, on ne se met pas en général à table tout de suite. Effectivement, avant l'entrée, le plat, les fromages et le dessert, on prend d'habitude l'apéritif, ou l'apéro. En général, c'est quelque chose de simple à boire et quelque chose à grignoter que l'on prend au salon ou dans le jardin s'il fait beau.

L Now, read the rest of the article and answer the questions.

Comme son nom l'indique, c'est pour faire venir l'appétit. Les choix des boissons varient selon la saison, la région et l'occasion, allant du champagne au pastis en passant par les vins de noix ou de fruits, le martini (une marque de vermouth rouge ou blanc), la bière, le soda et le whisky.

Il ne faut pas oublier la consommation de nourriture qui constitue un élément important de l'apéritif. Ce que l'on prend d'habitude, ce sont des petits amuse-bouches qui se mangent avec les doigts. Chips, olives, cacahuètes, rien de plus simple. Dans le sud de le France, on retrouve souvent la tapenade, un mélange d'olives noires ou vertes, anchois, câpres, ail et huile d'olive servi avec des rondelles de baguette ce qui ne donne pas envie d'embrasser son voisin à moins qu'il en ait dégusté, lui aussi!

Véritable signe du savoir-vivre français, l'apéritif est une activité largement partagée au sein de la société française. C'est une occasion de se retrouver en famille ou entre amis pour partager un verre, voire même deux, avant de s'installer à table. La conversation peut varier entre l'actualité, la politique, la vie de tous les jours, mais il est important que tout le monde puisse y participer. C'est un moment agréable où les hôtes reçoivent leurs invités et qui met le ton à l'après-midi ou à la soirée.

---

1   Pourquoi les gens servent-ils l'apéritif?
     _____

2   Quelles sont les boissons typiques de l'apéro? Parmi ces boissons, lesquelles aimez-vous?
     Lesquelles n'aimez-vous pas? Y en a-t-il que vous ne connaissez pas?
     _____

3   A votre avis, pourquoi les amuse-bouches se prennent normalement avec les doigts?
     _____

Writing

M   **There are likely to be some traditions in your family and in your region. Write a blog post
     in which you describe the importance of food in your daily life and for family celebrations.
     (80–100 words)**

     _____

     _____

     _____

     _____

     _____

     _____

Self-check

Tick the box that matches your level of confidence.

   1 = very confident   2 = need more practice   3 = not confident

Cochez la case qui correspond à votre niveau d'aisance.

   1 = très sûr(e) de vous   2 = j'ai besoin de plus de pratique   3 = pas sûr(e) du tout

	1	2	3
Can use relative pronouns.			
Can use relative pronouns with prepositions.			
Can understand and use vocabulary related to food, meals and restaurants.			
Can read and understand a cultural text about food and drink (CEFR A2).			
Can write about one's own culture and traditions (CEFR B1).			

8 Métro, boulot, dodo
The rat race

In this unit, you will learn how to:

✓ Use present tense verbs.

✓ Use negation.

CEFR: Can write about familiar matters having to do with work (A2); Can understand texts that consist of mainly high frequency everyday or job-related language. (B1).

Meaning and usage

The present tense

1   The present tense in French is similar to English. It is used to express actions and situations that are currently happening.

Je cherche un travail, donc je lis les petites annonces. *(I am looking for a job, so I am reading the classified ads.)*

 A   If je cherche *(I am looking for)* **is the present tense form for the first person singular (je) for the verb chercher** *(to look for),* **what would the equivalent be for these verbs?**

    1   parler _____

    2   marcher _____

    3   voyager _____

2   The present tense can be used to indicate a habitual action.

Tous les jours, je me lève tôt, parce que le trajet pour aller au boulot me prend plus d'une heure. *(Every day, I get up early, because the commute to get to work takes me over an hour.)*

3   The present tense is used to indicate absolute truth.

La terre est ronde. *(The earth is round.)*

4   In French there is no literal equivalent for *is* or *does*, as in *he is studying* or *he does study*, so the present tense in French has three English equivalents:

Il étudie le français.   { *(He is studying French.)*
                              (He studies French.)
                              (He does study French.)

How to form the present tense

Regular verbs

1   French verbs are classified into three main types according to the ending of the infinitive: **-er**, **-ir** and **-re**. To form the present tense of regular verbs, remove the **-er**, **-ir** or **-re** and add the personal ending of the noun to the stem of the verb.

Subject pronoun	Gagner *(to earn or win)*	Réussir *(to succeed)*	Perdre *(to lose)*
je	gagn-e	réuss-is	perd-s
tu	gagn-es	réuss-is	perd-s
il/elle/on	gagn-e	réuss-it	perd
nous	gagn-ons	réuss-issons	perd-ons
vous	gagn-ez	réuss-issez	perd-ez
ils/elles	gagn-ent	réuss-issent	perd-ent

Stem-changing verbs

1   Some verbs undergo changes in the stem. Verbs ending in **-cer** and **-ger** change the stem in the **nous** and **vous** forms for pronunciation reasons to maintain the soft 'c' and soft 'g' sounds.

Commencer *(to begin)*		Manger *(to eat)*	
je commenc-e	nous commenç-ons	je mang-e	nous mang-eons
tu commenc-es	vous commenç-ez	tu mang-es	vous mang-ez
il/elle/on commenc-e	ils/elles commenc-ent	il/elle/on mang-e	ils/elles mang-ent

2   Verbs ending in **-ayer** have an optional stem change, so there are two possible acceptable ways to conjugate these verbs.

B   **Consider the following two options for the conjugation of the verb payer. What are the differences? What stays the same?**

Payer *(to pay)*			
je pay-e	nous pay-ons	je pai-e	nous pay-ons
tu pay-es	vous pay-ez	tu pai-es	vous pay-ez
il/elle/on pay-e	ils/elles pay-ent	il/elle/on pai-e	ils/elles pai-ent

These two sets of conjugations are equally acceptable for verbs like **payer**. Other common verbs of this type include **balayer** *(to sweep)*, **effrayer** *(to frighten)* and **essayer** *(to try)*.

3   Verbs ending in **-oyer** and **-uyer** are conjugated with the same endings as regular **-er** verbs, but with a change to the stem.

C Compare the conjugation of **tutoyer** and **appuyer** with the regular -er verb conjugation. What is different for these verbs? What stays the same?

Tutoyer (to use the informal tu)		Appuyer (to lean, press)	
je tutoi-e	nous tutoy-ons	j'appui-e	nous appuy-ons
tu tutoi-es	vous tutoy-ez	tu appui-es	vous appuy-ez
il/elle/on tutoi-e	ils/elles tutoi-ent	il/elle/on appui-e	ils/elles appui-ent

 *The verbs **tutoyer** (to use **tu**) and **vouvoyer** (to use **vous**) do not have direct translations in English because the distinction between the informal **tu** and formal **vous** does not exist. Use **tu** with friends, family, children and animals and **vous** with people you don't know or with people like your boss to show respect. When you meet someone, start by using the **vous** form. Once you are more familiar, you can say, **Est-ce qu'on peut se tutoyer?** (Can we use **tu** with each other?)*

4 Some verbs, like **appeler**, double the consonant. Others, like **acheter** change the accent. In both cases, the changes are made for pronunciation purposes and the endings remain the same as for regular verbs.

 D Look at the table. Which forms of **appeler** have a double ll? Which forms of **acheter** add an accent? From what you know about their pronunciation, what makes these different?

Appeler (to call)		Acheter (to buy)	
j'appell-e	nous appel-ons	j'achèt-e	nous achet-ons
tu appell-es	vous appel-ez	tu achèt-es	vous achet-ez
il/elle/on appell-e	ils/elles appell-ent	il/elle/on achèt-e	ils/elles achèt-ent

5 Verbs like **considérer** (to consider), **compléter** (to complete), **espérer** (to hope), **régler** (to settle), etc., also have a stem change, where the -**é** before the ending changes to an -**è** in the je, tu, il/elle/on and ils/elles forms.

E Using this rule, conjugate the verb **préférer**.

Préférer (to prefer)	
1 je _____	4 nous _____
2 tu _____	5 vous _____
3 il/elle/on _____	6 ils/elles _____

 F Some verbs are called 'boot' verbs because of the changes in spelling and accents. Outline the forms of the verbs **appeler**, **acheter** and **préférer** that have stem changes. Which forms are part of the boot?

G Complete the sentences with the correct form of the verb in brackets.

1 Il _____ (agacer) ces collègues avec toutes ses questions.
2 Tu _____ (vouvoyer) le PDG (le président-directeur général).
3 Pour ce nouveau poste, nous _____ (déménager) en Europe.
4 Elles _____ (diriger) cette entreprise depuis 2016.
5 Vous _____ (envoyer) des CV.
6 Le patron _____ (ennuyer) ses employés avec ces histoires interminables.
7 Elle _____ (essayer) un nouveau logiciel de design.
8 Je/J' _____ (espérer) avoir des nouvelles sur mon nouvel emploi.

Irregular verbs

1 Some verbs do not follow the pattern of regular verbs and so are called irregular. Here are some of the most common irregular verbs in the present tense:

Subject pronoun	Aller *(to go)*	Avoir *(to have)*	Connaître *(to know)*	Être *(to be)*	Faire *(to do/make)*	Savoir *(to know)*	Venir* *(to come)*
je/j'	vais	ai	connais	suis	fais	sais	viens
tu	vas	as	connais	es	fais	sais	viens
il/elle/on	vait	a	connaît	est	fait	sait	vient
nous	allons	avons	connaissons	sommes	faisons	savons	venons
vous	allez	avez	connaissez	êtes	faites	savez	venez
ils/elles	vont	ont	connaissent	sont	font	savent	viennent

*__Devenir__ *(to become)*, __revenir__ *(to come back)* and __tenir__ *(to hold)* are conjugated like __venir__ *(to come)*. Be sure to note other irregular verbs as you come across them.

__Savoir__ *and* __connaître__ *both mean to know.* __Savoir__ *is used for knowing facts, things that are memorized or abilities.* __Connaître__ *is used for people and places and connotes familiarity.*

__Je sais la date de votre anniversaire.__ *(I know your birthdate.)*

__Vous connaissez son amie Julie?__ *(Do you know her friend Julie?)*

Special uses of the present

1 __Être en train de__ + infinitive
Since there is no real distinction in French between the notions of *he studies* and *he is studying* (right now), the expression __être en train de__ followed by an infinitive can be used to say that someone is currently in the process of doing the action.

__Il est en train d'étudier.__ *(He is studying [right now].)*

2 **Aller** + infinitive

   Actions that are going to take place in the near future can be expressed by using the verb **aller** in the present followed by an infinitive (the English equivalent of *going to* + infinitive).

   Elle va démissionner parce qu'elle a trouvé un nouvel emploi. *(She is going to quit because she found a new job.)*

3 **Venir de** + infinitive

   Venir *(in the present)* **de** followed by an infinitive can be used to describe an action that was just completed. This is referred to as the 'recent past'.

   Elle vient d'être embauchée par une nouvelle entreprise. *(She was just hired by a new company.)*

4 The present is used with certain expressions to indicate duration.

   Il y a dix ans que je travaille pour cette entreprise. *(It's been ten years that I have been working for this company.)*

   Ça fait trois mois qu'il est au chômage. *(He has been unemployed for three months.)*

H **Complete the sentences with the correct form of the verb in brackets.**

   1 Nous _____ (être) en retard pour la réunion.

   2 Elles _____ (faire) toujours des fautes d'orthographe dans leurs e-mails.

   3 Je _____ (aller) au travail en vélo tous les jours.

   4 Elle _____ (venir) de compléter 30 ans de service.

   5 Qu'est-ce que vous _____ (aller) faire pour les vacances?

   6 Il _____ (avoir) un diplôme en économie.

   7 Tu _____ (savoir) comment faire marcher cette imprimante?

   8 Vous _____ (aller) sortir comme ça?

   9 Elle _____ (être) très bonne en maths.

   10 Il _____ (connaître) beaucoup de monde, il est très bien connecté.

Negation

I **Look at the two sentences and indicate the elements that make the second one negative.**

   Elle regarde son écran. *(She is looking at her screen.)*

   Elle ne regarde pas son écran. *(She isn't looking at her screen.)*

1 To make a basic sentence negative in French, you add **ne … pas** around the verb.

   Elle ne travaille pas aujourd'hui. *(She is not working today./She doesn't work today.)*

2 **Ne** changes to **n'** before a vowel.

   Il n'a pas le numéro. *(He doesn't have the number.)*

Pas *can sometimes be used alone to make a negative statement.*

Pas du tout. *(Not at all.)* **Pas souvent!** *(Not often!)* **Pas beaucoup!** *(Not a lot!)*

In spoken French, **ne** *is often left out.*

Je sais pas! *(I don't know!)*

3 There are many other expressions that can be used to make sentences negative. Compare the following:

Affirmative statement	Negative statement
Il aime le travail. *(He likes work.)*	Il n'aime pas le travail. *(He doesn't like work.)*
Elle a un stylo. *(She has a pen.)*	Elle n'a pas de stylo. *(She doesn't have a pen.)*
Ils sont déjà arrivés. *(They already arrived.)*	Ils ne sont pas encore arrivés. *(They haven't arrived yet.)*
Tu as encore du travail à faire. *(You still have work to do.)*	Tu n'as plus de travail à faire. *(You don't have any more work to do.)*
Nous oublions tout. *(We forget everything.)*	Nous n'oublions rien. *(We don't forget anything.)*
Vous gardez quelque chose. *(You are keeping something.)*	Vous ne gardez rien. *(You aren't keeping anything./You don't keep anything.)*
Vous embauchez quelqu'un. *(You are hiring someone.)*	Vous n'embauchez personne. *(You aren't hiring anyone.)*
Elle voit tout le monde. *(She sees everyone.)*	Elle ne voit personne. *(She sees no one.)*
Elle m'appelle souvent au bureau. *(She often calls me at the office.)*	Elle ne m'appelle guère au bureau. *(She hardly ever calls me at the office.)*
Elle m'appelle toujours au boulot. *(She always calls me at work.)*	Elle ne m'appelle jamais au boulot. *(She never calls me at work.)*
Ils sont parfois en retard. *(They are sometimes late.)*	Ils ne sont jamais en retard. *(They are never late.)*
Vous voulez le vert et le bleu. *(You want the green one and the blue one.)*	Vous ne voulez ni le vert ni le bleu. *(You want neither the green one nor the blue one.)*
Ils sont partout. *(They are everywhere.)*	Ils ne sont nulle part. *(They are nowhere.)*
Ils sont quelque part. *(They are somewhere.)*	Ils ne sont nulle part. *(They are nowhere.)*

4 **Personne**, **rien** and **aucun** are negative pronouns and can be used as the subject of a sentence, the object of a sentence or with a preposition as the indirect object of a sentence.
Personne n'est là. *(No one is there.)*
Je ne vois personnne. *(I don't see anyone.)*
Tu ne parles à personne. *(You aren't speaking to anyone.)*
Rien n'est important. *(Nothing is important.)*
Elle ne fait rien. *(She isn't doing anything.)*
Je ne pense à rien. *(I'm thinking about nothing.)*
Aucun must agree in gender and number with the noun it is representing.
Aucun des films ne m'intéresse. *(None of the movies interest me.)*
Je n'ai reçu aucune lettre de lui. *(I didn't receive any letter from him.)*

J **Complete the sentence with the missing word. There's a hint in brackets.**

1 On ne paye _____ assez les employés. (never)
2 Je ne comprends _____ le travail des ingénieurs. (hardly)
3 Malheureusement, le patron n'est _____ là. (not)
4 Ils font la grève parce qu'ils ne veulent _____ travailler le dimanche. (no longer)
5 Les salariés ne comprennent _____ à la vie des ouvriers. (nothing)
6 _____ n'a de l'argent pour le projet. (no one/nobody)
7 Il cherche du travail, mais il ne trouve _____. (nothing)
8 Je cherche l'imprimante. Je ne la trouve _____. (nowhere)

You disagree! Use a different negative expression to answer each of the questions.

1 Est-ce que c'est possible d'aimer son travail? Non, _____.

_____

2 Les patrons, pensent-ils aux conditions de travail des ouvriers? Non, _____.

_____

3 Pouvez-vous faire des heures supplémentaires? _____.

_____

4 Vous êtes au chômage? Qu'est-ce que vous faites tous les jours? Non, _____.

_____

5 Est-ce qu'on doit être poli avec tout le monde? Non, _____.

_____

6 Est-ce qu'il faut toujours dire la vérité? Non, _____.

_____

Negation with questions

1 You can use the expression **n'est-ce pas?** to negate a statement and make it into a question.
Vous aimez bien votre nouveau travail, n'est-ce pas? *(You like your new job, don't you?)*
C'est difficile, n'est-ce pas? *(It's difficult, isn't it?)*

2 For questions using **est-ce que**, follow the regular rules.
Est-ce que tu ne veux pas travailler? *(Do you not want to work?)*
Est-ce qu'elle n'aime jamais le travail? *(Does she never like work?)*

3 With inversion, put the negative expression before and after the inverted verb and subject.
Ne veux-tu pas travailler? *(Do you not want to work?)*
N'aime-t-elle jamais le travail? *(Does she never like work?)*

To say *yes* to a negative question, use **si.**
Tu ne sais pas quoi faire? *(You don't know what to do?)*
Si, je sais quoi faire. *(Yes, I know what to do.)*

L **Match the question with the answer.**

1 Ne vas-tu pas venir à la réunion?   a Non, je ne les oublie pas.
2 Est-ce qu'elles ne sortent pas le soir?   b Si, tout le monde est là de bonne heure.
3 Personne ne vient au bureau tôt le matin?   c Parce qu'elle n'a rien dans la tête.
4 Ne faites-vous rien d'intéressant au travail? d Si, je vais venir à la réunion.
5 Ne fait-il rien de la journée?   e Si, je l'écris.
6 Pourquoi n'arrive-t-elle guère à s'organiser? f Pas souvent, elles ont trop de travail.
7 N'oubliez-vous pas les dossiers?   g Non, rien.
8 N'écris-tu pas le rapport?   h Non, il est paresseux.

Vocabulary

Languages often borrow expressions from one another. In French, the abbreviation **CV** *is used, it comes from the Latin* curriculum vitae. *English loan words are common in French.* **Un meeting** *is commonly used for* **une réunion.** **Un job** *is also used but is informal. In virtually all cases, the borrowed word is masculine.*

Here is a list of additional useful vocabulary for discussing work.

faire des études	*to study*	**un PDG**	*a CEO*
un stage	*an internship*	**un salaire**	*a salary*
un stagiaire	*an intern*	**un cadre**	*a manager*
une demande d'emploi	*a job application*	**être renvoyé**	*to be fired*
des débouchés (m.)	*the job opportunities*	**le chômage**	*unemployment*
l'entretien	*the interview*	**être au chômage**	*to be unemployed*
remplir un formulaire	*to fill out a form*	**prendre sa retraite**	*to retire*
un poste	*a position*	**un retraité**	*a [AmE] retiree, [BrE] pensioner*
un métier	*an occupation/trade*	**un jour férié**	*a bank holiday*
une formation	*job training*	**un congé**	*a holiday*
une affaire (f.)	*a transaction*	**un congé payé**	*a paid holiday*
gagner sa vie	*to earn a living*	**des vacances**	*the vacation/holiday*
faire (la) grève	*to go on strike*	**embaucher**	*to hire*

Être licencié *has more than one meaning: to be fired or laid off, to be licensed or to have an undergraduate degree. It is most commonly used to mean to be laid off. If used to say that one has an undergraduate degree, it is typically followed by the preposition* **en** *and a discipline:* **Claire est licenciée en biologie.** *(Claire has a degree in biology.)*

M **Find the odd one out.**

1 la formation | le congé | les vacances | le jour férié
2 être renvoyé | être licencié | travailler | être au chômage
3 la retraite | l'apprenti | le stagiaire | le PDG
4 le retraité | l'ouvrier | le salarié | l'employé

Reading

N Read the first paragraph of a story about Sylvie's job then answer the questions.

    1 Où est-ce que Sylvie travaille? _____

    2 Est-ce qu'elle aime son travail? Pourquoi ou pourquoi pas? _____

> Sylvie travaille pour une compagnie indépendante de production de films. Ça fait trois ans qu'elle y travaille. Elle aime beaucoup son travail parce que ce n'est jamais la routine comme dans d'autres boulots et elle adore le cinéma. De plus, elle aime bien ses collègues avec qui elle passe beaucoup de temps.

O Now read the rest of the story. Indicate if the following statements are V (**vrai**/true) or F (**faux**/false). If the statements are **false**, correct them.

> C'est un travail qui change selon les besoins de l'entreprise et chaque jour elle doit faire quelque chose de nouveau. Un jour elle travaille dans son bureau: elle organise les réunions entre les réalisateurs, les producteurs et les monteurs. Le jour suivant elle rencontre des stars et gère les employés qui s'occupent d'elles. Parfois, elle voyage pour chercher un site pour le tournage d'un film. C'est un travail fatigant et ce n'est pas toujours facile, mais c'est loin d'être embêtant.
>
> Cependant, Sylvie ne gagne pas bien sa vie. Son petit salaire ne lui permet pas de vivre comme elle le voudrait. Ses collègues sont d'accord avec elle, ils ne savent pas s'ils vont pouvoir trouver une meilleure situation ailleurs. Elle est en train de remettre son CV à jour pour l'envoyer à de plus grosses boîtes. Sylvie est ambitieuse et travailleuse. Régulièrement, elle sort tard du travail et souvent, elle se retrouve au boulot même le week-end. Elle économise quand elle le peut, mais c'est difficile comme elle ne gagne pas grand-chose. Elle aime beaucoup voyager à l'étranger mais c'est presque impossible sans congés ni argent. Alors, elle espère se trouver un autre emploi car elle ne tient pas à devoir encore être obligée de travailler quand il sera l'âge de prendre sa retraite.

1	She manages everyone in the office.	V/F
2	Her job is easy and boring.	V/F
3	She is updating her CV because she found a new job that interests her.	V/F
4	She is ambitious and hard working.	V/F
5	She often gets out of work late and works often at the weekend.	V/F
6	She has been able to save a lot of money.	V/F

P   Find the eight regular verbs that were used in this text. The English equivalents are listed to help you. Complete the table with the missing infinitives.

French infinitive	English infinitive	French infinitive	English infinitive
1 _____	to work	5 _____	to take care of
2 _____	to like	6 _____	to earn
3 _____	to organize	7 _____	to end up
4 _____	to meet	8 _____	to save

Q   Four stem-changing verbs were used in the text. Complete the table with the missing infinitives.

French infinitive	English infinitive	French infinitive	English infinitive
1 _____	to manage	3 _____	to travel
2 _____	to send	4 _____	to hope

✎ Writing

R   Describe your work life using the present tense. Try to include as much information as possible using a variety of verbs. (80–100 words)

_____

_____

_____

_____

_____

_____

_____

 Have you given any thought to this unit's title? **Métro, boulot, dodo** *is a commonly used expression referring to one's daily routine of* **métro** *(underground train),* **boulot** *(job),* **dodo** *(sleep). Native speakers use it to mean something halfway between the drudgery of commuting long hours and the rat race, but it is always a commentary on the negative aspects of suburban life.*

Self-check

Tick the box that matches your level of confidence.

1 – very confident   2 = need more practice   3 = not confident

Cochez la case qui correspond à votre niveau d'aisance.

1 = très sûr(e) de vous   2 = j'ai besoin de plus de pratique   3 = pas sûr(e) du tout

	1	2	3
Use present tense verbs.			
Use negation.			
Can write about familiar matters having to do with work (CEFR A2).			
Can understand texts that consist of mainly high frequency everyday or job-related language. (CEFR B1).			

9 Il pleut à verse

It's pouring rain

In this unit, you will learn how to:

✅ Understand and use impersonal verbal expressions.

✅ Understand and use modal verbs.

CEFR: Can describe the climate and weather and express preferences about them (A2); Can recognize significant points in straightforward weather reports (B1).

Meaning and usage

Impersonal verbal expressions

1   The impersonal pronoun **il** is used when an expression in French has no agent, meaning there is no actual subject of a sentence. It is called impersonal because there is no real subject. The verb in these expressions is always conjugated in the third person singular no matter what tense is used.

 A   **Look at the title of this unit, Il pleut à verse. The pronoun il is the subject. What does il refer to?**

2   Verbs used to express weather conditions in French require an impersonal subject and can't be conjugated with anything other than **il**.

geler *(to freeze)*	**Il gèle.** *(It's freezing.)*
grêler *(to sleet)*	**Il grêle.** *(It's sleeting.)*
neiger *(to snow)*	**Il neige.** *(It's snowing.)*
pleuvoir *(to rain)*	**Il pleut.** *(It's raining.)*

3 Other weather conditions can be expressed in French using the verb **faire** in an impersonal manner. Here again, the pronoun **il** does not refer to a person or thing.

Quel temps fait-il? *(What is the weather like?)*	**Il fait gris.** *(It's grey.)*
Il fait beau. *(It's nice.)*	**Il fait du soleil.** *(It's sunny.)*
Il fait mauvais. *(It's not nice.)*	**Il fait du vent.** *(It's windy.)*
Il fait chaud. *(It's hot.)*	**Il fait sec.** *(It's dry.)*
Il fait froid. *(It's cold.)*	**Il fait humide.** *(It's humid.)*

B **Join the two phrases to make a logical statement about the weather. For some items, more than one answer is possible.**

1 Il fait beau _____
2 Il neige _____
3 Il fait gris _____
4 Il fait du soleil _____
5 Il fait très chaud _____
6 Il pleut aujourd'hui _____

a et il fait du vent, restons chez nous aujourd'hui.
b mais ça va, j'ai mon parapluie.
c alors allons à la plage pour nous rafraîchir.
d mais pas trop mauvais quand même.
e et il n'y a pas un seul nuage.
f et le ciel bleu est magnifique!

4 The expression **Il y a** can be followed by a noun or by an expression of time.

Il y a des cerisiers en fleurs au printemps. *(There are cherry trees in blossom in the spring.)*
Il y a un an que j'ai fait du ski dans les Pyrénées! *(I skied in the Pyrenees a year ago!)*
Ça fait can be used to express how long ago something happened or has been happening:
Ça fait trois ans que nous sommes amis. *(It has been three years that we've been friends.)*
Ça fait longtemps qu'on n'a pas eu de neige. *(It's been a long time since it snowed.)*

5 **Ce/C'/Cela** can be used this way as well:

Ce n'est pas important. *(It's not important.)*
C'est beau. *(It's beautiful.)*
Cela est vrai. *(It's true.)*

6 Like **faire**, some other personal verbs can be used in impersonal constructions while some verbs can only be used that way. Here are some additional impersonal verbal expressions:

s'agir de *(to be about)*	**Il s'agit d'un énorme ouragan.** *(It's about a huge hurricane.)*
arriver *(to happen, to be a possibility)*	**Il est arrivé un accident.** *(An accident happened.)*
convenir *(to be advisable)*	**Il convient d'être vigilant.** *(It is advisable to be vigilant.)*
se faire *(to become)*	**Il se fait beau dehors.** *(It's starting to be nice outside.)*
importer* *(to be important, to matter)*	**Il importe qu'il le fasse.** *(It is important that he do it.)*
falloir *(to be necessary, to have to)*	**Il faut que nous sortions.** *(We have to go out.)*
paraître *(to appear)*	**Il paraît qu'il fera chaud.** *(It appears it will be hot.)*
se passer *(to happen)*	**Il se passe quelque chose.** *(Something is happening.)*
sembler* *(to seem)*	**Il semble qu'il fasse beau.** *(It seems that it's nice out.)*
suffire de/que* *(to suffice)*	**Il suffit d'un peu de soleil.** *(A little sun is enough.)*
se trouver *(to be, to happen to be)*	**Il se trouve toujours une foule.** *(There is always a crowd.)*
valoir mieux* *(to be better)*	**Il vaut mieux que tu le fasses.** *(It's better if you do it.)*

Some of these expressions must be followed by a verb in the subjunctive because they indicate an opinion or a doubt; they are indicated with an asterisk.

C **Pick an impersonal verbal expression from the box to complete the sentences. For some items, more than one answer might be correct.**

il faut	il s'agit	il paraît	il arrive	il vaut mieux
il se trouve	il y a	il importe	il suffit	il convient

1 _____ qu'il le fasse.
2 _____ de regarder la télévision pour savoir la météo.
3 _____ que vous notiez le temps avant de vous habiller le matin.
4 _____ qu'il va neiger, la température baisse.
5 _____ qu'un orage éclate d'un coup.
6 _____ de noter qu'on assiste à un réchauffement climatique.
7 _____ bien fermer toutes les fenêtres, il va faire froid ce soir.
8 Dans ce film, _____ d'un couple qui passe toute une année dehors sous tous les temps.
9 _____ très longtemps que je n'ai pas vu d'arc-en-ciel, pourtant ce n'est pas rare après la pluie.
10 _____ toujours des gens qui n'apprécient pas beaucoup la chaleur.

D **Which of the verbs from C can be used both personally and impersonally? Which ones cannot? Make two lists using the infinitive of these verbs.**

Personally	Impersonally

Modal verbs

1 A modal verb expresses possibility, desirability, will or obligation. French has fewer modal verbs than English. English has modal verbs such as *shall, will, might, can, ought to, must* and *to be able to,* and they are not conjugated. French has just three verbs used this way: **vouloir**, **devoir** and **pouvoir**, but they are conjugated and all three are irregular. Contrary to English usage, French does not use modal verbs to say that something will happen in the future.

2 **Vouloir** expresses desire and is practically a command when used in the present. It can be followed by an infinitive or by a noun.
Je veux du soleil. *(I want the sun.)*
Je veux bronzer. *(I want to suntan.)*

3 Here are the forms of **vouloir** in the present, the imperfect and the **passé composé**:

Present	
je veux	nous voulons
tu veux	vous voulez
il/elle/on veut	ils/elles veulent

Imperfect	
je voulais	nous voulions
tu voulais	vous vouliez
il/elle/on voulait	ils/elles voulaient

Passé composé	
j'ai voulu	nous avons voulu
tu as voulu	vous avez voulu
il/elle/on a voulu	ils/elles ont voulu

4 **Devoir** has multiple meanings and can express obligation, probability or supposition. When followed by a noun, it means *to owe*.

Elle doit aller au marché. *(She has to go to the market./She is supposed to go to the market.)*

Tu devrais mettre un pull, il fait froid. *(You should put on a jumper, it is cold outside.)*

Nous devions partir un peu plus tôt pour éviter la canicule.

(We were supposed to leave early to avoid the heatwave.)

Il lui doit dix euros. *(He owes him ten euros.)*

5 When used in the imperfect, **devoir** roughly translates as *was supposed to*. In the **passé composé**, or past perfect, it is *to have to* or *must have*. For *should have* or *would have*, use **devoir** in the conditional perfect.

Il devait partir vers dix heures ce matin. *(He was supposed to leave at 10 o'clock this morning.)*

Nous avons dû rentrer, il faisait trop froid dehors.

(We had to come back in, it was too cold outside.)

Il a dû pleuvoir cette nuit. *(It must have rained last night.)*

Il devait pleuvoir cette nuit. *(It was supposed to rain last night.)*

Elle aurait dû vous appeler, vous êtes sûr que le téléphone n'a pas sonné?

(She should have called you, are you sure the telephone didn't ring?)

6 Here are the forms of **devoir** in the present, the imperfect and the **passé composé**:

Present	
je dois	nous devons
tu dois	vous devez
il/elle doit	ils/elles doivent

Imperfect	
je devais	nous devions
tu devais	vous deviez
il/elle devait	ils/elles devaient

Passé composé	
j'ai dû	nous avons dû
tu as dû	vous avez dû
il/elle a dû	ils/elles ont dû

It might sometimes be confusing to tell when you should use **falloir** *or* **devoir**. **Falloir** *is stronger and indicates that something must be done.* **Devoir** *can be used to say that something should be done, is supposed to be done, or needs to be done.*

Il faut aller au travail pour gagner de l'argent. *(You must go to work to make money.)*

Il doit aller au travail ce week-end pour des heures supplémentaires.
(He has to go to work this weekend to do overtime.)

Il doit partir pour aller au travail maintenant. *(He has to [should] leave to go to work now.)*

7 **Pouvoir** means *to be able to do something*. It can also mean that one has the physical ability or the permission to do something.
   Est-ce que je peux venir avec vous? *(Can I come with you?)*
8 If you wish to translate *could* in the present into French, use **pouvoir** in the conditional. To say you could do something in the past, use the imperfect. To say it was not possible for you to do something in the past, use the **passé composé**.
   Elle pourrait y aller si elle le voulait. *(She could go if she wanted to.)*
   Il pouvait le faire facilement. *(He could do it easily.)*
   Il n'a pas pu sortir, il avait trop à faire. *(He wasn't able to go out, he had too much to do.)*

9   Here are the forms of **pouvoir** in the present, the imperfect and the **passé composé**:

Present	
je peux	nous pouvons
tu peux	vous pouvez
il/elle/on peut	ils/elles peuvent

Imperfect	
je pouvais	nous pouvions
tu pouvais	vous pouviez
il/elle/on pouvait	ils/elles pouvaient

Passé composé	
j'ai pu	nous avons pu
tu as pu	vous avez pu
il/elle/on a pu	ils/elles ont pu

E   **Complete the conversations with the correct form of vouloir, devoir or pouvoir to form logical sentences.**

Eugène: Dis donc, il fait froid aujourd'hui. Tu **(1)** _____ sortir au restaurant ce soir ou rester à la maison?

Pauline: Il fait tellement froid que je ne **(2)** _____ pas imaginer sortir, et toi?

Charlotte: Vous **(3)** _____ bien fermer la fenêtre? Il y a trop de vent.

Patrick: Est-ce que je **(4)** _____ le faire tout de suite? Je suis un peu occupé.

Dominique: Quelle heure est-il? Ne **(5)** _____-nous pas rentrer? Il commence à faire nuit.

Frédérik: Je ne sais pas, mais nous **(6)** _____ rentrer quand vous **(7)** _____.

Jeanne: Les filles ne **(8)** _____ pas aller chez leur grand-mère demain, elles **(9)** _____ faire leurs devoirs.

Charles: Qu'est-ce que nous **(10)** _____ dire à ma mère? Elle va être déçue.

10 Other than these verbs, there are other ways to express modality in French. Sometimes you need to use a particular verb, sometimes conjugate it in a particular tense and sometimes you can use an adverb.

To say *may* or *might* in French, you can use **peut-être** or **se pouvoir** with the subjunctive.
J'irai peut-être lui parler. *(I may/might speak to him.)*
Il se peut qu'elle vienne. *(She might come.)*
In French, *shall* and *will* are expressed using the future tense. *Shall have* and *will have* use the future perfect.

J'arriverai avant huit heures. *(I shall/will arrive before 8 o'clock.)*
Elle sera partie avant nous. *(She shall have/will have left before us.)*

To say *would have* in French, use the conditional perfect.
Nous aurions voulu aller à son concert. *(We would have wanted to go to his concert.)*

F Translate the following expressions into English.

1 Elle ne veut pas sortir, il fait trop mauvais. _____

2 Nous irons nous balader cet après-midi. _____

3 Jeanne ne peut pas nager. Elle n'a jamais appris. _____

4 Vous voulez aller à la plage sous cette pluie? Vous êtes fous. _____
_____

5 Souleymane a voulu nous rejoindre, mais il a raté son train. _____
_____

6 Tu as dû l'aimer beaucoup. _____

7 Qui devait venir vous aider? _____

8 Il lui doit combien? £100? C'est beaucoup, non? _____

Vocabulary

G Find the odd one out.

1 l'hiver | le printemps | le vent | l'automne
2 la pluie | la neige | le verglas | l'arc-en-ciel
3 le mois | la saison | le froid | le jour
4 les averses | le ciel dégagé | le soleil | le beau temps

Reading

H Read the first part of the weather forecast and answer the question.

Est-ce qu'il fait plus froid en France que d'habitude à cette époque? _____

---

le 25 décembre

Bulletin météorologique du vendredi 25 décembre

Aujourd'hui, le temps reste dans les normes pour la fin du mois de décembre. Le ciel sera couvert sur la moitié nord de l'Hexagone avec du brouillard de la Franche-Comté à la région Nord-Pas-de-Calais de même que sur les Midi-Pyrénées et l'Aquitaine. Attention au verglas sur ces régions ; après la neige, dans les hauteurs surtout, il va geler.

I   **Now continue reading and answer the questions.**

Sur la côte est allant de la Bretagne jusqu'en Aquitaine, on continue de voir des inondations dû aux intempéries de ces derniers jours, mais les perturbations se sont arrêtées et il règne maintenant un temps paisible dans cette partie du pays où il fait beau mais froid. Par ailleurs, il fait du soleil dans le quart sud-est du pays. Quant aux températures, elles varient entre 7 degrés et moins 4. Cet après-midi, il fera 2 degrés à Lille, 3 à Paris ainsi qu'à Strasbourg, 5 à Bordeaux, 6 degrés à Nice et 7 degrés à Ajaccio.

Demain, on peut s'attendre à une continuation de ce temps relativement calme. Certes, il y aura encore quelques précipitations surtout entre le Massif Central et les Alpes. Le matin, on retrouvera un temps gris avec des brouillards sur la majeure partie du pays, sauf sur la Méditerranée ou il fera encore du soleil avec des températures agréables. L'après-midi dans les régions de l'ouest et du sud-ouest il y aura une bonne évolution vers un temps ensoleillé par rapport au temps gris du matin. Par contre dans le nord, les grisailles ne se dégageront pas de la journée. Pour ce qui est des températures, toujours relativement douces près de la Méditerranée et proches de la normale, voire légèrement au-dessus dans la plupart du pays, notamment dans le sud.

1   Où est-ce qu'il va y avoir du verglas? Pourquoi? _____
2   Où et pourquoi y a-t-il eu des inondations? _____
3   Dans quelle partie de la France est-ce qu'il fait beau? _____
4   Où fait-il le plus froid? Le moins froid ? _____
5   Quel temps fera-t-il demain? _____

J   **Find all the impersonal and modal verbs in the text. List them and give the infinitives.**

_____
_____

Vocabulary

K   Categorize the weather expressions in the text into two columns, one for good weather, one for bad weather.

Beau temps	Mauvais temps

Writing

L   What is the weather like in the town where you live? Write an email to a person who lives in another country describing the climate in all its seasons and say which is your favourite and why. (100–120 words)

De:

À:

Sujet:

Self-check

Tick the box that matches your level of confidence.

1 = very confident   2 = need more practice   3 = not confident

Cochez la case qui correspond à votre niveau d'aisance.

1 = très sûr(e) de vous   2 = j'ai besoin de plus   3 = pas sûr(e) du tout
de pratique

	1	2	3
Understand and use impersonal verbal expressions.			
Understand and use modal verbs.			
Can describe the climate and weather and express preferences about them (CEFR A2).			
Can recognize significant points in straightforward weather reports (CEFR B1).			

10 Le shopping sera plus facile à l'avenir?

Will shopping be easier in the future?

In this unit, you will learn how to:

- ✅ Express future plans.
- ✅ Form the future tense.

CEFR: Can understand a blog post about the future of shopping (B1); Can write about personal shopping habits and preferences (B1).

Présent Je fais les courses. ⟩ **Futur proche** Je vais faire les courses. ⟩ **Futur** Je ferai les courses.

Meaning and usage

The future

There are several ways to express the future in French.

1 French has a construction to refer to an action in the near future that is the same as the English *to be going (to do something)*. It is called the *near future* or **futur proche** and is used to refer to something that will be happening soon.

   Je vais aller avec vous au supermarché. *(I am going to go with you to the supermarket.)*

   Tu vas sortir avec eux? *(Are you going to go out with them?)*

2 The *future* tense, or **futur simple** in French, is used to express intention and to refer to an action that will take place after the point in time of speaking. It is the equivalent of *will + infinitive* in English:

   Nous irons au marché ce samedi. *(We will go to the market this Saturday.)*

   Ahmed achètera un cadeau pour sa mère. *(Ahmed will buy a gift for his mother.)*

3 The future tense can also be used to make predictions, to say something might happen, and to state something will happen because of or in spite of current circumstances.

   Nous irons peut-être la semaine prochaine. *(We will probably/might go next week.)*

   Elle fera du shopping demain malgré les foules.

   (She will go shopping tomorrow in spite of the crowds.)

4 Expressions such as **croire que**, **espérer que**, **penser que**, **savoir que**, **ne pas savoir si** can be followed by either the present or the future tense:

   Je crois qu'elle vient. *(I think she is coming/will come.)*

   Je crois qu'elle viendra. *(I think she is coming/will come.)*

5 The future can also be used to express a command or order.

Tu feras tes devoirs! *(You will do your homework!)*

Georges ne conduira pas tout seul! *(Georges will not drive alone!)*

6 In French, the future is used both before and after expressions of time such as **au moment où**, **dès que, lorsque** and **quand**:

Elle sortira dès qu'il sera arrivé. *(She'll go out as soon as he arrives.)*

Nous ferons la lessive pendant que tu feras les courses.

(We'll do the laundry while you do the shopping.)

7 In sentences with **si**, the present + the future tense indicate that something is likely to happen:

Si elle a le temps, elle ira faire du shopping. *(If she has the time, she'll go shopping.)*

Claire passera à la caisse si elle trouve ce dont elle a besoin.

(Claire will go to the cash register if she finds what she needs.)

Be sure to distinguish between will *as used to express the future and the verb* **vouloir**, *which translates as* will *when it infers willingness.*

Je lui parlerai demain. *(I will talk to him tomorrow.)*

Voulez-vous me téléphonez ce soir? *(Will you/Are you willing to call me tomorrow?)*

A **Explain why the future tense is used in these sentences.**

1 Elle ira demain.

Reason: _____

2 Tu penses qu'ils viendront ?

Reason: _____

3 Si tu me le dis à l'avance, j'essaierai d'être là.

Reason: _____

4 Nous irons peut-être leur rendre visite.

Reason: _____

5 Vous irez au marché quand ils y seront?

Reason: _____

6 Tu rangeras ta chambre avant de sortir!

Reason: _____

How to form the future tense

Regular verbs

1 The future tense, or **futur simple**, is formed by using the root from the infinitive and adding the relevant future ending.

The following table shows the future tense forms of three common regular verbs.

Subject pronoun	Parler	Choisir	Attendre
je/j'	parlerai	choisirai	attendrai
tu	parleras	choisiras	attendras
il/elle/on	parlera	choisira	attendra
nous	parlerons	choisirons	attendrons
vous	parlerez	choisirez	attendrez
ils/elles	parleront	choisiront	attendront

Note that with regular verbs ending in **-re**, the final **-e** is dropped before adding the future endings.

2   Some regular verbs have spelling changes. Verbs that end in **-eler** and **-eter** double the **l** or **t**. Verbs that end in **-yer** change the **y** to **i**, though that change is optional for verbs that end in **-ayer**. Verbs like **acheter** have an **accent grave** on the e.
Il ficellera vos paquets. *(He'll tie up your packages.)*
Elle jettera ses reçus à la poubelle. *(She will throw her receipts in the bin.)*
Tu appuieras sur le bouton pour passer ta commande.
(You will push the button to complete your order.)
J'achèterai des chaussures. *(I will buy some shoes.)*

If you observe the endings for the future tense you will notice that they are the same as for the present tense of the verb **avoir: -ai, -as, -a, -avons, -avez, -ont.** *This is an easy way to remember the endings.*

B   Rewrite these sentences using the **futur proche** and then again in the **futur simple**.

1   Nous faisons les courses. _____

_____

2   Tu ne veux pas aller au supermarché. _____

_____

3   Vous choisissez vos vêtements la veille au soir. _____

_____

4   Ils multiplient leurs efforts. _____

_____

5   Je vais chez l'épicier acheter des fruits. _____

_____

6   Elle passe à la caisse pour régler ses achats. _____

_____

7   Vous payez par chèque ou en liquide? _____

_____

8   Nous achetons une voiture neuve. _____

_____

Irregular verbs

1   A number of verbs have irregular future forms, but the endings are the same as those of regular verbs. The following are the most common:

Infinitive	Future stem	First person singular form
avoir	aur-	j'aurai
aller	ir-	j'irai
courir	courr-	je courrai
devoir	devr-	je devrai
envoyer	enverr-	j'enverrai
être	ser-	je serai
faire	fer-	je ferai
falloir	faudr-	il faudra
mourir	mourr-	je mourrai
pleuvoir	pleuvr-	il pleuvra
pouvoir	pourr-	je pourrai
recevoir	recevr-	je recevrai
savoir	saur-	je saurai
tenir	tiendr-	je tiendrai
venir	viendr-	je viendrai
voir	verr-	je verrai
vouloir	voudr-	je voudrai

 Note that the verbs **pleuvoir** *(to rain) and* **falloir** *(to have to, to be necessary to) can only be conjugated with the impersonal subject pronoun* **il**.

 C   Look at the irregular verbs in the previous table and answer the following questions.

1   Which verbs drop the **-ir** from the infinitive and double the **r** before the future ending?

_____

2   Which verbs are completely irregular? _____

D   Use the following words to form sentences in the future. Say what will happen in the future for people to be healthier and happier.

1   (aller à la gym demain matin/je) _____

2   (sortir seulement le vendredi soir/mes amis et moi) _____

3   (ne pas manger trop/tu) _____

4   (arrêter de boire des boissons sucrées/elle) _____

5   (appeler sa mère le dimanche/il) _____

6 (quitter le travail à une heure raisonnable/je) _____

7 (dépenser moins en vêtements/il) _____

8 (se lever plus tôt/elles) _____

E Philippe and Jean are discussing possible plans for the coming weekend. Use the verbs in brackets in the future to complete the sentences.

1 **Philippe:** Dis-moi Jean, que _____ (faire)-vous ce week-end?

2 **Jean:** Si c'est moi qui décide, j'_____ (avoir) envie de rester à la maison, mais ma femme veut sortir.

3 **Philippe:** La mienne aussi. Nous _____ (aller) faire des courses samedi matin, mais nous _____ (être) disponibles l'après-midi et dans la soirée.

4 **Jean:** Vous pourriez venir dîner chez nous si ma femme est d'accord. Vous _____ (venir) vers 19 heures?

5 **Philippe:** Tu es sûr? Ma femme _____ (être) ravie! Nous aimerions tous les deux pouvoir vous voir.

6 **Jean:** Oui oui, j'en suis sûr, je _____ (voir) avec elle et je _____ (rappeler) plus tard pour confirmer, d'accord?

Vocabulary

F Match the French time phrases with the English.

1	la veille	**a**	right away
2	demain matin	**b**	next week
3	la semaine prochaine	**c**	the following weekend
4	le week-end d'après	**d**	in three months
5	tout de suite	**e**	the day before
6	dans trois mois	**f**	tomorrow morning

G Here is a list of places where you can go to buy certain things. Match the places from the box with the items. Use a dictionary to look up any new words if needed.

la pharmacie	l'épicerie	la banque	la bijouterie
le kiosque à journaux	l'opticien	l'horloger	la librairie

1 des lunettes _____

2 un magazine _____

3 de l'argent _____

4 une montre _____

5 des enveloppes _____

6 des boucles d'oreille _____

7 des pansements _____

8 une pomme _____

 # Reading

H Read the first paragraph of the article on the future of shopping and answer the question in the article's title.

Le shopping sera plus facile à l'avenir?

Pour ceux qui n'aiment ni faire la queue, ni passer un temps interminable dans les rayons à la recherche du lait de soja, ni renvoyer par la poste pour la énième fois un pantalon qui ne va pas, il y a de bonnes nouvelles. Le shopping de l'avenir sera très différent. Entre téléphones mobiles de plus en plus connectés et magasins équipés des dernières technologies, nous entrons dans une ère où la vente au détail se fera de façon plus rapide, plus simple et plus personnalisée.

I Now continue reading and answer the questions in French.

Des études démontrent bien que les clients recherchent avant tout la rapidité dans les achats. C'est la raison pour laquelle les magasins ayant des points de vente physiques ne fermeront pas bientôt leurs portes. Effectivement, si l'on peut monter dans sa voiture et acheter ce que l'on désire en une heure de temps, on est content d'avoir son blouson, ses baskets ou sa robe à mettre le soir même. À l'avenir, on pourra entrer dans un magasin et se connecter avec un clic. Par ailleurs, les réseaux sociaux ont un réel pouvoir dans les décisions des clients, une tendance qui ira croissant dans les années à venir. Que le client veuille faire son shopping chez lui sur Internet ou en magasin, les entreprises auront besoin d'améliorer la communication et le marketing afin de mieux façonner l'expérience du client et d'assurer les achats futurs.

Dans tout ceci, ce que l'on redoutera avant tout, ce sera la fraude à distance, l'usurpation d'identité et le manque de confidentialité. Inévitablement, nous aurons besoin de partager nos informations personnelles pour pouvoir effectuer des achats par carte bancaire que ce soit en magasin ou en ligne et de nouvelles formes de paiement par téléphone mobile sont en voie de développement. Dans les situations où le distributeur gardera nos coordonnées et l'histoire de nos commandes, les banques de données auront besoin d'une protection de plus en plus vigilante. Toujours est-il que le consommateur devra rester attentif à sa propre sécurité. L'évolution du shopping vers de nouvelles technologies et de nouvelles formes d'expérience ne fait pas de doute, mais ne se fera pas sans danger.

1 En quoi le shopping sera-t-il différent à l'avenir?

_____

2 Qu'est-ce que les clients recherchent avant tout?

_____

3 Pourquoi dit-on que les magasins ne fermeront plus bientôt leurs portes?

_____

4 Quels sont les risques des nouvelles technologies?

_____

Vocabulary

J Match the synonyms from the article. Look up any words that you do not know.

1	acheter	**a**	le consommateur
2	l'avenir	**b**	la sécurité
3	en ligne	**c**	un point de vente
4	le client	**d**	les achats
5	un magasin	**e**	le futur
6	la protection	**f**	sur Internet
7	les commandes	**g**	faire du shopping

K Find the opposites of these expressions. They are all in the article.

1 danger _____

2 déconnecté _____

3 négligent _____

4 le vendeur _____

Some French verbs can be used as nouns. **Pouvoir,** _for example, when used as a noun means_ power _and_ **devoir** _means_ duty.

Leur pouvoir d'achat ne cesse d'augmenter. _(Their buying power hasn't stopped growing.)_

Voter est un devoir de tous les citoyens. _(Voting is a duty of all citizens.)_

# Writing

L   How do you generally do your shopping? Do you shop online or in shops? What kinds of items do you usually buy? How do you think this will be different for you in the future? Write a blog post on this topic. [100–120 words]

_____

_____

_____

_____

_____

_____

_____

_____

_____

_____

Self-check

Tick the box that matches your level of confidence.

    1 = very confident   2 = need more practice   3 = not confident

Cochez la case qui correspond à votre niveau d'aisance.

    1 = très sûr(e) de vous   2 = j'ai besoin de plus de pratique   3 = pas sûr(e) du tout

	1	2	3
Express future plans.			
Form the future tense.			
Can understand a blog post about the future of shopping (CEFR B1).			
Can write about personal shopping habits and preferences (CEFR B1).			

11 N'oubliez pas de faire vos tâches ménagères!

Don't forget to do your chores!

In this unit, you will learn how to:

✓ Give commands and instructions using the imperative.

✓ Use the imperative with pronouns.

CEFR: Can understand simple user instructions for equipment (A2); Can describe how to do something giving detailed instructions (B1).

Meaning and usage

The imperative

1   The *imperative*, or **impératif**, is a verb form used to express commands, instructions or suggestions. It is one of four moods in French (the indicative, the conditional and the subjunctive are the others).
    Range ta chambre. *(Clean your room.)*
    Faites votre lit tous les jours. *(Make your bed every day.)*
    Allons faire les commissions. *(Let's go grocery shopping.)*

 A   **Look again at the three examples. How is this form different from other verb conjugations in French?**

2   The imperative is quite direct. You can add **s'il te plaît** or **s'il vous plaît** *(please)* to make it sound more polite or you can use the conditional.
    S'il te plaît, donne à manger au chat. *(Please feed the cat.)*

    Pourrais-tu donner à manger au chat? *(Could you feed the cat?)*

How to form the imperative

The imperative has just three forms: **tu**, **nous** and **vous**. This is because you can't give orders or directions to yourself, him, her or them.

1   To form the imperative, take the present tense form of the verb and drop the subject pronouns.

finir (*to finish*)	
Present	Imperative
tu finis	finis
vous finissez	finissez
nous finissons	finissons

2 For verbs that have an infinitive ending in **-er**, drop the **-s** in the **tu** form.

Mange des pommes. *(Eat some apples.)*

This also applies to **-ir** verbs conjugated like **-er** verbs such as **ouvrir** *(to open)* and **offrir** *(to offer).*

Offre un cadeau. *(Offer a gift.)*

Ouvre la bouteille de Champagne. *(Open the bottle of Champagne.)*

However, when followed by the object pronouns **y** or **en**, the **-s** stays. This is for pronunciation purposes.

Mange des pommes. *(Eat some apples.)*   **Manges-en.** *(Eat some.)*

*Don't forget **aller** (to go) has an infinitive ending in **-er**, so it is formed like other **-er** verbs.*

Va au supermarché *(Go to the supermarket.)*

Vas-y! *(Go there!/Go on!)*

B **Decide which form of the imperative of the verb laver (to wash) you would use in these situations and why.**

    1 An adult tells the new cleaning lady to wash the kitchen floor. _____

    2 A brother wants to clean the bathroom with his sister. _____

    3 A parent tells her daughter to wash her clothes. _____

In spoken French, the present sometimes replaces the imperative.

Tu me passes le sel, s'il te plaît? *(Can you pass the salt, please?)*

Imperative of irregular verbs

1 Expressions like **sortir la poubelle** *(to take out the rubbish)* and **mettre la table** *(to set the table)* both use verbs that are irregular in the present indicative, but they are formed as with other verbs in the imperative.

C **Translate the following into French.**

    1 Take out the rubbish. (informal form) _____

    2 Take out the rubbish. (formal/plural form) _____

    3 Let's take out the rubbish. _____

    4 Set the table. (informal form) _____

    5 Set the table. (formal/plural form) _____

    6 Let's set the table. _____

2 Four verbs do not follow the pattern and are irregular in the imperative.

avoir (*to have*)	être (*to be*)	savoir (*to know*)	vouloir (*to want*)
aie	sois	sache	veuille
ayons	soyons	sachons	voulons
ayez	soyez	sachez	veuillez

D Turn these statements into commands. The first one is done for you.

1 Tu balayes la cuisine. Balaye la cuisine.

2 Nous changeons les draps. _____

3 Vous repassez les chemises. _____

4 Tu passes l'aspirateur. _____

5 Nous nettoyons la salle de bains. _____

6 Vous avez une chambre propre. _____

7 Tu finis la lessive. _____

8 Vous tondez le gazon. _____

9 Nous recyclons les canettes. _____

10 Tu es pratique. _____

Pronouns with imperatives

1 In the affirmative, direct and indirect object pronouns follow the verb, and **me** and **te** become **moi** and **toi** and are preceded by a hyphen.
Tu m'aides à nettoyer la maison. (*You help me clean the house.*)
Aide-moi à nettoyer la maison! (*Help me clean the house!*)

2 This is also the case with pronominal verbs like **se lever** (*to get up*).
Vous vous levez. (*You get up.*)
Levez-vous. (*Get up!*)

E Tell your housemates what to do for a party you are having this evening using the expressions in brackets. Repeat the commands to them both in the plural, and then to just one of them using the singular.

1 _____ _____ (s'occuper des courses)

2 _____ _____ (se débrouiller pour faire un gâteau)

3 _____ _____ (arrêter de se disputer)

4 _____ _____ (se dépêcher)

5 _____ _____ (s'habiller)

6 _____ _____ (s'amuser à la fête)

3 In the negative, the pronoun precedes the verb.
Ne la salis pas. (*Do not dirty it.*)
Ne les laissez pas par terre. (*Don't leave them on the floor.*)
Ne te lave pas les mains. (*Don't wash your hands.*)

4 Like with other imperative forms, the **-s** is removed for **-er** verbs in the negative.

Ne repasse pas la robe. *(Don't iron the dress.)*   **Ne la repasse pas.** *(Don't iron it.)*

Ne mange pas de sucre. *(Don't eat any sugar.)*   **N'en mange pas.** *(Don't eat any.)*

F Aurélie asks Marc what they should do for dinner, but they can't agree. Answer using the negative imperative and use the expression in brackets in the affirmative imperative.

1 **Aurélie:** Est-ce que nous devons sortir au restaurant du coin? (préparer le dîner chez nous)

   Marc: <u>Non, n'y sortons pas, préparons le dîner chez nous.</u>

2 **Aurélie:** Est-ce que je dois faire le plat avec une recette? (faire le plat sans recette)

   Marc: _____

3 **Aurélie:** Est-ce je dois couper tous les légumes en julienne? (couper les légumes en dés.)

   Marc: _____

4 **Aurélie:** Est-ce que nous devons mettre du poivre? (mettre du sel)

   Marc: _____

5 **Aurélie:** Est-ce que je dois repasser les serviettes? (utiliser des serviettes en papier)

   Marc: _____

6 **Aurélie:** Est-ce que nous devons nous mettre à table? (manger dans le salon)

   Marc: _____

In formal written instructions, such as on signs and in recipes, the infinitive is often used instead of the imperative.

Défense d'entrer. *(Do not enter.)*

Ne pas marcher sur la pelouse. *(Do not walk on the grass.)*

Mélanger les œufs et la crème. *(Mix the eggs and the cream.)*

Vocabulary

les tâches ménagères	the household chores	balayer	to sweep
tondre la pelouse	to mow the lawn	un chiffon	a rag
passer l'aspirateur	to vacuum	le désordre	the mess
le linge	the laundry	une éponge	a sponge
le sèche-linge	the clothes dryer	essuyer	to wipe, to wipe down
plier	to fold	le ménage	the household
l'appareil ménager	the household appliance	s'occuper de	to take care of
un balai	a broom	les ordures (f.)	the rubbish

G Read the note with a list of household chores that a mother left for her children Mohamed and Lana. Indicate if the following statements are V (**vrai**/true) or F (**faux**/false).

	Les enfants,
	Quand vous rentrez, n'oubliez pas de faire vos tâches ménagères avant
	de vous installer devant la télé.
	Mohamed, tonds la pelouse, sors le chien, donne à manger aux chats et
	lave la voiture.
	Lana, passe l'aspirateur en haut, mets le linge sale dans la machine à
	laver, sors le linge du sèche-linge et plie-le.
	Tous les deux, videz le lave-vaisselle et mettez la table et n'oubliez pas,
	faites vos devoirs!
	Merci et à ce soir,
	Maman

1 Mohamed has to take out the dog.   V/F
2 Mohamed has to vacuum.   V/F
3 Lana has to fold the laundry.   V/F
4 Lana has to empty the dishwasher.   V/F
5 Both of them have to clear the table.   V/F
6 Both of them have to do their homework.   V/F

Go back over the unit and look at all the expressions that were used to discuss household chores and responsibilities. Look up any expression you don't know already.

H Sort the following into the activities that you like to do and those you don't.

changer les draps (*to change the sheets*)	**laver les vitres** (*to wash the windows*)
donner à manger au chat (*to feed the cat*)	**faire la vaisselle** (*to do the dishes*)
faire le lit (*to make the bed*)	**vider le lave-vaisselle** (*to empty the dishwasher*)
faire les commissions (*to go grocery shopping*)	**faire la lessive** (*to do the laundry*)

faire les poussières (*to dust*)	**plier le linge** (*to fold the laundry*)
payer les factures (*to pay the bills*)	**recycler** (*to recycle*)
passer la serpillère (*to mop the floor*)	**repasser** (*to iron*)
mettre la table (*to set the table*)	**sortir la poubelle** (*to take out the rubbish bin*)
passer l'aspirateur (*to vacuum*)	**tondre le gazon** (*to mow the lawn*)

J'aime	Je n'aime pas

To say something is messy, use the expression **être en désordre**. *This can't be used for people though, just places or things.*

Sa chambre est en désordre. (*His room is messy.*)

To say that a person is messy or not tidy, use **désordonné**.

Ils sont tellement désordonnés! (*They are so messy!*)

I   **Use the verbs and pronouns to make sentences about what needs to be done in the house.**

1   faire/nous _____

2   ranger/tu _____

3   plier/vous _____

4   essuyer/vous _____

5   s'occuper de/nous _____

6   balayer/tu _____

# Reading

J   Anne-Sophie Picard has bought a new electrical appliance. Read the first few lines of the user manual to figure out what it is for.

NOTICE

Lisez attentivement le mode d'emploi avant la première utilisation de votre appareil et conservez-le pour les utilisations futures.

UTILIZATION

- Avant d'utiliser l'appareil, nettoyez les récipients à l'eau chaude savonneuse ou au lave-vaisselle.

- Branchez l'appareil.

- Versez le lait dans les pots. N'utilisez pas de lait froid, il est préférable d'utiliser du lait à température ambiante.

- Utilisez un yaourt nature et distribuez-le dans chacun des pots.

- Placez les récipients dans le corps de l'appareil sans les couvrir pour laisser l'eau s'évaporer.

- Mettez le couvercle sur l'appareil.

- Appuyez sur l'interrupteur à la position marche.

- Le temps estimé de la fermentation du yaourt est de huit à dix heures.

- Conservez les yaourts au réfrigérateur et mangez-les dans les huit jours.

NETTOYAGE ET ENTRETIEN

- Assurez-vous que l'appareil est débranché avant de le nettoyer.

- Ne plongez pas l'appareil dans de l'eau, nettoyez-le avec un simple coup d'éponge.

- Pour ranger l'appareil, enroulez le câble et placez-le dans le ramasse câble qui se trouve sous la base de l'appareil.

RECOMMANDATIONS

- Vous pouvez ajouter du lait en poudre pour rendre le yaourt plus onctueux.

- Ne déplacez pas l'appareil pendant son fonctionnement.

- N'ouvrez pas le couvercle pendant le fonctionnement de l'appareil.

- Ne placez pas l'appareil dans des endroits exposés au courant d'air.

- Évitez de le mettre à côté d'appareils ménagers qui font des vibrations, sinon le yaourt ne prendra pas.

- N'utilisez pas l'appareil dehors.

K   Answer the questions in French.

1   Quels ingrédients doit-on utiliser pour faire du yaourt? _____

2   Combien de temps faut-il pour faire du yaourt? _____

3   Que faut-il faire avant de nettoyer l'appareil? _____

4   Qu'est-ce qu'il ne faut pas faire? _____

5   Qu'est-ce qu'on peut ajouter au yaourt pour qu'il soit meilleur? _____

6   Pourquoi ne faut-il pas mettre la yaourtière à côté d'appareils qui font des vibrations? _____

L **Find the following verbs in the text. If they are in the imperative, put them in the infinitive.**

1 to clean _____
2 to use _____
3 to pluq in _____
4 to put away _____

5 to keep _____
6 to pour _____
7 to add _____
8 to avoid _____

Writing

M **What household task are you good at doing? Write an email to a friend explaining the best way to do it. Try to use the imperative. (80–100 words)**

_____

_____

_____

_____

_____

_____

_____

_____

_____

_____

_____

Self-check

Tick the box that matches your level of confidence.

1 = very confident   2 = need more practice   3 = not confident

Cochez la case qui correspond à votre niveau d'aisance.

1 = très sûr(e) de vous   2 = j'ai besoin de plus de pratique   3 = pas sûr(e) du tout

	1	2	3
Give commands and orders using the imperative.			
Use the imperative with pronouns.			
Can understand simple user instructions for equipment (CEFR A2).			
Can describe how to do something giving detailed instructions (CEFR B1).			

12 Pour être heureux

In order to be happy

In this unit, you will learn how to:

✅ Indicate your attitude.

✅ Use infinitives and past infinitives.

CEFR: Can write accounts of experiences, describing feelings and reactions in simple connected text (B1); Can understand fairly complex texts about personal problems and express own emotions (B2).

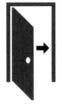  

Fermer la porte   À vendre   Ne pas nourrir les animaux

Meaning and usage

Infinitives

The infinitive is a verb in its non-conjugated, or 'dictionary', form. In English this is *to* + verb, e.g. *to eat, to see, to be, to have*, etc. This form has no tense and no gender or number. Infinitives in French end in **-er**, **-ir** or **-re**.

1 The infinitive can also sometimes function as a noun and may serve as the subject of a sentence.

   Parler est parfois difficile. *(Speaking is sometimes difficult.)*

   Sortir seul peut être dangereux. *(Going out alone can be dangerous.)*

   Dire la vérité est important. *(Telling the truth is important.)*

2 The infinitive is used in impersonal commands in such places as cookbooks, instruction manuals and with posted rules and safety instructions.

   Préchauffer le four à 200 °C/400 °F. *(Preheat the oven to 200 °C/400 °F.)*

   En cas d'incendie, appeler le 18. *(In case of fire, call 18.)*

   Ne pas marcher sur la pelouse. *(Don't walk on the grass./Keep off the grass.)*

3 Many verbs in French are commonly followed by an infinitive. Here are some common ones.

aimer	détester	falloir	sembler
adorer	désirer	pouvoir	sentir
aller	devoir	préférer	sortir
compter	espérer	savoir	vouloir

Nous allons _regarder_ la télévision pour nous détendre. *(We are going to watch TV to relax.)*
Il ne faut pas _être_ méchant avec vos frères. *(You mustn't be mean to your brothers.)*
Je peux vous _donner_ des conseils? *(Can I give you some advice?)*
Il sait _faire_ la cuisine. *(He knows how to cook.)*

 A Check to make sure you know these verbs, then use a dictionary to find ten more infinitives and their meanings.

 Note that an adverb, a negative or a direct or indirect object pronoun may separate the conjugated verb from the infinitive.

Il sait bien faire la cuisine. *(He knows how to cook well.)*

Nous ne pouvons pas venir. *(We can't come.)*

Elle vous a dit de vous taire. *(She told you to be quiet.)*

 B Many French proverbs and common expressions use infinitives. Look and identify the verbs used in the infinitive. Guess the proverb's meaning and try to find an equivalent in English.

1 Mettre la charrue avant les bœufs. _____
2 Donner un œuf pour avoir un bœuf. _____
3 Donner c'est donner, reprendre c'est voler. _____
4 Bien faire et laisser dire. _____
5 C'est la goutte d'eau qui fait déborder le vase. _____
6 Déshabiller Paul pour habiller Jacques. _____
7 Il faut se méfier de l'eau qui dort. _____
8 J'ai d'autres chats à fouetter. _____

C Complete the sentences using the verbs in brackets. The first verb will need to be conjugated in the present, the other left in the infinitive.

1 Elle _____ (aimer, sentir) le vent sur sa peau.
2 Ils _____ (adorer, partir) le week-end.
3 Je _____ (aller, faire) de la randonnée samedi matin.
4 Jean _____ (détester, faire) ses devoirs.
5 Nous _____ (désirer, se voir) plus souvent.
6 Je _____ (devoir, rappeler) plus tard, quelqu'un est à la porte.
7 Nous _____ (espérer, avoir) le plaisir de vous revoir.
8 Il _____ (sortir, voir) un concert ce soir.

D Translate the sentences in C into English.

1 _____
2 _____
3 _____
4 _____
5 _____
6 _____
7 _____
8 _____

Infinitives with prepositions

Infinitives with à

Some verbs have the preposition **à** between the conjugated verb and the infinitive. The conjugated verb must have the preposition added to it before the infinitive can be used.

aider à	*to help to*	**encourager à**	*to encourage to*
s'amuser à	*to have fun at*	**s'habituer à**	*to get used to*
apprendre à	*to learn to*	**hésiter à**	*to hesitate to*
arriver à	*to succeed in, to manage to*	**inviter à**	*to invite to*
s'attendre à	*to expect to*	**se mettre à**	*to start to*
avoir du mal à	*to find it difficult to*	**se préparer à**	*to prepare (oneself) to*
chercher à	*to try to, to attempt to*	**renoncer à**	*to give up*
commencer à	*to begin to*	**réussir à**	*to succeed at*
continuer à	*to continue to*	**servir à**	*to be used for*
se décider à	*to make up one's mind to*	**tenir à**	*to really want to, to be attached to*

Infinitives with de

Other verbs have the preposition **de** between the conjugated verb and the infinitive.

arrêter de	*to stop + –ing*	**mériter de**	*to deserve to*
choisir de	*to choose to*	**oublier de**	*to forget to*
conseiller de	*to advise to*	**permettre (à quelqu'un) de**	*to allow someone to*
se contenter de	*to content oneself with*	**persuader de**	*to persuade to*
continuer de (or à)	*to continue to*	**se presser de**	*to hurry to*
décider de	*to decide to*	**promettre de**	*to promise to*
s'efforcer de	*to try hard to*	**proposer de**	*to propose to*
essayer de	*to try to*	**refuser de**	*to refuse to*
être obligé de	*to be obligated to*	**rêver de**	*to dream about*
s'excuser de	*to apologize for*	**se soucier de**	*to care about*
finir de	*to finish*	**se souvenir de**	*to remember to*

Avoir expressions with de

Many idiomatic expressions with **avoir** also take **de** + an infinitive after them.

avoir besoin de	*to need*
avoir envie de	*to feel like*
avoir honte de	*to be ashamed*
avoir peur de	*to be afraid*
avoir raison de	*to be right*
avoir tort de	*to be wrong*

In all of these cases of verbs with prepositions, most people find it useful to memorize the verb with its preposition and to try to remember to use it when speaking and writing. Write these out on flashcards if necessary to try and remember which verbs need these prepositions.

E Complete the sentences with **à, de, d'** or **ø** (no preposition).

1 Tu arrêtes _____ fumer? C'est bien pour ta santé.
2 Nous ne voulons pas _____ vous déranger.
3 Rachid cherche _____ embaucher quelqu'un dans son entreprise.
4 Elles n'ont pas envie _____ nous rejoindre. C'est dommage.
5 Vous permettez _____ votre enfant _____ jouer tout seul dans le jardin?
6 Elle a promis _____ ne plus le faire.
7 J'ai du mal _____ parler de mes problèmes.
8 Nous nous efforçons _____ aller à la gym au moins trois fois par semaine.

The infinitive with other prepositions

The infinitive is sometimes used with other prepositions.

Nous lui parlerons _afin de résoudre_ le problème. _(We'll talk to him in order to solve the problem.)_

Il dort _au lieu de travailler._ _(He is sleeping instead of working.)_

Dites au revoir _avant de partir!_ _(Say goodbye before leaving!)_

Vous devez vous coucher tôt _pour ne pas être_ fatigué demain.
(You should go to bed earlier in order to not be tired tomorrow.)

Entrez _sans faire_ de bruit. _(Come in without making noise.)_

Avoiding the subjunctive using infinitives

The infinitive can be used to avoid the subjunctive, the mood used to express doubt or uncertainty. The subjunctive almost always follows **que**. In impersonal expressions, you can replace **que** with **de** and change the verb to an infinitive. You can also sometimes rewrite a sentence using an infinitive instead of the subjunctive. The pronouns might need to change as well.

Il est important que tu viennes. → **Il est important de venir.** _(It's important to come.)_

Il faut que nous soyons là. → **Il faut être là.** _(We have to be there.)_

Elle demande qu'il parte. → **Elle lui demande de partir.** _(She is asking him to leave.)_

F   Rewrite the sentences using an infinitive in place of the subjunctive. Remember to use the appropriate preposition if necessary.

1   Il est essentiel _que tu boives_ au moins un verre de vin rouge par jour. _____
_____

2   Vous défendez _que nous sortions?_ _____

3   Il ne faut pas _que tu manges_ de trop. _____

4   Nous sommes tristes de voir _qu'il parte._ _____

5   Il est nécessaire _que vous acceptiez_ vos défauts. _____

6   Elle demande _que tu_ y _ailles_ avec eux. _____

Using infinitives in the negative

In the negative **ne … pas**, **ne … plus**, **ne … jamais** and **ne … rien** all precede the infinitive verb.

J'essaie de ne pas rire. _(I'm trying not to laugh.)_

Nous avons peur de ne plus vous voir. _(We are afraid to not see you anymore.)_

Il a promis de ne rien fumer ce week-end. _(He promised not to smoke anything this weekend.)_

You might sometimes see that pas is omitted when used with verbs like cesser, oser, pouvoir and savoir, especially in written or formal French. This does not usually affect the meaning of the sentence, but it may make the negation weaker and not as certain.

Elle ne cesse d'y penser. *(She can't stop thinking about it.)*

Je n'ose y croire. *(I don't dare believe it.)*

Paul ne saurait dire la vérité. *(Paul wouldn't know how to tell the truth.)*

 G Look at these instances of **ne … personne** and **ne … que** and indicate how they are different from the examples.

Elle a décidé de ne sortir avec personne. *(She decided to not go out with anybody.)*

Vous rêvez de ne travailler que quatre jours par semaine?
(You dream about working only four days a week?)

H Put the following sentences in the negative using the expression in brackets. Remember to put the negation with the infinitive.

1 Nous choisissons de sauter nos séances de gym. (ne … pas)

_____

2 Elle veut arrêter de manger le matin. (ne … rien)

_____

3 On m'a conseillé de fumer. (ne … plus)

_____

4 Tu t'habitues à voir tes amis tous les jours. (ne … personne)

_____

5 Il décide d'être si perfectionniste. (ne … pas)

_____

6 Vous vous efforcez de boire des bières tous les soirs. (ne … plus)

_____

7 Claire promet de nourrir ses émotions hostiles. (ne … jamais)

_____

8 Nous cessons de faire attention à nos défauts. (ne … que)

_____

 If you want to say that you enjoy something, you can use the verb aimer (to like or love), apprécier (to appreciate) or s'amuser (to enjoy oneself, to have fun).

Elle aime jouer au tennis. *(She enjoys playing tennis.)*

Nous avons beaucoup apprécié le dîner qu'elle a préparé.
(We really enjoyed the dinner she prepared.)

Ils se sont vraiment amusés. *(They truly enjoyed themselves.)*

Past infinitives

In the past tense, the infinitive is formed with **avoir** or **être** along with the past participle of the verb in question. It is generally used after **après**. The rules of agreement in the past apply.

Après avoir réfléchi, j'ai décidé de ne pas y aller. *(After thinking about it, I decided not to go.)*

Nous sommes contents d'être venus ici. *(We are happy to have come here.)*

Merci de m'avoir écrit cette lettre. *(Thanks for having written me that letter.)*

I **Combine the two sentences using a past infinitive as in the model.**

1 Je regrette. Je n'ai pas continué mes études.
   Je regrette de ne pas avoir continué mes études.

2 Elle est déçue. Elle n'a pas pris la bonne décision.
   _____

3 Nous sommes quand même heureux. Nous avons acheté notre propre maison.
   _____

4 Paul n'est pas content. Il n'est pas arrivé à vaincre ses émotions.
   _____

5 Elles sont désolées. Elles ne sont pas venues hier, elles ont eu un empêchement.
   _____

6 Ce n'était pas une bonne idée. On a fait une fête surprise pour l'anniversaire de Robert. Il n'était pas du tout content.
   _____

7 Il est au désespoir. Il a été licencié hier.
   _____

Vocabulary

J **Match the emotion that goes with the expressions. Look up any new words in a dictionary if needed.**

l'amour	la surprise	la colère	le désir	le bonheur	la haine	la peur	la tristesse

1 _____: l'affection, l'amitié, la passion
2 _____: l'enthousiasme, la satisfaction, le plaisir
3 _____: l'étonnement, la stupéfaction, le saisissement
4 _____: l'animosité, l'aversion, le dégoût
5 _____: la terreur, la crainte, l'effroi
6 _____: la fureur, l'indignation, la rage
7 _____: le chagrin, le désespoir, la mélancolie
8 _____: l'envie, l'attirance, la concupiscence

K Find an equivalent verb for each of the nouns in the box in J.

1 _____   5 _____

2 _____   6 _____

3 _____   7 _____

4 _____   8 _____

Reading

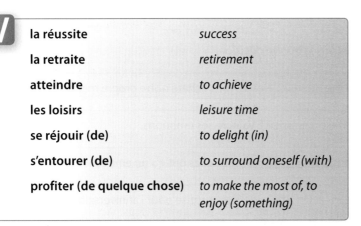

la réussite	success
la retraite	retirement
atteindre	to achieve
les loisirs	leisure time
se réjouir (de)	to delight (in)
s'entourer (de)	to surround oneself (with)
profiter (de quelque chose)	to make the most of, to enjoy (something)

L Read the first paragraph of the article and answer the questions.

1 Quelles sont « les marques extérieures d'une belle vie » mentionnées ici?

_____

2 Pourquoi dit-on que le bonheur n'est pas quelque chose à atteindre?

_____

Pour être heureux

Existe-t-il une recette pour le bonheur? Vous avez tout ce dont vous avez besoin, mais le sentiment de ne pas être tout à fait satisfait de la vie persiste. On mesure souvent son bonheur en termes de réussite professionnelle, de l'achat d'une voiture de luxe ou bien selon le montant d'argent qu'on aura épargné avant de pouvoir prendre sa retraite. Mais enfin, on peut avoir toutes les marques extérieures d'une belle vie et ne pas se sentir heureux. Sachez que le bonheur n'est souvent autre chose que le choix d'accepter sa vie et apprendre à l'aimer. C'est une façon de vivre et non pas quelque chose à atteindre.

M   Now read the rest of the article and answer the questions.

On sait que la famille, la santé, l'amour, les amis, les loisirs et la vie professionnelle peuvent contribuer au bonheur, mais on peut encore prendre des démarches pour se rendre plus heureux. Il faut se demander si on doit changer son attitude envers ses obligations professionnelles, ses relations personnelles et même les conditions de sa vie. Apprécier les petits détails de la vie est également important. Il faut prendre son temps pour se faire plaisir, pour faire plaisir aux autres, pour faire de nouvelles découvertes. Si vous voulez être plus satisfait en général, vous pouvez vous fixer des objectifs, que ce soit à court ou à long terme. Après avoir atteint votre but, vous vous féliciterez d'avoir réussi et vous serez de bonne humeur tout au long de l'expérience. Effectivement, se réjouir à l'avance vous permet d'être encore plus heureux. Finalement, il faut savoir s'entourer de personnes positives. Le bonheur n'existe pas dans la solitude et on a besoin de le partager pour en profiter pleinement.

1   Qu'est-ce qui peut contribuer au bonheur? _____
2   Qu'est-ce qu'on a besoin de changer si on n'est pas heureux? _____
3   Dites au moins trois choses qu'on peut faire pour être plus heureux selon cet article. _____

N   Identify the infinitives and the past infinitives in the article.

Infinitives	Past infinitives

 # Writing

O   What do you do to be happy? Write a diary entry in which you describe your emotional state and your efforts at relaxing and being happy. (80–100 words)

_____

_____

_____

_____

_____

_____

_____

_____

_____

 Many online magazines and blogs are geared towards improving your lifestyle and increasing health and happiness. You can look them up online to further enhance your vocabulary.

Self-check

Tick the box that matches your level of confidence.

1 = very confident   2 = need more practice   3 = not confident

Cochez la case qui correspond à votre niveau d'aisance.

1 = très sûr(e) de vous   2 = j'ai besoin de plus de pratique   3 = pas sûr(e) du tout

	1	2	3
Indicate your attitude.			
Use infinitives.			
Use past infinitives.			
Can write accounts of experiences, describing feelings and reactions in simple connected text (CEFR B1).			
Can understand fairly complex texts about personal problems and express your own emotions (CEFR B2).			

13 J'habitais dans un petit village tranquille

I lived in a small, quiet village

In this unit, you will learn how to:

✔ Understand a narrative.

✔ Use the imperfect.

> CEFR: Can understand short narratives about someone's childhood (A2); Can write simple texts about experiences or events in the past (B1).

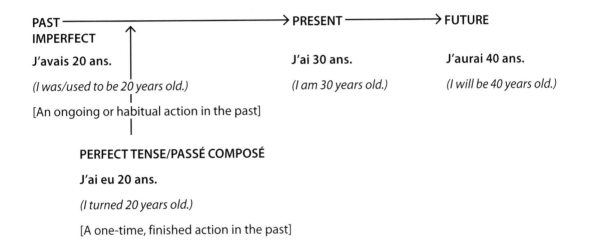

PAST ─────────────────→ PRESENT ───────────→ FUTURE
IMPERFECT

J'avais 20 ans.
(I was/used to be 20 years old.)

[An ongoing or habitual action in the past]

PERFECT TENSE/PASSÉ COMPOSÉ

J'ai eu 20 ans.
(I turned 20 years old.)

[A one-time, finished action in the past]

J'ai 30 ans.
(I am 30 years old.)

J'aurai 40 ans.
(I will be 40 years old.)

Meaning and usage

French tenses

The imperfect

The *imperfect*, or **imparfait**, is a simple tense used to provide description and background information in the past. It can answer these questions:

Qu'est-ce qui se passait? *(What was going on?)*

Comment étaient les gens ou les choses? *(What were people or things like?)*

*A simple tense means a tense that does not need an auxiliary. The imperfect is a simple tense—***vous aimiez** *(you used to love/you loved)—unlike the* **passé composé**, *which is a compound tense, formed of two components, the auxiliary and past participle:* **vous avez aimé** *(you loved).*

1   The imperfect can be translated in several ways into English. For example, **il parlait** can be translated as *he was speaking, he would speak, he used to speak, he spoke*.

Be sure to differentiate between would *used in the imperfect and in the conditional, as in these two sentences:*

J'<u>*allais*</u> **au travail tous les jours à neuf heures du matin.** *(I* <u>would go</u> *to work every day at nine in the morning.)*

Si je n'étais pas malade, j'<u>*irais*</u> **au travail.** *(If I weren't sick, I* <u>would go</u> *to work.)*

2   The imperfect can be used to provide descriptions of settings and to present background information.
Quand nous <u>*étions*</u> **jeunes, nous** <u>*habitions*</u> **dans une petite maison de ville avec un jardin de rien du tout.** *(When we were young we lived in a small townhouse with a tiny garden.)*

3   It is used to discuss ongoing past actions that might be interrupted, often by an event or action where the **passé composé** is used.
Ses frères la <u>*poussaient*</u> **sur la balançoire quand elle est tombée.** *(Her brothers were pushing her on the swing when she fell.)*

4   It is used to describe habitual or repeated actions that occurred in the past.
Tous les ans, ma famille et moi, nous <u>*allions*</u> **dans le sud de la France pour y passer nos vacances.** *(Every year, my family and I used to go to the South of France to spend our holiday there.)*

If a specific number of times is given, the imperfect is not used, but rather the **passé composé**.

Il a fait le voyage quatre fois. *(He made the trip four times.)*

A   **Decide if you would use the imperfect if you were to translate the following into French.**

		Yes	No
1	I <u>went</u> out to the movies this weekend.		
2	Habitually, he <u>would travel</u> during the summer.		
3	We <u>called</u> them.		
4	He <u>was watching</u> television when the storm started.		
5	The twins <u>were</u> simply adorable.		
6	They <u>visited</u> Paris three times.		

5   The imperfect is used when referring to date and time in the past.

Il était 8h30 en ce jour du 27 décembre lorsqu'elle est finalement arrivée.

(It was on the 27th of December, at 8.30 when she finally arrived.)

*Note that it is as if the day and time were ongoing actions that were interrupted by the arrival, which is why **elle est finalement arrivée** (she finally arrived) is in the **passé composé**.*

6   It is used for describing emotions, physical traits, a state of being or a state of mind in the past. These are things that don't have a specific beginning or end.

Emotions	Les gamins étaient terrifiés par les films d'horreur, mais cela ne les empêchait pas de les regarder. *(The kids were terrified by horror films but that did not stop them from watching them.)*
Physical traits	Quand elle était petite, elle était blonde et elle avait de grands yeux verts. *(When she was little, she had blonde hair and big green eyes.)*
State of being	Quand tu étais jeune, tu étais toujours si polie. *(When you were young, you were always so polite.)*
State of mind	Il ne pensait qu'à faire des bêtises. *(He only thought to do stupid things.)*

Verbs commonly associated with emotions, physical traits, a state of being or a state of mind are:

aimer *(to like)*   **pouvoir** *(to be able to)*

avoir *(to have)*   **réfléchir** *(to ponder)*

être *(to be)*   **savoir** *(to know)*

penser *(to think)*   **vouloir** *(to want)*

*If there were a change in the emotions, physical traits, state of being or state of mind, the **passé composé** would be used.*

Il avait toujours des idées lumineuses. *(He always had bright ideas.)*

Il réfléchissait au problème quand il a eu une bonne idée.
(He was thinking about the problem when he had a good idea.)

*In the first example, this reflects a habitual action, not something that happened just one time. In the second, the verb **réfléchir** (to think/to reflect) was ongoing when it was interrupted by the action of having a good idea.*

7   The imperfect can also be used to express wishes or desires.

Oh, si j'étais président! *(If only I were President!)*

Si nous allions au cinéma ce soir? *(How about going to the cinema tonight?)*

B Read your French friend's email and underline the sentence which describes what she thought about her recent trip.

De:	Agnès
À:	Toi
Sujet:	Toulouse

Bonjour!

Je rentre de mon voyage à Toulouse. C'était trop beau! Ce n'est pas pour rien qu'on l'appelle « la ville rose ». Tous les vieux immeubles en brique étaient magnifiques. Le soir, on est sorti dans des restaurants qui servaient de la bonne nourriture et on est resté tard à se promener en centre ville. Bref, on a bien fait de venir! Et toi, ça va? Réponds-moi quand tu pourras.

Bises!

Agnès

How to form the imperfect

Most imperfect forms are regular. To form the imperfect, take the first person plural present tense form (**nous**) and remove the ending. Then add **-ais**, **-ais**, **-ait**, **-ions**, **-iez**, **-aient**.

Jouer nous jouons	Grandir nous grandissons	Sortir nous sortons	Perdre nous perdons
je jouais	je grandissais	je sortais	je perdais
tu jouais	tu grandissais	tu sortais	tu perdais
il/elle/on jouait	il/elle/on grandissait	il/elle/on sortait	il/elle/on perdait
nous jouions	nous grandissions	nous sortions	nous perdions
vous jouiez	vous grandissiez	vous sortiez	vous perdiez
ils/elles jouaient	ils/elles grandissaient	ils/elles sortaient	ils/elles perdaient

 C **Sortir** is an irregular verb in the present. What do you notice about its conjugation in the imperfect?

Irregular verbs in the imperfect

Irregular verbs like **sortir** *(to go out)* are formed in the same way as other verbs in the imperfect by using the first personal plural of the present tense **nous** form.

1 Some verbs have spelling changes in the **tu, il/elle/on** and **ils/elles** forms in the present. Verbs that change the accent or double a consonant don't have those changes in the imperfect because the present tense **nous** form doesn't have them.

Acheter nous achetons	Appeler nous appelons	Préférer nous préférons
j'achetais	j'appelais	je préférais
tu achetais	tu appelais	tu préférais
il/elle/on achetait	il/elle/on appelait	il/elle/on préférait
nous achetions	nous appelions	nous préférions
vous achetiez	vous appeliez	vous préfériez
ils/elles achetaient	ils/elles appelaient	ils/elles préféraient

2   The present tense **nous** form of verbs like **étudier** *(to study)* and **rire** *(to laugh)* already have -**ions** at the end. These verbs are still formed in the same way as other regular verbs, so they have a double -**ii**-.

Le soir, nous étudiions pendant des heures. *(In the evening, we used to study for hours.)*

Vous riiez trop. *(You were laughing too much.)*

Likewise, verbs ending in -**ayer**, -**oyer** and -**uyer** have -**yi**- in the imperfect with **nous** and **vous**.

Nous essayions de nous voir toutes les semaines. *(We tried to see each other every week.)*

Avant, vous envoyiez souvent des lettres, maintenant vous envoyez des e-mails. *(Before, you sent letters, now you send emails.)*

3   Verbs ending in -**ger** like **manger** *(to eat)* have two stems in the imperfect. The reason for this change is pronunciation. The third person plural ending -**eaient** might look off, but the -**e**- is there to keep the -**g**- soft, just like in the **je**, **tu** and **il/elle/on** forms. For the **nous** and **vous** forms, the -**i**- serves that purpose, so an -**e**- is not needed.

manger nous mangeons	
je mangeais	nous mangions
tu mangeais	vous mangiez
il/elle/on mangeait	ils/elles mangeaient

 D   Using the example of manger, try to conjugate the verb **commencer** *(to begin)* in the imperfect. What do you notice?

4   The only verb that is truly irregular in the imperfect is **être** *(to be)*. Its stem is **ét**-, but it has the same endings as other verbs in the imperfect.

être	
j'étais	nous étions
tu étais	vous étiez
il/elle/on était	ils/elles étaient

E Complete the sentences using the imperfect of the verb in brackets.

1 Pendant notre enfance, nous _____ (habiter) dans une vieille ferme.
2 Quand Lucien _____ (être) petit, il _____ (avoir) une peur bleue des serpents.
3 Tous les ans, vous _____ (aller) en colonie de vacances.
4 Les enfants _____ (adorer) regarder les dessins animés.
5 Je _____ (taquiner) mes frères tout le temps, c'_____ (être) drôle.
6 Quand tu _____ (devoir) faire les devoirs de vacances, qu'est-ce que tu _____ (s'ennuyer)!

 The expression **qu'est-ce que** *in sentence 6 of Activity E in this context is not used to form a question, rather it is used to put emphasis on the verb* **s'ennuyer** *(to be bored). One of the ways to translate that sentence would be:* When you had to do your summer homework, how bored you were!

F Change these sentences from the present to the imperfect.

1 Vous attendez quelqu'un. _____
2 Est-ce que tu me poses une question? _____
3 Pourquoi est-ce qu'elle est là? _____
4 Nous venons pour vous demander quelque chose. _____
5 Je ne sais pas quoi lui dire. _____
6 Vous avez besoin de quelque chose? _____

Vocabulary

Expressions of time used with the imperfect

The following adverbs of frequency that denote habitual or repetitive actions are commonly found with the imperfect.

tous les (matins, jours, soirs, etc.)	*every (morning, day, evening, etc.)*	**parfois**	*sometimes*
chaque (semaine, mois, etc.)	*each (week, month, etc.)*	**régulièrement**	*regularly*
en général, généralement	*in general, generally*	**toujours**	*always*
d'habitude, habituellement	*usually, habitually*	**souvent**	*often*

Use of these expressions of time with the imperfect is based on context and how the speaker chooses to frame it. Consider the following:

Chaque matin, je prenais un café et un pain au chocolat comme petit déjeuner.
(Every morning, I used to have a coffee and chocolate croissant for breakfast.)

Pendant mon voyage, chaque matin, j'ai pris un expresso au café du coin.
(During my trip, every morning, I had an espresso at the café on the corner.)

*In the first example, the imperfect is used since this refers to an undefined length of time; there is no precise beginning or ending. In the second example, the notion is that the trip is over and done with, therefore the **passé composé** is used and not the imperfect.*

G   **Put the following sentences into French using the imperfect.**

   1   His son was always difficult. _____
   2   When we were young, we regularly went to school on foot. _____
   3   You (singular, familiar) often played outside with your friends. _____
   4   We went to the park every week. _____
   5   Usually you (plural, formal) were talkative and friendly. _____
   6   I read the newspaper every morning while I had breakfast. _____

Reading

V	à la hâte	*hastily*	se comporter	*to behave*
	de bonne heure	*early*	**s'occuper de**	*to take care of*
	faire un caprice	*to have a tantrum*	**se salir**	*to get dirty*
	se déguiser	*to dress up*		

H   **Read the first paragraph of your friend Jerôme's description of his childhood. Indicate if the following statements are V (vrai/true) or F (faux/false).**

   1   Jérôme had a good childhood.   V/F
   2   He lived in a big city.   V/F
   3   He liked animals.   V/F

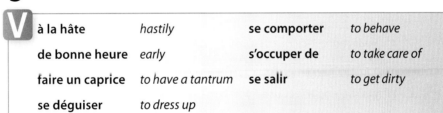

Mon enfance était merveilleuse. J'habitais dans un petit village tranquille qui s'appelait Fretin. J'adorais y vivre. Nos voisins étaient fermiers, je passais beaucoup de temps avec eux. Le matin, je me réveillais de bonne heure, je m'habillais à la hâte et je descendais prendre mon petit déjeuner aussi vite que possible pour pouvoir m'occuper des poules, des lapins et des jeunes vaches avant d'aller à l'école. Je les adorais!

I Now, continue reading and answer the questions in French.

À l'école, je travaillais bien et j'avais de bonnes notes et beaucoup d'amis. Nous jouions au foot pendant la récréation, mais nous essayions toujours de ne pas nous salir. La maîtresse était sympathique, mais exigeante et parfois sévère. Le soir, après le dîner, mes parents m'aidaient avec mes devoirs. Je me couchais toujours de bonne heure.

Ma petite sœur n'était pas comme moi. Elle était égoïste, mal polie et capricieuse. Tout le monde disait qu'elle était un petit diable, surtout quand nous allions régulièrement passer nos grandes vacances chez nos grands-parents. Elle faisait tout le temps des caprices si ma grand-mère ne la laissait pas se déguiser. Pour la distraire, souvent, ma grand-mère nous disait:

- Et, si nous allions à la plage? Si vous êtes sages, je vous achèterai une glace.

En ce qui me concerne, je me comportais toujours bien, mais pour ma petite sœur ce n'était pas toujours le cas. Alors, elle n'avait pas le droit à sa glace et elle avait tellement de chagrin qu'à la fin, je partageais la mienne avec elle.

1 Quelle sorte d'élève Jérôme était-il?

_____

2 Qu'est-ce que Jérôme faisait avec ses amis à l'école pendant la récréation?

_____

3 Comment était la sœur de Jérôme?

_____

4 Pourquoi est-ce que Jérôme partageait sa glace avec sa sœur?

_____

J Why is the imperfect used when the grandmother is quoted:

- Et, si nous allions à la plage?

K Find the French equivalents in the text to these phrases in English.

1 I spent a lot of time with them _____

2 I loved them _____

3 My parents helped me with my homework _____

4 Everyone said she was a little devil _____

5 She threw tantrums all the time _____

6 I always behaved well _____

*Many French people feel a strong regional connection, calling themselves **Breton** (from Bretagne), **Normand** (from Normandy) or **Franc-comtois** (from Franche-Comté) for example. Throughout the last century, many French people moved from the countryside, **la campagne**, away from their ancestral region to the city, in order to find work. Many people keep a second home in the region where they are from as a retreat from city life where they can maintain their regional identity.*

Writing

L   Write a short account in French about your childhood. You could write about your friends, your family, what you did with them, your school, where you lived, what you did during the summer, etc. Include some specific memories. (80–100 words)

_____

_____

_____

_____

_____

_____

_____

_____

_____

_____

_____

_____

_____

_____

_____

_____

Self-check

Tick the box that matches your level of confidence.

1 = very confident   2 = need more practice   3 = not confident

Cochez la case qui correspond à votre niveau d'aisance.

1 = très sûr(e) de vous   2 = j'ai besoin de plus   3 = pas sûr(e) du tout
de pratique

	1	2	3
Understand a narrative.			
Use the imperfect.			
Can understand short narratives about someone's childhood (CEFR A2).			
Can write simple texts about experiences or events in the past (CEFR B1).			

14 Marie-Ange a loué un appartement
Marie-Ange rented an apartment

In this unit, you will learn how to:

✔ Understand and use vocabulary related to housing.

✔ Use the **passé composé**.

> CEFR: Can understand short texts describing events in some detail (A2); Can express events and ideas related to home and living arrangements (B1).

Meaning and usage

The passé composé

1 The perfect tense, or **passé composé**, is used to tell what happened in the past and can be translated in three different ways in English.

Il _a trouvé_ un nouveau locataire.
{
(He _found_ a new tenant.)

(He _did find_ a new tenant.)

(He _has found_ a new tenant.)
}

2 The **passé composé** is used to describe actions that happened at a specific time in the past. There is a clear beginning and end to the action.
Nous avons acheté notre nouvelle maison en 2016. *(We bought our new house in 2016.)*

3 It is used to discuss a past action that happened a specific number of times.
Ils ont appelé l'agent immobilier cinq fois! *(They called the estate agent five times!)*

4 It is also used to relate a series of events that happened over a limited period of time.
J'ai rencontré l'architecte. Nous avons discuté du projet. Le soir même, Il m'a envoyé le devis. *(I met with the architect. We discussed the project. That very night, he sent me the estimate.)*

How to form the passé composé

1 The **passé composé** is made up of two parts: the auxiliary and the past participle. Two-part tenses such as this are called *perfect*.

2 An auxiliary is a word that is used in the conjugation of certain tenses.

> *Auxiliary verbs are sometimes called 'helping verbs'. In this case, they 'help' put the verb in the past.*

The two auxiliaries used with the **passé composé** are: **avoir** *(to have)* and **être** *(to be).*
J'_ai fini_ **de peindre.** *(I finished painting.)*
Paul _est allé_ **chez son amie.** *(Paul went to his friend's house.)*

Verbs conjugated in the passé composé with avoir

1   Most French verbs use **avoir** in the **passé composé**. These are known as *transitive verbs*.

> *Transitive verbs are verbs that can be followed by a direct object. They are action verbs that do something to someone or something. For example:*
>
> **Il a donné** <u>la clé</u> **à Jean.** *(He gave* <u>the key</u> *to Jean.)*
> **La clé** *(the key) is the thing that is given, so it is the direct object.*

2   The verb **avoir** is conjugated in the present tense when used as the auxiliary verb of the **passé composé**.
J'ai acheté un jean. *(I bought some jeans.)*
Nous avons mangé du pain. *(We ate some bread.)*

A   **Complete the following sentences with the correct form of the auxiliary verb avoir.**

1   Nous _____ finalement choisi la nouvelle couleur pour les murs du salon.
2   Pendant trois ans, ma famille _____ habité à Purley, en Angleterre.
3   Ils _____ loué une maison de campagne pour y passer les grandes vacances.
4   _____-vous vendu votre maison?
5   J'_____ emménagé dans mon nouvel appartement la semaine dernière.
6   Tu _____ réussi à tout emballer toi-même.

B   **Find the infinitives of the verbs used in the passé composé in A.**

1   _____   4   _____
2   _____   5   _____
3   _____   6   _____

3   The past participle is the form of the verb used. In English, it is the equivalent of *-ed* for regular verbs.
Les nouveaux locataires ont _téléphoné_. *(The new tenants called.)*
Il a _acheté_ **un nouvel appartement.** *(He bought a new apartment.)*

C   **Look again at the verbs in A and B and indicate how past participles of regular verbs ending in -er, -ir and -re are formed.**

4   The past participle of verbs that use **avoir** as their auxiliary does not usually change. It remains the same, regardless of the subject.
J'ai installé le parquet dans la salle à manger. *(I installed wood floors in the dining room.)*
Nous avons installé le parquet dans la salle à manger.
(We installed the wood floors in the dining room.)
Elles ont installé le parquet dans la salle à manger.
(They installed the wood floors in the dining room.)

D Complete the following sentences with the correct past participle of the verb in brackets.

1 Nous avons _____ (vider) tous les cartons.

2 J'ai _____ (finir) de lire les annonces immobilières.

3 Elles ont _____ (vendre) leur maison de ville.

4 Il a _____ (bâtir) sa nouvelle maison en Lausanne.

5 Vous avez _____ (restaurer) cette ferme.

6 Tu as _____ (attendre) que le prêt soit approuvé.

5 As in English, many past participles in French are irregular. The most common irregular past participles in French are:

avoir	to have	eu	mourir	to die	mort
boire	to drink	bu	ouvrir	to open	ouvert
conduire	to drive	conduit	pleuvoir	to rain	plu
croire	to believe	cru	pouvoir	to be able to	pu
devoir	to have to	dû	prendre	to take	pris
dire	to tell	dit	recevoir	to receive	reçu
écrire	to write	écrit	rire	to laugh	ri
être	to be	été	suivre	to follow	suivi
faire	to do	fait	tenir	to hold	tenu
lire	to read	lu	vivre	to live	vécu
mettre	to put	mis	vouloir	to want	voulu

E Verbs from the same families share the same irregularities. If **mettre** is irregular and its past participle is **mis**, state what the past participles of the following verbs are.

1 admettre (*to admit*) _____

2 émettre (*to emit*) _____

3 omettre (*to omit*) _____

4 permettre (*to allow*) _____

5 promettre (*to promise*) _____

6 remettre (*to put back*) _____

F Conjugate the following verbs in the **passé composé**.

1 entendre   tu _____

2 grandir   elles _____

3 interdire   nous _____

4 perdre   vous _____

5 rénover   il _____

6	découvrir	j'_____
7	avoir	tu _____
8	comprendre	vous _____
9	pousser	ils _____
10	rendre	nous _____

6 When the direct object precedes a verb conjugated with the auxiliary **avoir** in the **passé composé**, the past participle that follows must agree in number and gender with that object. If the direct object is masculine singular, nothing changes.

J'ai cherché le numéro de l'artisan carreleur, mais je ne l'ai pas <u>trouvé</u>.
(I looked for the tiler's number, but I did not find it.)
If the direct object is feminine singular, an **-e** gets added.
Pendant notre absence, la pelouse a bien poussé, alors il l'a tond<u>ue</u> hier.
(The grass grew a lot during our absence, so he mowed it yesterday.)
If the direct object is masculine plural, an **-s** gets added.
J'ai parlé aux voisins hier, je les ai v<u>us</u> à la piscine.
(I spoke to the neighbours yesterday; I saw them at the pool.)

> If a past participle ends in an **-s** and a masculine plural direct object precedes, do not add an extra **-s**.
>
> **Tu as pris les documents?** *(Did you take the documents?)*
>
> **Oui je les ai pris.** *(Yes, I took them.)*

If the direct object is feminine plural, an **-es** gets added.
Il n'a pas oublié les clés, il les a pris<u>es</u>. *(He did not forget the keys, he took them.)*
If there is an indirect object, or the pronoun **y** or **en** that precedes the verb, there is no agreement.
Tu as téléphoné à ta mère? *(Did you call your mother?)*
Oui, je lui ai téléphoné. *(Yes, I called her.)*
Tu as mis les photos sur la table? *(Did you put the pictures on the table?)*
Oui, j'y ai mis les photos. *(Yes, I put the photos there.)*
Il a acheté du lait? *(Did he buy some milk?)*
Oui, il en a acheté. *(Yes, he bought some.)*

G Decide whether agreement is needed. Add **-e**, **-s**, or **-es** if needed.

1 La maison de ville à Paris, ils l'ont finalement visité _____?
2 Les photos que tu as pris _____ sont magnifiques!
3 Tous les meubles qui étaient dans son loft, Claire les a vendu _____ en ligne.
4 Ils ont rénové _____ le premier étage l'été dernier.
5 Chantal, de l'agence immobilière? Oui, je l'ai appelé _____.
6 Nous avons fait _____ le tour du lotissement.

Adverbs in the **passé composé** *are most often found in between the auxiliary and the past participle.*

Nous avons patiemment attendu pour pouvoir emménager.
(We patiently waited to be able to move in.)

With longer adverbs or for emphasis, the adverb can come at the beginning or end of the sentence.

Elle l'a regardé longuement. *(She looked at it for a long time.)*

Verbs conjugated in the passé composé with être

1   Verbs in the **passé composé** that are intransitive, meaning they cannot or do not have a direct object, use **être** as their auxiliary.

2   Here is a list of these verbs along with their past participle:

Infinitive	Past participle
aller *(to go)*	allé
arrive *(to arrive)*	arrivé
descendre *(to go down, to descend)*	descendu
entrer *(to enter, to go in)*	entré
monter *(to go up, to ascend)*	monté
mourir *(to die)*	mort
naître *(to be born)*	né
partir *(to leave)*	parti
passer *(to pass, to spend time)*	passé
rester *(to stay)*	resté
retourner *(to return)*	retourné
sortir *(to go out)*	sorti
tomber *(to fall)*	tombé
venir *(to come)*	venu

Descendre, monter, passer, rentrer, retourner *and* **sortir** *are conjugated with* **avoir** *when they have a direct object. When this happens, the past participle does not agree with the subject.*

J'ai descendu l'aspirateur. *(I brought the vacuum cleaner down/downstairs.)*

Elle a monté un verre d'eau pour son mari qui était malade. *(She took up a glass of water upstairs for her husband who was sick.)*

Tu as passé la nuit là-bas. *(You spent the night there.)*

Ils ont rentré le chien. *(They brought the dog in.)*

Nous avons rendu les livres à la bibliothèque. *(We returned the books to the library.)*

Vous avez sorti la poubelle. *(You took out the bin.)*

H Complete the following sentences with the correct form of the auxiliary verb **être**.

1 Nous _____ allés chez elle hier soir.

2 Tu _____ retourné à ta maison d'enfance.

3 Je/J' _____ restée toute la nuit.

4 Elle _____ passée devant la maison des voisins.

5 Vous _____ tombés dans les escaliers.

6 Ils _____ entrés après les autres.

I Look at the past participles in H and see if you can understand the changes from one subject to another.

3 With verbs that have the auxiliary **être**, the past participle agrees in gender and number with the subject of the verb. The past participle doesn't change with masculine singular subjects, but takes an **-e** for feminine singular, an **-s** for masculine plural and an **-es** for feminine plural.

Pierre est rentré chez lui tard. *(Pierre went home late.)*

Yvonne est allée chez toi. *(Yvonne went to your house.)*

Les femmes sont arrivées en avance. *(The women arrived early.)*

Ils ne sont pas encore morts. *(They are not dead yet.)*

J Make full sentences using the passé composé with the elements provided.

1 il / partir / après nous _____

2 nous / rentrer / hier matin _____

3 vous (masculine plural) / monter / dans votre chambre _____

4 tu / naître / au mois de mars _____

5 je / tomber / par terre _____

6 elles / aller / cet après-midi _____

7 ils / descendre / au sous-sol _____

8 elle / sortir / vers quatre heures _____

Forming negatives and questions in the passé composé

Negation in the passé composé

1 When using the **passé composé** for an affirmative statement, the word order is:
subject + auxiliary + past participle + rest of the sentence.
Nous avons fait une offre d'achat. *(We have made a purchase offer.)*

2 When negating a statement, the negation **ne ... pas** *(not)*, **ne ... jamais** *(never)*, **ne ... rien** *(nothing)*, **ne ... plus** *(anymore, any longer)*, etc. surround the auxiliary:
*subject + **ne/n'** + auxiliary + **pas** (or other negation word) + past participle + rest of the sentence.*
Nous n'avons pas fait d'offre d'achat. *(We have not made any purchase offer.)*
Elle n'est jamais retournée avec les clés. *(She never came back with the keys.)*

3   When **personne** (nobody) or **rien** (nothing) are used as the subject, they go before **ne**.
    Personne or **Rien** + **ne** + auxiliary + past participle.
    Personne n'a vu le propriétaire aujourd'hui. (Nobody has seen the owner today.)
    Rien ne s'est passé. (Nothing happened.)
4   The following negations surround both the auxiliary and past participle: **ne … personne**
    (nobody), **ne … que** (only), **ne … aucun** (not one, not any, none), **ne … nulle part** (nowhere).
    Tu n'as vu personne? (You saw nobody? You didn't see anybody?)
    Il n'a trouvé que du papier peint sur les murs. (He only found wallpaper on the walls.)
5   When **personne** is used with a preposition, use the following word order:
    ne + verb + preposition + **personne.**
    Elle n'a parlé à personne. (She spoke to nobody. She didn't speak with anybody.)

K   **Translate the following.**

1   I have never lived in a country home. _____
2   We have not yet rented an apartment in Paris. _____
3   You had never been there? (masculine plural you) _____
4   They only liked this mattress. _____
5   She didn't talk to anyone. _____
6   He said nothing. _____

Question formation in the passé composé

1   The long form can be used to ask questions by using **est-ce que**.
    Est-ce que tu as aimé la couleur du vestibule? (Did you like the colour of the entrance hall?)
    Comment est-ce qu'il a eu les moyens d'acheter cet immeuble?
    (How did he afford to buy this building?)
    Est-ce que Marie et Luc t'ont aidé à déménager? (Did Marie and Luc help you move?)
2   Inversion can also be used to ask questions in the **passé composé**. The subject and auxiliary
    are inversed and linked by a hyphen.
    As-tu aimé la couleur du vestibule? (Did you like the colour of the entrance hall?)
    Comment a-t-il eu les moyens d'acheter cet immeuble? (How did he afford to buy
    this building?)
    Marie et Luc t'ont-ils aidé à déménager? (Did Marie and Luc help you move?)

Note that when doing inversion with **elle**, **il**, **on** while using **avoir** as the auxiliary, a **-t-** has to be
added for pronunciation purposes.

When proper names (e.g. **Marie et Luc**) are used, the corresponding subject pronoun (**ils**) is added for
the inversion and the proper names stay in their place.

3   For negative questions, either the long form or inversion can be used.
    Est-ce qu'ils n'ont rien trouvé d'intéressant? (Did they not find anything interesting?)
    N'ont-ils rien trouvé d'intéressant?

L Read the following answers. Come up with a corresponding question using either **est-ce que** or inversion.

1 _____?

Non, je n'ai pas vu la piscine.

2 _____?

Oui, Théo a habité ce quartier pendant plusieurs années.

3 _____?

Non, elle n'est pas passée nous voir.

4 _____?

Non, nous n'avons pas reçu d'offre d'achat.

5 _____?

Oui, nous sommes rentrés dans la maison.

6 _____?

Non, je ne l'ai pas appelée hier.

Meaning and usage

The passé composé vs. the imperfect

The **passé composé** is often used in conjunction with the imperfect. Make sure to differentiate between them.

1 The **passé composé** presents actions completed at very specific moments and answers the question, 'What happened?'
2 The imperfect is used for habitual, repeated, ongoing actions and can answer the questions, 'What was going on?' or 'What were things like?'
3 The **passé composé** and the imperfect can appear in the same sentences. The imperfect sets the stage and gives description and background information whereas the **passé composé** is used for an event or occurrence.

M Which of the verbs in these sentences would translate as imperfect and which as **passé composé**?

1 It was 10 o'clock when someone knocked on the door. _____
2 When you left the office, it was raining. _____
3 When she was little, her family lived in a farmhouse in the country. _____

 *Most of the time, **avoir**, **connaître**, **être**, **pouvoir**, **savoir** and **vouloir** are in the imperfect. They are only used in the **passé composé** when there is a change involved. For example, to say how old you were in the past, you usually use the imperfect:*

Quand j'avais dix ans, je jouais dehors tout le temps. *(When I was ten, I played outside all the time.)*

But, when your birthday comes around and your age changes:

J'ai eu 20 ans en 2016. *(I turned 20 years old in 2016.)*

N Jacqueline and her family are moving tomorrow, but nobody is helping her. Say what the others were doing while she worked on the move using the words provided.

1 mettre les affaires dans des boîtes en carton / les enfants / jouer dehors

Elle a mis les affaires dans des boîtes en carton pendant que les enfants jouaient dehors.

2 fermer les boîtes en carton / son mari / promener le chien

_____

3 nettoyer la cuisine / son mari / faire les courses

_____

4 couvrir les meubles avec des draps / sa fille / regarder la télé

_____

5 monter au grenier pour le vider / son mari / faire la cuisine

_____

6 sortir chercher les clés de la nouvelle maison / sa mère / tricoter

_____

7 téléphoner au fournisseur d'Internet pour changer l'adresse / son fils / bricoler au sous-sol

_____

8 confirmer l'arrivée des déménageurs le lendemain / son père / lire le journal

_____

> *Try looking up Francophone property ads of interest to you. Read them and see if you can understand them. This would be great practice.*

O Complete the story of how Jacqueline and her family found their new home. Use the verb in brackets in the imperfect or **passé composé**.

Jacqueline (**1** être) _____ contente de chercher une nouvelle maison. Ils (**2** vouloir) _____ plus de place et ils (**3** chercher) _____ une maison plus grande que celle où ils (**4** habiter) _____ jusqu'à présent avec une chambre pour sa fille, une chambre pour son fils, une grande chambre pour elle et son mari plus une chambre d'amis. Quand Jacqueline (**5** rencontrer) _____ l'agent immobilier, elle lui (**6** expliquer) _____ ce dont ils (**7** avoir) _____ besoin. Quand ils (**8** voir) _____ la maison pour la première fois, toute la famille en (**9** tomber) _____ amoureuse. Elle (**10** dit) _____ tout de suite à son mari, « Achetons-la! ». C'était la maison idéale pour eux!

Vocabulary

P   Match the French with the English.

1	acheter	**a**	the key
2	approuver	**b**	the lease
3	avoir les moyens	**c**	the grass/lawn
4	la boîte en carton	**d**	a purchase offer
5	la clef/clé	**e**	the loan
6	emballer	**f**	to approve
7	une offre d'achat	**g**	the owner
8	la pelouse	**h**	the neighbourhood
9	déménager	**i**	to have the means
10	le prêt	**j**	the neighbour
11	le quartier	**k**	to buy/purchase
12	le voisin/la voisine	**l**	the cardboard box
13	le propriétaire	**m**	to move
14	le bail	**n**	to pack

Q   List six expressions used to refer to different types of lodgings.

_____ _____ _____

_____ _____ _____

*In French **le rez-de-chaussée** (the ground floor) is equivalent to the first floor in North America. Therefore, Americans must remember to adjust their thinking when speaking French, since for them, **le deuxième étage** is really the third floor, etc.*

Reading

R   Read the first paragraph of Marie-Ange's story and answer the question.

Je suis de la Guadeloupe, mais pendant trois ans, j'ai fait des études à Grenoble, en France. J'ai beaucoup aimé y habiter. Avant de déménager, plusieurs fois, j'ai lu les annonces immobilières en ligne. C'est comme ça que j'ai trouvé Jean-Baptiste, le propriétaire qui louait son appartement.

Où est-ce que Marie-Ange est allée? Pourquoi? _____

L'année où j'ai déménagé, Jean-Baptiste devait voyager au Canada pour son travail, c'est la raison pour laquelle il louait son appartement. De plus, il me l'a loué meublé, ce qui était bien pratique. Je ne voulais pas me préoccuper d'avoir à acheter de nouveaux meubles ni dépenser trop d'argent. J'ai beaucoup aimé son appartement. Comme beaucoup d'apparts en France, il était petit, mais Jean-Baptiste l'avait très bien décoré.

Pendant mon séjour, Jean-Baptiste a été très sympa avec moi, il m'a dit que si je voulais, je pouvais réarranger les meubles et j'ai même eu le droit de repeindre la chambre.

Jean-Baptiste a toujours aimé les Antilles, alors avant de partir, pour le remercier de sa gentillesse, et d'avoir été si conciliant, j'ai fait imprimer des photos que j'avais prises de la plage et de la nature à la Guadeloupe. Je les ai faites encadrer, et je les ai mises au mur de son salon. Quand il est rentré chez lui, il m'a envoyé un e-mail, il avait adoré la surprise.

1   Comment a-t-elle trouvé son appartement?
_____

2   Est-ce qu'elle a acheté des meubles? Pourquoi ou pourquoi pas?
_____

3   Est-ce qu'elle a aimé son appartement? Pourquoi ou pourquoi pas?
_____

4   Qu'est-ce qu'elle a changé dans l'appartement?
_____

5   Quelle surprise a-t-elle laissée quand elle est partie?
_____

Writing

T Write a blog post similar to Marie-Ange's about a place where you have lived, how you found it and why you lived there. Use the **passé composé** to say what you did and what happened and the imperfect to give background about what was going on. (80–100 words)

_____

_____

_____

_____

_____

_____

_____

_____

Self-check

Tick the box that matches your level of confidence.

1 = very confident   2 = need more practice   3 = not confident

Cochez la case qui correspond à votre niveau d'aisance.

1 = très sûr(e) de vous   2 = j'ai besoin de plus de pratique   3 = pas sûr(e) du tout

	1	2	3
Use vocabulary related to housing and the home.			
Use the **passé composé**.			
Can understand short texts describing events in some detail (CEFR A2).			
Can express events and ideas related to home and living arrangements (CEFR B1).			

15 Nous devrions être écolo

We should be green

In this unit, you will learn how to:

✅ Use the present conditional.

✅ Form **si** (*if*) clauses.

CEFR: Can read and understand information about the environment in which the writer expresses specific attitudes and points of view (B2); Can write clear and detailed texts on environmental issues expressing an opinion and including supporting details (B2).

Meaning and usage

Present conditional

The conditional is used to express what might happen or what could happen. It is also used as a form of politeness. It is one of four moods in French (the indicative, the imperative and the subjunctive are the others).

1   There is no direct translation of the word *would* in French. Using the conditional in French is equivalent to the English use of *would* + verb.

Si nous gagnions à la loterie, nous _créerions_ une ferme bio où on _ne se servirait pas_ de pesticides et où les animaux _vivraient_ en plein air, pas dans des cages.

(If we won the lottery, we _would create_ an organic farm, where we _would not use_ pesticides and the animals _would live_ outdoors, not in cages.)

A   Look at the following sentences and give the English equivalent of the underlined verbs.

1   Elle _recyclerait_ si elle avait plus de place. _____

2   Je _prendrais_ le train au lieu de prendre ma voiture pour réduire les émissions de CO2.

   _____

3   Vous _réduiriez_ votre consommation d'énergie en allant à vélo. _____

To say should or could in French, use the verbs **devoir** *(to have to) and* **pouvoir** *(to be able to) in the conditional.*

Tu devrais faire du covoiturage. *(You should carpool.)*

Pourriez-vous réutiliser vos sacs plastiques? *(Could you reuse your plastic bags?)*

2   Use the conditional to make polite requests or express desires.

Pourriez-vous fermer la porte s'il vous plaît? Il fait froid dehors. *(Could you please close the door? It's cold outside.)*

J'aimerais manger de la nourriture bio. *(I would like to eat organic food.)*

*You cannot use the expression **si vous voudriez** to say if you would like in French as the conditional cannot follow **si** (if). Instead, you can use the present, **si vous voulez** (if you want) or use the verb **souhaiter** (to wish) in the present: **si vous souhaitez** (if you wish).*

3   You may find the conditional used in the media when journalists present uncertain events or in statements expressing a possibility.
    Il semblerait que les ours polaires soient en voie de disparition. *(It would seem that polar bears are in danger of extinction.)*

4   The conditional can express future plans stated in the past.
    Le patron de l'entreprise a dit qu'il ferait réduire leur production de déchets nocifs. *(The company's boss stated that he would reduce their production of toxic waste.)*

5   It can be used in reported speech (indirect discourse).
    Il nous a dit qu'il prendrait les transports en commun pour se rendre au travail. *(He told us he would use public transport to go to work.)*

6   Use the conditional to discuss a hypothetical situation using *if* or **si** clauses.
    Si nous avions de l'argent, nous achèterions une voiture électrique. *(If we had the money, we would buy an electric car.)*

B   Look at the sentences and say what tense or mood the underlined verbs are in (present, imperfect, imperative, future or conditional). Then translate the sentences.

1   Si tu <u>recycles</u> present, tu <u>réduis</u> present les gaz à effet de serre.
    If you recycle, you reduce greenhouse gases.

2   Si tu <u>recycles</u> _____, tu <u>réduiras</u> _____ les gaz à effet de serre.
    _____

3   Si tu <u>veux</u> _____ <u>réduire</u> _____ les gaz à effet de serre, <u>recycle</u> _____!
    _____

4   Si tu <u>recyclais</u> _____, tu <u>réduirais</u> _____ les gaz à effet de serre.
    _____

The English would is sometimes used to express a habitual action in the past. In this case, the imperfect is used in French.

Quand j'étais petit, j'emportais mon déjeuner à l'école. *(When I was little, I would bring my lunch to school.)*

How to form the present conditional

1   To form the present conditional of regular verbs, take the infinitive of **-er** or **-ir** verbs and add the appropriate ending. For verbs ending in **-re**, remove the **-e** before adding the ending. All verbs use the same endings.

*When forming the conditional, the stem of the verb should always end in an **-r** before adding the endings.*

Subject pronouns	Recycler (to recycle)	Réussir (to succeed)	Pendre (to hang)
je	recycler-ais	réussir-ais	pendr-ais
tu	recycler-ais	réussir-ais	pendr-ais
il/elle/on	recycler-ait	réussir-ait	pendr-ait
nous	recycler-ions	réussir-ions	pendr-ions
vous	recycler-iez	réussir-iez	pendr-iez
ils/elles	recycler-aient	réussir-aient	pendr-aient

Another easy way to remember how to form the conditional is by using the following formula:

Infinitive (without the -e for -re verbs) + imperfect endings = present conditional

C **Complete the sentences by choosing the correct form of the present conditional.**

1 J'_____ savoir comment préserver nos ressources naturelles.

   a aimais   b aimes   c aimeraient   d aimerais

2 _____-vous faire du covoiturage avec moi?

   a Aimerais   b Aimeriez   c Aimez   d Aimerait

3 Si Théo avait un jardin, il _____ un poulailler.

   a construirais b construisait c construisais   d construirait

4 Vous _____ votre linge dehors, pour ne plus vous servir de votre lave-linge?

   a étendrez   b étendrait   c étendriez   d étendaient

5 Cathy n'aime pas conduire mais elle _____ bien une petite voiture électrique.

   a conduiriez   b conduirais   c conduirait   d conduisait

6 Les filles _____ leurs légumes s'il ne pleuvait pas.

   a planteraient b planteriez   c plantaient   d planterait

D **Put the subject and verb in brackets into the present conditional.**

1 (je / réduire) _____

2 (nous / réussir) _____

3 (il / prendre) _____

4 (tu / finir) _____

5 (elle / économiser) _____

6 (vous / croire) _____

7 (ils / planter) _____

8 (nous / rendre) _____

2 Some verbs that have spelling changes in the present indicative do not change in the present conditional. Examples of such verbs are **commencer**, **manger** and **préférer**.

Je préférerais mettre les épluchures dans le bac à compost.

(I would prefer to put the peel in the compost bin.)

Vous commenceriez un nouveau programme de recyclage.

(You would start a new recycling programme.)

Nous mangerions plus sainement si on avait plus de temps.

(We would eat more healthily if we had the time.)

E Conjugate the verbs in brackets in the present conditional.

1   S'ils pensaient à la protection de l'environnement, ils _____ (lancer) une campagne pour éduquer les jeunes.

2   Je _____ (nager) dans le lac si l'eau était plus propre.

3   Est-ce que vous _____ (préférer) un sac en plastique ou un sac en papier?

4   Nous _____ (manger) bio mais ça coûte très cher.

5   Elle _____ (répéter) l'expérience de faire du bénévolat sans hésitation.

6   Tu _____ (avancer) les efforts de réduire les émissions du CO2 si tu pouvais.

3   Just like in the present and the future, verbs that end in -**eler** and -**eter** double the **l** or **t** (e.g. je renouve*ll*erais, je je*tt*erais). Verbs like **acheter** have an accent grave on the **e** (e.g. **nous achèterions**). Most verbs that end in -**yer** change **y** to **i** (e.g. **il pa***i***erait**).

Je renouvellerais mes efforts d'emmener de l'eau avec moi au lieu d'acheter des bouteilles en plastique si je pouvais.

(I would renew my efforts to bring water with me instead of buying plastic bottles if I could.)

Tu ne jetterais pas tes mégots par terre si tu savais comme c'est mal.

(You wouldn't throw your cigarette butts on the ground if you knew how bad it is.)

Nous mènerons l'effort en faveur des réductions d'émissions.

(We'll lead the effort in favour of reducing emissions.)

Elle paierait une amende si elle ne triait pas ses ordures.

(She would pay a fine if she didn't separate her rubbish.)

---

*Verbs that end in -**ayer** have the option to keep the **y**. **Payer** (to pay) is one of them, so you could also write:*

Elle payerait une amende si elle ne triait pas ses ordures.

(She would pay a fine if she didn't separate her rubbish.)

*Either one is correct. Other verbs like this include **balayer** (to sweep), **effrayer** (to frighten), **essayer** (to try) and **rayer** (to cross out).*

F Put the verbs in brackets in the present conditional.

1   Les enfants ont dit qu'ils _____ (nettoyer) le parc.

2   Nous _____ (acheter) bien une voiture hybride mais nous ne savons pas où commencer nos recherches.

3   J'_____ (appeler) Arthur mais j'ai perdu son numéro.

4   S'il n'était pas si fatigué, il se _____ (lever) plus tôt.

5   Si vous étiez écolo, vous ne _____ (jeter) pas cela par terre.

6   Pour économiser de l'eau, nous _____ (essayer) de ne pas arroser pendant la journée quand le soleil la fait s'évaporer.

Irregular verbs in the present conditional

A number of verbs have irregular conditional forms. They are the same as the irregular verbs in the future, but with the conditional endings. Here are the most common ones.

Infinitive	Conditional stem	First-person singular form
aller	ir-	j'irais
avoir	aur-	j'aurais
courir	courr-	je courrais
devoir	devr-	je devrais
envoyer	enverr-	j'enverrais
être	ser-	je serais
faire	fer-	je ferais
falloir*	faudra-	il faudrait
mourir	mourr-	je mourrais
pleuvoir*	pleuvr-	il pleuvrait
pouvoir	pourr-	je pourrais
recevoir	recevr-	je recevrais
savoir	saur-	je saurais
tenir	tiendr-	je tiendrais
venir	viendr-	je viendrais
voir	verr-	je verrais
vouloir	voudr-	je voudrais

*__Falloir__ and __pleuvoir__ do not have first-person singular forms.

G Put the subject and verb in brackets in the present conditional.

1 (pouvoir / vous) _____
2 (avoir / il) _____
3 (courir / nous) _____
4 (envoyer / tu) _____
5 (être / elle) _____
6 (aller / ils) _____

H Complete the sentences with either the conditional or the infinitive form of the verbs in brackets. The first one is done for you.

1 J'_aimerais_ (aimer) te voir jardiner sans pesticides.
2 Tu devrais _____ (prendre) les transports en commun au lieu de conduire.
3 Notre planète _____ (pouvoir) être une planète propre et sans pollution.
4 Tout le monde dans notre voisinage _____ (aimer) que la centrale nucléaire soit inspectée plus souvent.

5   Si Richard était vraiment concerné par la protection de l'environnement, il _____ (faire) plus attention à son empreinte carbone.

6   Les gouvernements devraient _____ (mettre) en place plus de réglementations pour protéger notre planète.

7   Nous _____ (pouvoir) réduire notre consommation d'électricité en nous assurant d'éteindre les appareils électriques le plus souvent possible.

8   Ils ont dit qu'ils nous _____ (apprendre) comment réduire nos déchets de 40%.

Vocabulary

I   Decide if the following are **bon** (*good*) or **mauvaise** (*bad*) for the planet.

1   les sacs (m) en plastique _____   5   les déchets (m) nocifs _____
2   le covoiturage _____   6   une ferme bio _____
3   une voiture électrique _____   7   les transports (m) en commun _____
4   les panneaux (m) solaires _____   8   une empreinte carbone _____

French and English share many words. The following words (cognates) have common origins and are not defined, as it is not necessary to speak fluent French to understand them. Notice the minor differences in spelling:

l'énergie (f)	**recycler**	**la centrale nucléaire**
les pesticides (m)	**le lac**	**la consommation**
planter	**la planète**	**l'électricité**

J   Rearrange the letters to find other cognates relating to the environment.

1   sle coursesres _____
2   l' reinventmenno _____
3   l' derbyhi _____
4   al touonlipl _____

Though words that are the same or similar can help comprehension when acquiring a language, faux amis (false friends) can be tricky. For example, biologique or bio in French means organic and not biological.

K Complete the sentences using the expressions in the box.

| des panneaux solaires | planter | ferme bio |
| des sacs en plastique | en voie de disparition | poulaillers |

1 Quand Louise va au centre commercial, elle prend son panier. Elle ne veut pas utiliser
   _____ parce qu'ils ne sont pas biodégradables.
2 Dans la _____, toutes les poules sont libres. Elles vivent en plein
   air et dans leurs _____, il n'y a pas de cages.
3 Dominique a décidé d'installer _____ sur le toit de sa maison.
4 Tu devrais _____ des légumes dans ton jardin pour manger bio.
5 Vous savez que le thon rouge est _____. On ne devrait plus en manger.

L Match the French with the English.

1 les ordures ménagères   a a chicken coop
2 un jardin potager   b outside
3 ramasser   c to build
4 construire   d to pick/to pick up
5 la récolte   e to reduce
6 réduire   f the household waste
7 un poulailler   g the harvest/crop
8 dehors   h a vegetable garden

 Reading

M You have just come across a blog on an environmentally friendly website. Read the first
   paragraph of the blog post and answer the questions.

Qu'est-ce que la jeune femme voudrait faire pour aider la planète? Quel serait le bénéfice?

_____

Blog quotidien

Des poules pour réduire les ordures ménagères et un petit potager.

J'aimerais faire un peu plus pour aider à conserver notre planète. Je viens d'acheter une petite
maison qui a un grand jardin. Je voudrais adopter des poules. Les poules pourraient manger
la plupart de mes ordures ménagères. Elles m'aideraient à réduire tout ce que je jette à la
poubelle donc j'aiderais la planète!

N **Now read the rest of the blog post and answer the questions.**

De plus, je me disais que je devrais leur construire un poulailler parce que dans le nord de la France, il fait frais, donc je ne voudrais pas laisser les poules tout le temps dehors. Je ne sais pas comment faire. Si mes amis ne travaillaient pas le week-end, je leur demanderais de m'aider. Je ne voudrais pas l'acheter tout prêt parce que ça coûterait trop cher.

Comme je suis plutôt débrouillarde et qu'il me resterait assez de place dans le jardin, je pourrais même faire un petit jardin potager. Je planterais mes légumes, je les cultiverais et je les cuisinerais. J'aimerais aussi les partager avec mes amis et ma famille. Qui sait, peut-être que j'aurais de la chance et que j'aurais de bonnes récoltes! Je pourrais même vendre mes légumes et mes œufs au marché.

En plus de mon projet d'avoir des poules et un jardin potager, je pense souvent à réduire la consommation d'eau et d'énergie de la maison. Je fais attention à couper l'eau quand je prends une douche ou quand je me brosse les dents et j'attends que le lave-vaisselle soit entièrement rempli avant de le mettre en marche. Si j'avais assez d'argent, j'installerais des panneaux solaires. C'est un projet pour plus tard.

Et vous, que pourriez-vous faire pour aider la planète?

1 Qu'est-ce que la jeune femme demanderait à ses amis s'ils ne travaillaient pas le week-end?
   _____

2 Qu'est-ce que la jeune femme aimerait faire dans le reste de son jardin?
   _____

3 Si les récoltes étaient bonnes, que ferait-elle des légumes?
   _____

4 Qu'est-ce qu'elle pourrait faire de plus si elle avait assez d'argent?
   _____

O **Find all the verbs conjugated in the present conditional in the blog post.**

_____

_____

 # Writing

P   Write a comment in response to the question that was asked at the end of the blog, Que pourriez-vous faire pour aider la planète? Use the conditional as much as possible. (80–100 words)

_____

_____

_____

_____

_____

_____

_____

_____

_____

_____

_____

_____

_____

Self-check

Tick the box that matches your level of confidence.

1 = very confident   2 = need more practice   3 = not confident

Cochez la case qui correspond à votre niveau d'aisance.

1 = très sûr(e) de vous   2 = j'ai besoin de plus de pratique   3 = pas sûr(e) du tout

	1	2	3
Use the present conditional.			
Form **si** (*if*) clauses.			
Can read and understand information about the environment in which the writer expresses specific attitudes and points of view (CEFR B2).			
Can write clear and detailed texts on environmental issues expressing an opinion and including supporting details (CEFR B2).			

16 Martin se lève encore de bonne heure

Martin still gets up early

In this unit, you will learn how to:

✔ Use pronominal verbs (reflexive, reciprocal and idiomatic).

CEFR: Can understand short texts that convey information about past and present everyday routines and relationships (B1); Can write simple connected text on everyday routines (B1).

Meaning and usage

Pronominal verbs

Pronominal verbs are verbs that use pronouns. They fall into three categories: reflexive, reciprocal and idiomatic.

1   Reflexive verbs express something that the subject does to itself.
    Lucas _se brosse_ les dents tous les matins. (*Lucas brushes his teeth every morning.*)

Common reflexive verbs		
s'arrêter (*to stop*)	se coucher (*to go to bed*)	se maquiller (*to put on make-up*)
s'asseoir (*to sit down*)	s'habiller (*to get dressed*)	se préparer (*to get ready*)
se brosser (*to brush hair or teeth*)	se laver (*to wash*)	se promener (*to take a walk*)
	se lever (*to get up*)	se réveiller (*to wake up*)
se changer (*to change*)		

 A   Underline the reflexive pronouns. When and how do they change?

1   Tu te lèves à six heures du matin? C'est tôt!
2   Ils se changent en rentrant du boulot.
3   Nous nous promenons dans le parc.
4   Je me réveille de bonne heure pour aller à la pêche.
5   Vous vous couchez après avoir regardé un film.
6   Elle s'habille dans des vêtements chic pour aller au bureau.

2 Reciprocal verbs indicate that two or more individuals do something to each other.

Ils s'écrivent souvent. *(They write to each other often.)*

Common reciprocal verbs		
s'aimer *(to love each other)*	s'embrasser *(to kiss each other)*	se rencontrer *(to meet with each other)*
se détester *(to detest/to hate each other)*	se parler *(to talk to each other)*	se retrouver *(to meet up/to get together with each other)*
se disputer *(to fight each other)*	se quitter *(to leave each other)*	se sourire *(to smile at each other)*
s'écrire *(to write to each other)*	se regarder *(to look at each other)*	se téléphoner *(to call each other on the phone)*

B **With many verbs, you can add the reflexive or reciprocal pronouns. This causes a change in meaning. Translate the following.**

1 Nous préparons la valise. _____

2 Nous nous préparons. _____

3 Ils regardent l'émission. _____

4 Ils se regardent dans les yeux. _____

The meaning of a sentence can change completely depending on whether or not you are using a pronominal expression or a direct object pronoun.

Je m'ennuie. *(I am bored.) (pronominal)*

Je t'ennuie. *(I am boring you.) (direct object)*

3 With idiomatic pronominal verbs, the pronoun is included, but it doesn't indicate that the action is being done to oneself or to one another.

Je me demande si elle est là. *(I wonder if she is there.)*

Common pronominal verbs used idiomatically		
s'en aller *(to go away)*	se demander *(to wonder)*	se sentir *(to feel)*
s'amuser *(to have fun)*	se dépêcher *(to hurry)*	se souvenir de *(to remember)*
s'apercevoir *(to notice)*	se marier *(to get married)*	se tromper *(to be mistaken)*
s'appeler *(to be called)*	se passer *(to happen)*	se trouver *(to be located)*

C **Verbs like this usually have a different meaning when used without the pronoun. State what that meaning is for each of the idiomatic verbs in the table, without the reflexive pronoun. If you don't know it, look it up.**

1 aller

2 amuser

3 apercevoir

4 appeler

5 demander

6 dépêcher

7 marier

8 passer

9 sentir

10 souvenir (se souvenir is the only verb form, souvenir is a noun, meaning memory)

11 tromper

12 trouver

4 Pronominal verbs are also sometimes used to express the passive voice. Here again, the pronoun does not always translate literally.

En Angleterre, manger des cuisses de grenouille ne se fait pas.

(In England, eating frogs' legs is not done.)

Le steak tartar se mange cru. *(Steak tartare is eaten raw.)* The **se** does not translate as *itself*.

Ça se voit. *(It's noticeable.)*

How to form pronominal verbs

Pronominal verbs in simple tenses

1 In the present, the pronoun changes to align with the subject. It goes before the verb.

Se raser *(to shave)*	
je *me* rase	nous *nous* rasons
tu *te* rases	vous *vous* rasez
il/elle/on *se* rase	ils/elles *se* rasent

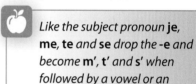
Like the subject pronoun je, me, te and se drop the -e and become m', t' and s' when followed by a vowel or an unaspirated h.

D **Conjugate the verbs in the present indicative, using the subject indicated.**

1 se laver / elle _____

2 s'aimer / nous _____

3 se disputer / ils _____

4 s'asseoir / je _____

5 s'écrire / vous _____

6 se coucher / nous _____

7 se tromper / tu _____

8 se téléphoner / elles _____

E **Complete with the best option.**

1 Inès _____ parce qu'elle a un rendez-vous amoureux.

   a se maquille   **b** te maquilles   **c** se maquillent

2 Les enfants _____ dès qu'ils arrivent à la plage.

   a nous baignons   **b** se baignent   **c** me baigne

3 Nous _____ au téléphone tous les soirs.

    a vous parlez   **b** se parlent   **c** nous parlons

4 Je _____ aux cultures étrangères.

    a t'intéresses   **b** s'intéresse   **c** m'intéresse

5 Quand tu n'as rien à faire, tu _____.

    a t'ennuies   **b** nous ennuyons   **c** s'ennuient

6 Vous _____ tout le temps.

    a te plains   **b** vous plaignez   **c** nous plaignons

2 In the imperative, drop the subject pronoun and put the reflexive pronoun after the verb with a hyphen. **Te/t'** becomes **toi**. Remember to drop the **-s** in the **tu** form where necessary.

Amuse-toi! *(Have fun!)*

Embrassez-vous! *(Kiss each other!)*

Levons-nous! *(Let's get up!)*

F **Jacqueline tells her children what they have to do in the morning. Put the verb in brackets in the imperative to complete the sentences.**

    1 Les enfants, _____, c'est l'heure! (se réveiller)

    2 Les enfants, _____, venez prendre le petit déjeuner! (se lever)

    3 Simon, _____, tu es sale! (se laver)

    4 Edith, _____, mets le pantalon bleu avec la chemise blanche. (s'habiller)

    5 Tous les deux, _____ les cheveux. (se brosser)

    6 Tous les deux _____, vous allez être en retard! (se dépêcher)

3 When the pronominal verb is in the infinitive, the pronoun still needs to agree with the subject of the sentence.

J'aime me maquiller. *(I like to put make-up on.)*

Nous allons nous revoir en juin. *(We will see each other again in June.)*

4 With simple verb tenses, the placement of the pronoun follows the rules of direct object pronouns.

Ils vont s'en aller demain. *(They are going to go away tomorrow.)*

Léo et Camille s'écrivaient tout le temps.

(Léo and Camille used to write to each other all the time.)

Tu te méfieras d'eux. *(You will be wary of them.)*

Vous vous souririez si vous pouviez vous voir.

(You would smile at each other if you could see each other.)

5 When forming questions using pronominal verbs, the rules remain the same. For questions using **est-ce que**, the pronoun goes before the verb.

Comment est-ce que tu t'appelles? *(What's your name?)*

For question inversion, the reflexive pronoun remains before the verb.

Comment t'appelles-tu? *(What's your name?)*

G Rewrite the following questions using question inversion.

  1 Est-ce que tu te trompes souvent? _____

  2 Est-ce qu'ils s'aiment? _____

  3 Est-ce que vous vous amusez? _____

  4 Est-ce que tu te maquilles? _____

  5 Est-ce que nous allons nous habituer à ce genre de vie? _____

  6 Est-ce qu'elles se parleront? _____

H Complete the sentences by adding the missing reflexive pronoun in the appropriate place.

  1 Thomas et Juliette sont très athlétiques, ils _____ ne _____ fatiguent pas _____ facilement.

  2 Je _____ ne _____ souviens _____ pas très bien de mon enfance.

  3 Nous _____ sommes _____ promenés _____ toute la journée.

  4 Vous ne/n'_____ allez pas _____ disputer _____ encore une fois.

  5 _____ Dépêche-_____, nous sommes en retard!

  6 Tu _____ débrouilles _____ très bien.

Pronominal verbs in the passé composé

1 In the **passé composé**, **être** is the auxiliary and the pronoun goes before it.
   Il s'est levé en retard, il s'est habillé et il est parti tout de suite. *(He woke up late, got dressed and left right away.)*

I Using what you know about direct object agreement in the **passé composé,** read these sentences and indicate why the past participle changes.

  1 Elle s'est reveillée. _____

  2 Nous nous sommes regardés. _____

  3 Ils se sont vus. _____

  4 Tu ne t'es pas habillée. _____

2 In most cases, the pronoun is the direct object of the sentence, so the past participle has to agree in gender and number with the pronoun.
   Elle s'est amusée. *(She had fun.)*
   Vous vous êtes disputés. *(You fought with each other. /You had a fight.)*

3 The past participle does not agree if there is a direct object after the verb in the **passé composé**. This happens most often with body parts, including hair.
   Hélène s'est coupée. *(Hélène cut herself.)*
   Hélène s'est coupé le doigt. *(Hélène cut her finger.)*
   Nous nous sommes lavés. *(We washed [ourselves].)*
   Nous nous sommes lavé les cheveux. *(We washed our hair.)*

> *When reflexive verbs are used with a body part, the possessive adjective (***mon, ton, son,*** etc.) is not used. Instead of a possessive adjective, the definite article (***le, la, les***) is used.*
>
> **Il s'est lavé les mains.** *(He washed his hands.)*

4 The past participle also does not agree when the pronoun is an indirect object.

Elles se sont vu_es_ dans la rue mais elles ne se sont pas parlé. *(They saw each other on the street but they did not speak to each other.)*

Verbs like **parler** *(to talk to)* are followed by **à** when they are not used pronominally.

Elle a parlé à son amie, son amie lui a parlé. *(She talked to her friend, her friend talked to her.)*

Other common verbs that have a reflexive pronoun that is an indirect object include: **se dire** *(to tell each other)*, **se téléphoner** *(to call on the phone)*, **se plaire** *(to please)*, **se ressembler** *(to look like)*, **se nuire** *(to hurt)*, **se sourire** *(to smile)*.

J **Add the necessary ending to the past participle.**

1 Sarah, tu t'es lavé_____ la figure?
2 Ils se sont tout dit_____.
3 Elle s'est inquiété_____.
4 Nous nous sommes parlé_____.
5 Vous vous êtes souri_____.
6 Elle s'est débrouillé_____.

Vocabulary

Expressions of frequency can be used to describe your daily routine.

chaque matin/jour/soir	each morning/day/evening
d'habitude	usually
de temps en temps	from time to time
rarement	rarely
souvent	often
tous les jours	every day

K **Match the French with the English.**

1 se faire
2 se retrouver
3 se connaître
4 s'établir
5 se forcer
6 se parler de tout et de rien
7 se prendre en main
8 s'occuper

a to establish oneself (in business)
b to pick oneself up
c to stay busy, to busy oneself
d to talk about this and that
e to make oneself
f to find oneself
g to meet (to get acquainted)
h to make the effort

# Reading

L Read the first paragraph of Martin's description about his current life compared with how it used to be, and answer the questions.

1 Où est-ce que Martin et sa femme se sont rencontrés? _____
_____

2 Qu'est-ce qu'ils étudiaient? Quelles carrières ont-ils choisies? _____
_____

M Now read the rest of Martin's story and answer the questions.

1 Pourquoi Martin est-il déprimé? _____
   _____

2 Quelle est sa routine le matin? _____
   _____

3 Comment est-ce que Martin et Anne se font-ils plaisir? _____
   _____

4 Qu'est-ce qu'Anne a dit pour que Martin décide de trouver un travail? ___
   _____

N **Find the pronominal verbs in the text and write them out in the infinitive. Indicate if they are reflexive, reciprocal or neither.**

Writing

O **Write a note to a friend to describe your daily routine now and when you were younger. What changes have you made? (80–100 words)**

_____

_____

_____

_____

_____

_____

Self-check

Tick the box that matches your level of confidence.

   1 = very confident   2 = need more practice   3 = not confident

Cochez la case qui correspond à votre niveau d'aisance.

   1 = très sûr(e) de vous   2 = j'ai besoin de plus de pratique   3 = pas sûr(e) du tout

	1	2	3
Use pronominal verbs (reflexive, reciprocal and idiomatic).			
Can understand short texts that convey information about past and present everyday routines and relationships (CEFR B1).			
Can write simple connected text on everyday routines (CEFR B1).			

17 Elle veut que tout le monde soit bien dans sa peau

She wants everyone to feel good about themselves

In this unit, you will learn how to:

- ✓ Form the present subjunctive.
- ✓ Understand when to use the subjunctive.
- ✓ Use medical vocabulary.

CEFR: Can understand detailed medical information (B2); Can write clear and detailed descriptions of health needs (B2).

Meaning and usage

The present subjunctive

1 The subjunctive is one of four moods in French along with the indicative (all present, future and past tenses), the imperative and the conditional. The subjunctive is used to express subjectivity and to convey such ideas as wishes, desires, emotions, uncertainty, doubt or obligation. In French, it is commonly used in the present and less commonly in the past.

2 The subjunctive itself does not imply any time reference (present, future, past), but its different tenses are determined by context or by the main verb in a sentence in which the subjunctive is the subordinate clause. The imperfect and pluperfect subjunctive are used infrequently and can mostly be found in formal, literary writing.

 A Identify which sentence expresses a fact, which conveys uncertainty, and which conveys an obligation. Which forms of aller (to go) are the same?

　1　Il sait qu'elle va chez le médecin cet après-midi.
　2　Il faut qu'elle aille chez le médecin cet après-midi.
　3　Je doute qu'elle aille chez le médecin cet après-midi.

3 In English, the subjunctive is rarely used, but you can find it in sentences such as *It is important that you be on time* or *If I were you, I'd call first*. It is used more often in French than in English.

4 While most indicative tenses in French are easily translated by using the equivalent English tense, e.g. **je chante** *(I sing)*, **j'ai chanté** *(I sang)*, the subjunctive and the indicative are often translated in English with the same verb forms:
Je sais que tu _comprends_. *(I know that you _understand_.)* (a fact, therefore indicative)
Je préfère que tu _comprennes_. *(I prefer that you _understand_.)* (an uncertainty, therefore subjunctive)
Nous voulons qu'elles _viennent_. *(We want them _to come_.)* (a preference, therefore subjunctive)

How to form the present subjunctive

1   You can form the present subjunctive by adding the following endings to the verb stem:

Singular	Plural
-e	-ions
-es	-iez
-e	-ent

2   For most of these verbs, you remove the third person plural ending **-ent** to find the stem. These are called one-stem verbs.
Elles ~~chantent~~ → chant-, **elles** ~~finissent~~ → finiss-, **elles** ~~attendent~~ → attend-.

Subject pronoun	Chanter	Finir	Attendre
je/j'	chante	finisse	attende
tu	chantes	finisses	attendes
il/elle/on	chante	finisse	attende
nous	chantions	finissions	attendions
vous	chantiez	finissiez	attendiez
ils/elles	chantent	finissent	attendent

*For **-er** verbs, the endings are the same as for the present indicative, except for the first and second person plural.*

3   The following one-stem verbs have an irregular stem, but the endings remain the same:

Subject pronoun	Faire	Pouvoir	Savoir
je	fasse	puisse	sache
tu	fasses	puisses	saches
il/elle/on	fasse	puisse	sache
nous	fassions	puissions	sachions
vous	fassiez	puissiez	sachiez
ils/elles	fassent	puissent	sachent

4   Some verbs have two stems. One for the singular and third person plural, and one for the first and second person plural. These verbs, such as **appeler**, **venir** and **boire**, also have two stems in the present indicative.

Subject pronoun	Appeler	Venir	Boire
je/j'	appelle	vienne	boive
tu	appelles	viennes	boives
il/elle/on	appelle	vienne	boive
nous	appelions	venions	buvions
vous	appeliez	veniez	buviez
ils/elles	appellent	viennent	boivent

With these verbs, the stems are different because of the number of spoken syllables in the conjugated verbs. The first and second person plural conjugations have two syllables and the other forms only have one when they are pronounced.

5   **Aller**, **avoir**, **être** and **vouloir** are two-stem verbs that are irregular in the subjunctive.

Subject pronoun	Aller	Avoir	Être	Vouloir
je/j'	aille	aie	sois	veuille
tu	ailles	aies	sois	veuilles
il/elle/on	aille	ait	soit	veuille
nous	allions	ayons	soyons	voulions
vous	alliez	ayez	soyez	vouliez
ils/elles	aillent	aient	soient	veuillent

B   **Fill in the gaps using the correct subjunctive form of the verbs in brackets.**

1   Nous avons peur qu'elle _____ (tomber).
2   Tu ne veux pas qu'il _____ (savoir) ce que tu as fait.
3   Elle n'a pas voulu qu'on _____ (aller) la voir à l'hôpital.
4   Pierre est content qu'elle _____ (pouvoir) marcher.
5   Il est important que vous _____ (faire) de l'exercice tous les jours. Il faut garder la forme!
6   Nous sommes désolés qu'il _____ (avoir) des pertes de mémoire.
7   Le médecin exige qu'elle _____ (prendre) des vitamines supplémentaires pendant sa grossesse.
8   Elle ne veut pas qu'il _____ (attraper) un virus.
9   L'infirmière va te donner une piqûre, que tu le _____ (vouloir) ou non.
10   Il faut que tous les enfants _____ (recevoir) les soins nécessaires.

The present subjunctive after que

1   The subjunctive is most commonly used in subordinate clauses (clauses introduced by **que**) where the subject of the subordinate clause is different from the subject of the main verb (e.g. **Elle veut que tu sois là**, *She wants you to be there*). The use of the subjunctive is determined by the meaning conveyed by the main verb.

2   Some verbs are always followed by the subjunctive. There are distinct categories when the subjunctive is always used. Here are some of them.

C   **Finish the sentences in the table using a verb in the subjunctive.**

Feelings		
Emotion	aimer mieux, être content, être déçu, être heureux, avoir honte, être ravi	**1** Tu es content qu'*il vienne*.
Judgement	il est dommage, il est regrettable, il est bon, il est juste, il est important, il vaut mieux	**2** Il est important que _____ _____
Surprise	s'étonner, être étonné, être surpris	**3** Elle est surprise que _____ _____
Fear	avoir peur, craindre	**4** J'ai peur que _____
Obligation	il faut, il ne faut pas, il est essentiel, il est nécessaire, il est obligatoire, il suffit	**5** Il est nécessaire que _____ _____

Will		
Commands	s'attendre à, commander, demander, dire, écrire, ordonner, proposer	**6** Nous proposons que _____ _____
Wishes	vouloir, vouloir bien, tenir à, souhaiter	**7** Vous souhaitez que _____
Permission and prohibition	accepter, défendre, interdire, empêcher, s'opposer à, refuser	**8** J'accepte que _____ _____
Advice	conseiller, recommander	**9** Elle recommande que _____ _____

Possibility		
Supposition	il est impossible, il se peut, il est possible, il n'est pas possible	**10** Il est possible _____ _____
Doubt	douter, il est douteux, il est peu probable, il est improbable	**11** Il est peu probable que _____ _____
Denial	nier, il est exclu	Il est exclu que tu les fasses.

After certain conjunctions		
Goal (when expressing a goal and not a consecutive result)	pour que, afin que, de façon que, de manière à, de sorte que	**12** Nous écrivons pour que _____ _____
Time	avant que, jusqu'à ce que, en attendant que	Tu lui parles jusqu'à ce qu'il soit d'accord avec toi.
Condition	à condition que, à supposer que, pourvu que	Je te donne les clés à condition que tu reviennes avant minuit.
Concession	bien que, quoi que	Elle vient quoi que tu veuilles.
Restriction	à moins que	Je le fais à moins que ce soit déjà fini.
Fear	de peur que, de crainte que	Je laisse la lumière allumée de peur que tu te perdes en rentrant.

With certain expressions when negated	
ça ne veut pas dire que, ce n'est pas que, il ne me semble pas que, il n'est pas certain que, il n'est pas clair que, il n'est pas évident que, il n'est pas vrai que, ne pas dire que, ne pas être sûr que, ne pas penser que, ne pas croire que, ne pas trouver que…	Il n'est pas certain que je vienne.

While **souhaiter** (to wish) is always used with the subjunctive when followed by **que**, **espérer** (to hope) is not. It is usually followed by the future.

J'espère qu'elle viendra. (I hope she will come.)

D **Put the following sentences into the negative.**

1 Elle croit que c'est important. _____

2 Vous pensez que les vaccins doivent être obligatoires. _____

3 Tu trouves qu'il a l'air blême. _____

4 Il est vrai que nous devons faire moins de sport. _____

5 Nous sommes sûrs que Claire est malade. _____

6 Elles disent que c'est bon. _____

3 The indicative can be used after the negative and in questions with **croire** and **penser** to convey the idea that you are certain about the action.

Je ne crois pas que tu as raison. (I don't believe you're right – I think you are wrong.)

Je ne crois pas que tu aies raison. (I don't believe you're right – I might be mistaken though.)

Je ne pense pas que tu as raison. (I don't think you're right – I think you are wrong.)

Je ne pense pas que tu aies raison. (I don't think you're right – I might be mistaken though.)

4 The subjunctive is used with superlatives or with **le premier**, **le seul**, **le dernier** in the main clause and to express you are uncertain something can happen or even exists.

C'est le plus bel hôpital qui soit. *(It's the most beautiful hospital there is.)* (This is an opinion, but it might not be true.)

Ce sont les seuls patients qu'il ait vus. *(Those are the only patients he saw.)* (There may have been others, he didn't see them.)

Ils cherchent une infirmière qui soit parfaitement bilingue. *(They are looking for a perfectly bilingual nurse.)* (They are looking, but what they are looking for might not exist.)

5 The subjunctive is used in independent clauses introduced with **que** and expressing an order or a wish.

Qu'il aille tout de suite aux urgences! *(Let him/He should go immediately to A&E.)*

Que je meurs si je mens. *(Hope to die if I'm lying.)*

In certain fixed expressions, there is no **que**.

Ainsi soit-il! *(So be it!)*   **Sauve qui peut!** *(Every man for himself!)*

Dieu soit loué! *(Praise be to God!)*   **Vive la République!** *(Long live the Republic!)*

It's a good idea to add these kinds of idiomatic expressions to your repertoire to improve your proficiency level.

6 There are several ways to avoid the subjunctive in French.
- Use a noun.
  Elle y va avant le départ de son mari. *(She's going there before her husband's departure.)*

- Make a general statement. Instead of saying:
  Il faut que tu prennes tes médicaments. *(You have to take your medicine.)*

  Say: **Il faut prendre ses médicaments.** *(One must take one's medicine.)*

- Find a different way of saying something. Make two sentences if necessary.
  Tu dois prendre tes médicaments. *(You have to take your medicine.)*
  Prends tes médicaments maintenant. Je l'exige. *(Take your medicine now. I demand it.)*

E **Cross out the incorrect form of the verb (indicative or subjunctive). If the forms look the same, say which one it is.**

1 Nous attendons que tu nous dis/dises la vérité.
2 Le père voit que son fils a/ait de la fièvre.
3 Je t'affirme que le médecin veut/veuille te parler.
4 Nous cherchons une maison qui est/soit accessible aux personnes handicapées.
5 Tu vas subir l'opération que le médecin commande/commande?
6 Elle a peur que ses blessures ne sont/soient pas guérissables.
7 Je ne pense pas qu'elle a/ait besoin de se faire opérer.
8 Vous êtes surpris qu'elle y arrive/arrive?

*The past subjunctive is used when the action in the subordinate clause happened before the action in the main clause. It is formed by using the auxiliary **être** or **avoir** along with the past participle of the verb. Compare these sentences:*

J'avais peur qu'elle tombe. *(I was afraid she would fall.)*

J'avais peur qu'elle soit tombée. *(I was afraid she had fallen.)*

F **Complete the sentences with the verb in brackets in either the indicative or the present subjunctive, depending on what is needed.**

1 Vous êtes contents que les résultats de la visite médicale _____ (arriver) si vite?

2 Elles veulent que tu _____ (aller) voir un médecin spécialiste.

3 Le chirurgien l'a vue ce matin. Il a dit qu'il faut qu'elle _____ (maigrir) avant de pouvoir se faire l'opérer.

4 J'ai un médicament périmé. Est-ce que je _____ (devoir) le jeter?

5 Il a besoin de faire renouveler son ordonnance? Qu'il le _____ (faire)!

6 Nous avons téléphoné pour qu'une ambulance _____ (venir) l'emmener aux urgences.

7 Ma grand-mère n'a pas besoin de lunettes puisqu'elle _____ (avoir) la vue presque parfaite.

8 Le médecin lui a donné une ordonnance pour des béquilles afin qu'il qu'il _____ (pouvoir) marcher avec sa jambe dans le plâtre.

Remember not to use the subjunctive when the main clause and the subordinate clause have the same subject. In these instances, you should use an infinitive.

Je veux que tu viennes. *(I want you to come.)*

Je veux venir. *(I want to come.)*

Vocabulary

G **Complete the conversation with the words in the box.**

rhume	consultation	fièvre	digestion	mal à la gorge
comprimés	médicament	(se) reposer	toux	

André: Bonjour Madame. Pourriez-vous m'aider avec quelque chose pour un (1) _____?

La pharmacienne: Vous avez de la (2) _____?

André:	Non, j'ai juste **(3)** _____ et j'ai un peu de **(4)** _____.
La pharmacienne:	D'accord, prenez ces **(5)** _____, mais attention, il ne faut pas conduire après.
André:	Merci. J'ai l'intention de rentrer chez moi pour me **(6)** _____.
La pharmacienne:	Vous désirez autre chose, monsieur?
André:	Oui, vous pourriez m'indiquer un **(7)** _____ pour ma femme? Elle a des problèmes de **(8)** _____.
La pharmacienne:	Cela dépendrait de beaucoup de choses. Il vaudrait mieux qu'elle vienne pour une **(9)** _____.
André:	D'accord, je lui dirai de venir si ça continue. Merci! Au revoir!
La pharmacienne:	Oui monsieur, au revoir!

H   Find the odd one out.

1   un hôpital | une clinique | un cabinet médical | un thermomètre | un centre de rééducation physique
2   le dentiste | l'infirmier | la radiographie | la radiologue | l'oculiste
3   une piqûre | suivre un traitement | se faire soigner | subir une opération | prendre des médicaments
4   donner une ordonnance | attraper la grippe | soigner | guérir | rééduquer
5   un comprimé | une pilule | une pastille | une gélule | un pansement
6   le dermatologue | le gynécologue | le pédiatre | le cancer | le psychiatre

📖 Reading

I   Read the introduction to an interview with Dr Marie Perez Siscar. Indicate if the following statements are V (vrai/true) or F (faux/false).

1   France Thalasso est le syndicat officiel de thalassothérapie en France.   V/F
2   Docteur Perez Siscar a commencé sa carrière comme médecin généraliste.   V/F
3   Docteur Perez Siscar n'a pas de salariés sous sa direction.   V/F

Directrice et médecin conseil des centres Côté Thalasso Banyuls sur Mer et Ile de Ré, le Docteur Marie Perez Siscar a récemment été élue Présidente de France Thalasso, le Syndicat officiel de la thalassothérapie en France. Ce médecin-ostéopathe qui a commencé sa carrière médicale comme urgentiste est également chef d'entreprise et gère une cinquantaine de collaborateurs. Nous l'avons interrogée pour que vous puissiez bénéficier de ses conseils.

J   Now read the interview and answer the questions that follow.

I: En quoi le travail que vous faites maintenant et le travail comme urgentiste sont-ils différents?

Dr PS: Le métier de médecin en thalassothérapie permet de conjuguer prévention et bien-être au lieu de traumatismes et stress; de prendre le temps d'écouter avec les patients qui restent longuement dans nos établissements.

I: Qu'est-ce que la thalassothérapie?

Dr PS: La thalassothérapie est définie comme étant « l'utilisation combinée des bienfaits du milieu marin, qui comprend le climat marin, l'eau de mer, les boues marines, les algues, les sables et autres substances extraites de la mer. »

I: Qui sont vos clients?

Dr PS: Les gens qui viennent dans nos centres ne sont pas malades. On parle de prévention santé, ou d'amélioration de la santé. Toutes les personnes pour qui le bien-être constitue aussi la santé sont nos clients; toutes les personnes qui ont des douleurs (y compris après une intervention chirurgicale) sont nos clients, toutes les personnes qui veulent passer un bon moment en se faisant du bien sont nos clients.

I: Quels sont les bienfaits de la thalassothérapie?

Dr PS: La thalassothérapie procure des bienfaits physiques: réadaptation progressive à l'effort, amélioration de la circulation veineuse, diminution ou disparition des tensions liées à des douleurs musculaires de stress, d'arthrose … Amélioration de la qualité du sommeil … Meilleure résistance aux infections microbiennes par stimulation des défenses immunitaires par la « recharge » en oligo-éléments, vitamines et minéraux contenus dans l'eau de mer, la boue et les algues, et des bienfaits psychiques grâce aux soins relaxants, l'effet des ions négatifs naturels du bord de mer …

I: Que faut-il faire pour être en forme et bien dans sa peau?

Dr PS: Il faut avoir une bonne hygiène de vie. Bien se nourrir, bouger et ne pas se croire seul au monde, s'intéresser aux autres …

1   Comment le travail actuel de Docteur Perez Siscar est-il différent du travail qu'elle a fait aux urgences? _____

2   Comment est-ce que la thalassothérapie aide les gens? _____

3   Qu'est-ce que le docteur veut dire quand elle dit « Il faut avoir une bonne hygiène de vie? »
_____

K Match the following terms from the interview with the English.

1 le bienfait   **a** marine (adj.), of the sea
2 l'urgentiste (m.)   **b** the seaweed
3 chirurgical(e)   **c** the benefit
4 marin   **d** the sleep
5 le sommeil   **e** surgical
6 les algues (f.)   **f** the A&E doctor

Writing

L Write an e-mail to the doctor to ask for her opinion about what you can do to improve your health. Describe what you currently do for your health and what you could be doing to make it better. Use the subjunctive where possible. (80–100 words)

_____

_____

_____

_____

_____

_____

_____

_____

_____

Self-check

Tick the box that matches your level of confidence.

1 = very confident   2 = need more practice   3 = not confident

Cochez la case qui correspond à votre niveau d'aisance.

1 = très sûr(e) de vous   2 = j'ai besoin de plus de pratique   3 = pas sûr(e) du tout

	1	2	3
Forming the present subjunctive.			
Understanding when to use the subjunctive.			
Can understand detailed medical information (CEFR B2).			
Can write clear and detailed descriptions of health needs (CEFR B2).			

18 La rage au volant
Road rage

In this unit, you will learn how to:

- Understand and use the passive voice.
- Understand and use indirect speech.

CEFR: Can express personal views and opinions about modes of transportation (B1); Can read reports concerned with current issues about transportation (B2).

Meaning and usage

The passive voice

1   The subject of the sentence in the passive voice, or **la voix passive**, receives the action.

Active: **La voiture renverse le piéton.** *(The car runs over the pedestrian.)*

Passive: **Le piéton est renversé par la voiture.** *(The pedestrian is run over by the car.)*

2   The passive voice is used to emphasize an action or state when the person or thing doing the action is unimportant, unknown or assumed to be known already.

 A   Identify the instances of the passive voice in these sentences and rewrite them in the active voice.

1   Le camion est conduit par Paul. _____

2   Le train est pris par les voyageurs. _____

3   Michelle est respectée de tout le monde. _____

4   La moto a été renversée par un camion sur l'autoroute. _____

How to form the passive voice

1   In order to form the passive voice, use the auxiliary **être** along with the past participle, which must agree in gender and number with the subject.

Le véhicule _est poursuivi_. *(The vehicle _is being followed_.)*

Les stars de cinéma sont aimées de leurs fans. *(Film stars are loved by their fans.)*

2   If present, the person or thing doing the action is preceded by **par**, except with the verbs **aimer**, **connaître** and **respecter**, which take **de**.

Le véhicule est poursuivi par la police. *(The vehicle is being chased by the police.)*

Les stars sont poursuivies par leurs fans. *(The stars are chased by their fans.)*

3 Conjugate **être** in the passive voice in the same tense as you would conjugate the verb in the active voice.

L'utilisation du téléphone portable _est_ interdite au volant. (*Using a mobile phone while driving _is_ prohibited.*)

L'utilisation du téléphone portable _a été_ interdite au volant. (*Using a mobile phone while driving _has been_ prohibited.*)

L'utilisation du téléphone portable _sera_ interdite au volant. (*Using a mobile phone while driving _will be_ prohibited.*)

B **Complete the sentences with the verbs in brackets in the passive. Use the verb tense indicated.**

  1 Son roman _____ (lire, passé composé) par des millions de personnes.

  2 Le trophée _____ (remporter, passé composé) par celui qui a conduit le plus vite.

  3 Sa mobylette _____ (voler, passé composé).

  4 Les pompiers _____ (avertir, passé composé) par le propriétaire que sa maison avait pris feu.

  5 Il _____ (aimer, présent) de tout le monde.

  6 Puisque tu as fui la scène de l'accident, tu _____ (rechercher, futur) par la police.

  7 La circulation _____ (affecter, présent) par l'accident sur la route.

  8 Espérons que la loi sur les pistes cyclables _____ (voter, futur).

4 French uses the passive voice much less than English. If a sentence seems awkward in the active voice, you can make sentences less awkward by using **on** in the active voice.

On a cassé le parebrise. (*Someone broke the windscreen.*)

On ne m'a pas dit qu'il aimait les bateaux. (*I wasn't told he likes boats.*)

Another way to avoid the passive voice is to use a pronominal verb.

La portière de la voiture a été ouverte. (*The car door was opened.*)

La portière de la voiture s'est ouverte. (*The car door opened.*)

There isn't really any other way to translate this into English because The door opened itself *has a different meaning.*

C **Rewrite the sentences to avoid the passive voice.**

  1 Les accidents sont évités en faisant attention à la route. _____

  2 L'arrivée de l'avion est attendue. _____

  3 Les bagages seront déposés à la gare. _____

  4 Le clignotant n'a pas été mis. _____

  5 Le pneu a été crevé. _____

6 Le code de la route n'a pas été respecté. _____

7 Une voiture a été arrêtée par un auto-stoppeur. _____

8 Des témoins de l'accident sont recherchés par la police. _____

> *Unlike in English, the passive voice is not possible in French in sentences with indirect objects. For instance, you cannot say in French,* Stephanie was spoken to. *Instead, use* **on**: **On a parlé à Stéphanie.**

Indirect speech

1 In French, there are two ways of reporting what someone has said, directly or indirectly. In direct speech, you quote someone.

Il m'a dit, « Tu ne conduis pas très bien ». *(He said to me, 'You don't drive very well.')*

In indirect speech, you report what the person has said without quoting them.

Il m'a dit que je ne conduisais pas très bien. *(He told me that I wasn't driving very well.)*

D **Fill in the gaps to form sentences using direct speech.**

1 Le capitaine dit qu'il faut mettre les gilets de sauvetage.
   Le capitaine a dit, « Il _____ ».

2 Elle a dit qu'elle n'aimait pas du tout conduire.
   Elle a dit, « Je _____ ».

3 Vous déclarez que vous serez prêts à partir dans dix minutes.
   Vous déclarez, « Nous _____ ».

Here are a number of verbs that can be used with indirect speech:

affirmer	*to affirm*	**expliquer**	*to explain*
ajouter	*to add*	**insister**	*to insist*
annoncer	*to announce*	**prétendre**	*to claim*
déclarer	*to declare, to state*	**répondre**	*to answer*
dire	*to say*	**soutenir**	*to maintain*

2 If the sentence being relayed has a conjugated verb, use **que** to join the two clauses. You may need to change the verb conjugation to agree with the new subject.
   Direct speech: **Jean dit, « Je vois un bateau à voile. »** *(Jean says, 'I see a sailing boat.')*
   Indirect speech: **Jean dit qu'il voit un bateau à voile.** *(Jean says that he sees a sailing boat.)*

3 You may also need to change the pronouns and possessives.

Direct speech: **Stéphane insiste, « Je veux voir ta nouvelle voiture. »** *(Stéphane insists, 'I want to see your new car.')*

Indirect speech: **Stéphane a insisté qu'il voulait voir ma nouvelle voiture.** *(Stéphane insisted that he wanted to see my new car.)*

E **Read what Thomas has to say about his commute and then summarize what he says using indirect speech. The first one is done for you.**

> J'habite à Villeurbanne dans la banlieue proche de Lyon et je travaille en centre-ville. Heureusement, ce n'est pas trop loin. D'habitude, je fais la navette à vélo pour me rendre au boulot. Normalement, le trajet me prend près d'une demi-heure. Dans la ville de Lyon et en région lyonnaise, on a aménagé l'espace urbain pour mieux l'adapter aux piétons et aux cyclistes. Il y a un réseau important de pistes cyclables et je me sens en sécurité quand je prends mon vélo. Toutefois, les jours où il fait trop mauvais, je prends les transports en commun. Si elle est disponible, ma femme me dépose à la station de métro. Nous avons de la chance d'habiter si près. C'est pratique, propre et rarement bondé.

Il dit qu'il habite à Villeurbanne dans la banlieue proche de Lyon et qu'il travaille en centre-ville.

_____

_____

_____

_____

_____

_____

_____

4 In sentences with the imperative, replace the order or command with **de** + the infinitive.

Direct speech: **Votre père: « Apprenez le code de la route! »**

(Your father: 'Learn the Highway Code!')

Indirect speech: **Votre père a dit d'apprendre le code de la route.**

(Your father said to learn the Highway Code.)

F **Jeanne is teaching Charles how to drive a car. Report on what she told him to do.**

Jeanne: Relâchez le frein à main.

Charles: D'accord.

Jeanne: Posez votre pied sur la pédale du frein.

Charles: D'accord.

Jeanne: Mettez la clé de contact et tournez-la.

Charles: C'est fait.

Jeanne: Enclenchez le levier de vitesse.

Charles: OK.

Jeanne: Levez votre pied du frein et appuyez sur la pédale d'accélérateur.

_____

_____

_____

_____

_____

_____

_____

_____

5   When using indirect speech, the tenses change as follows:

Direct speech			Indirect speech		
Présent	Jean: « J'*achète* une moto. » Jean: (I am buying a motorcycle.)		**Imparfait**	Jean a dit qu'il *achetait* une moto. (Jean said he was going to buy a motorcycle.)	
Futur	Marie: « Nous *louerons* une voiture. » Marie: (We will rent a car.)		**Conditionnel**	Marie a dit qu'ils *loueraient* une voiture. (Marie said that they would rent a car.)	
Passé composé	Paul: « Elle *a reçu* un PV. » Paul: (She got a ticket.)		**Plus-que-parfait**	Paul a dit qu'elle *avait reçu* un PV. (Paul said that she got a ticket.)	

G   **Rewrite the sentences using indirect speech.**

1   Elle affirme, « Toutes les voitures doivent passer une inspection annuelle ».

_____

2   Nous avons dit, « Nous nous méfions des systèmes de géolocalisation. »

_____

3   Le policier lui demande, « Donnez-moi vos papiers d'identité ».

_____

4   Nous avons expliqué, « Faites attention quand il fait nuit parce qu'il y a des cerfs dans le coin».

_____

5   Le conducteur de la voiture a assuré, « Je ne roulais pas à 160 kilomètres à l'heure ».

_____

6   Il a crié, « Venez au secours! »

_____

7   Vous avez dit, « Je prendrai un café quand je serai arrivé ».

_____

8   Tu as répondu, « J'ai réussi à faire un créneau ».

_____

6 Reporting questions happens in different ways depending on the type of question.

When reporting questions with **est-ce que,** use **si:**

Direct speech: Il demande, « **Est-ce que tu prends le train?** »

(He asks, 'Are you taking the train?')

Indirect speech: Il a demandé si tu prenais le train. *(He asked if you were taking the train.)*

For questions with **où, quand, combien, comment, pourquoi** and **qui,** just undo the inversion.

Direct speech: **Chantal demande, « Où est-il? »** *(Chantal asks, 'Where is he?')*

Indirect speech: **Chantal demande où il est.** *(Chantal asks where he is.)*

In questions with **qu'est-ce que** or **qu'est-ce qui,** use **ce que/ce qu'** or **ce qui.**

Direct speech: **Elle demande, « Qu'est-ce que tu veux? »** *(She asks, 'What do you want?')*

Indirect speech: **Elle a demandé ce que tu voulais.** *(She asked what you wanted.)*

H Iris calls her friend Antoine because her car has a flat tyre. Antoine tells his mother and asks to borrow her car. Change the statements made by Iris into indirect speech.

1 **Iris:** Bonjour Antoine, tu m'entends? Je suis au bord de l'autoroute.

Antoine: Oui, oui, qu'est-ce qui se passe?

Antoine à sa mère: <u>Iris me demande si je peux l'entendre. Elle dit qu'elle est au bord de l'autoroute.</u>

2 **Iris:** Ecoute Antoine, pourrais-tu m'aider? J'ai eu un pneu crevé.

Antoine: Oh là là, c'est terrible!

Antoine à sa mère: _____

3 **Iris:** Oui, c'est terrible. Est-ce que tu sais comment mettre une roue de secours? J'en ai une.

Antoine: Oui, je sais mettre une roue de secours. Heureusement que tu en as une.

Antoine à sa mère: _____

4 **Iris:** Super! Tu peux me rejoindre? Je suis sur le périphérique en allant vers l'est juste après la porte d'Orléans?

Antoine: Je crois que oui.

Antoine à sa mère: _____

5 **Iris:** Ta mère te laissera-t-elle prendre sa voiture pour venir m'aider? Je lui en serais très reconnaissante.

Antoine: Je vais lui demander.

Antoine à sa mère: _____

Antoine: Iris, c'est bon, je peux prendre sa voiture.

Vocabulary

I Complete the sentences with the appropriate expression in the box. Look up new words in a dictionary if needed.

obtenir son permis	un train de banlieue	faire du covoiturage
défaut de ceinture	faire la navette	les transports en commun

    1 Céline prend _____ pour aller au travail tous les jours. Le trajet lui prend 45 minutes aller-retour.

    2 Eric n'a pas pu _____ du premier coup. Il l'aura certainement la prochaine fois.

    3 J'ai arrêté de _____ avec mes collègues. Ils étaient tout le temps en retard.

    4 Elle a reçu une amende pour _____. Pourtant, je lui avais dit de la mettre.

    5 Marianne n'aime pas prendre _____. Elle trouve que c'est trop lent et qu'il y a trop de monde.

    6 Pierre doit _____ entre sa maison et son bureau tous les jours. Aller au travail, c'est fatigant, mais nécessaire.

J Put the words in the appropriate category. Look up new words in a dictionary if needed.

un kayak	une moto	une montgolfière
un taxi	un paquebot	un canoë
une péniche	une barque	un avion
une voiture	une camionnette	un bus
un hélicoptère	un bateau	un autocar
un camion	un tramway	le métro

Transport aérien	Transport terrestre	Transport maritime

 Un autobus *or* **bus** *is the French word for a bus that circulates within a city.* **Un autocar** *or* **car** *is the French word for a bus that transports people from one city to another or that is privately hired.*

K Here are some useful verbs for discussing transportation. Write sentences using them.

1 monter *(to board, to get into)* _____

2 descendre *(to get out of)* _____

3 attendre *(to wait for)* _____

4 arriver *(to arrive)* _____

5 changer *(to change)* _____

6 s'arrêter *(to stop)* _____

7 se dépêcher *(to hurry)* _____

8 manquer *(to miss)* _____

9 présenter son ticket *(to present one's ticket)* _____

10 décoller *(to take off)* _____

11 atterrir *(to land)* _____

12 prendre l'avion/un vol *(to take a plane)* _____

13 démarrer *(to start [a vehicle])* _____

14 stationner *(to park)* _____

📖 Reading

L Read the first paragraph of the following online article below and find two ways to say *road rage* in French.

1 _____

2 _____

◄ | ► | www.journalquotidien.fr

Vous êtes dans la voiture aux heures de pointe ou bien vous êtes en retard pour un rendez-vous et on vous coupe le chemin. Dans ces situations, il est difficile de maîtriser ses émotions. Il est parfois impossible d'éviter que les esprits s'échauffent et la conduite agressive, ou ce qu'on appelle maintenant « la rage au volant », est devenue habituelle. Effectivement, le talonnage, les vitesses excessives, les coups de klaxon, les changements de voie dangereux, les gestes et les paroles désobligeantes ou même obscènes font partie maintenant de nos déplacements quotidiens.

M Now read the rest of the article and answer the questions that follow.

www.journalquotidien.fr

Pour rester calme au volant, prenez votre temps. Essayez de vous donner suffisamment de temps pour le déplacement. Pardonnez et oubliez autant que possible. Tout conducteur est un être humain comme vous. Si l'on vous coupe le chemin, soyez reconnaissant qu'il n'y ait pas eu d'accident. Minimisez les gestes et les cris afin d'éviter que les esprits s'échauffent. Si le klaxon est utilisé trop facilement, on risque d'énerver les autres conducteurs. Utilisez le clignotant, ne suivez pas les autres voitures de trop près, partagez la route, soyez patient et courtois.

Comment faut-il réagir quand on est agressé par d'autres conducteurs? En premier lieu, il faut éviter de provoquer le conducteur en question. Restez calme, ne sortez pas de votre véhicule, prenez une bonne description de la personne et notez le numéro de la plaque d'immatriculation du véhicule de l'agresseur si possible. Ne suivez pas le véhicule de l'agresseur afin d'éviter que la situation dégénère. Par la suite, contactez la police et surtout ne rentrez pas directement chez vous, vous pourriez être suivi.

L'agressivité au volant est dangereuse et met en danger l'ensemble des automobilistes. Pour garantir la sécurité de tous, il faut respecter le code de la route et faciliter le passage de tous.

1 Qu'est-ce qu'on peut faire pour éviter le stress et la colère quand on est au volant?

2 Qu'est-ce qu'il ne faut pas faire si on est victime d'une agression sur la route?

3 Que faut-il faire pour la sécurité de tout le monde sur la route?

 Writing

N Have you ever experienced road rage? Write a comment to the online news article describing your experience with this phenomenon. What do your friends and family think? Report their opinions using indirect speech and say whether or not you agree with them. (80–100 words)

_____

_____

_____

_____

_____

_____

Self-check

Tick the box that matches your level of confidence.

1 = very confident   2 = need more practice   3 = not confident

Cochez la case qui correspond à votre niveau d'aisance.

1 = très sûr(e) de vous   2 = j'ai besoin de plus   3 = pas sûr(e) du tout
                                de pratique

	1	2	3
Can understand and use the passive voice.			
Can understand and use indirect speech.			
Can express personal views and opinions about modes of transportation (CEFR B1).			
Can read reports concerned with current issues about transportation (CEFR B2).			

19 Pourquoi financer le cinéma français?

Why finance the French film industry?

In this unit, you will learn how to:

- ✓ Use the pluperfect.
- ✓ Use the past conditional.
- ✓ Use the future perfect.

CEFR: Can understand detailed texts about the world of media (B2); Can write a clear and detailed text about the realm of media (B2).

Meaning and usage

The pluperfect

Plus-que-parfait	Passé	Présent
Il avait fini	*Vous avez fini*	*Elle finit*

1 In narration in the past, **the pluperfect**, also known as **the past perfect**, or **plus-que-parfait**, serves to indicate actions in the past that precede other past actions. In the examples given, **Il avait fini** *(He had finished)* happened before **Vous avez fini** *(You finished)*, which happened before the present **Elle finit** *(She finishes/She is finishing)*. In English, the pluperfect is formed with *had* + past participle.

A **Look at these sentences in the pluperfect. Say what tense the auxiliary verbs (être or avoir) are in and give the infinitive of the main verb.**

1 Nous avions mangé avant son arrivée. *(We had eaten before his arrival.)*

_____

2 Tu avais appris le français avant d'aller à Paris. *(You had learned French before going to Paris.)*

_____

3 Elle était sortie au spectacle. *(She had left for the show.)*

_____

How to form the pluperfect

1. The pluperfect is formed with the auxiliary in the imperfect followed by the past participle. The choice of auxiliary (**être** or **avoir**) is the same as for the **passé composé**, as are the rules for agreement in gender and number. Here are two examples:

Regarder (*to watch*)	
j'avais regardé (*I had watched*)	nous avions regardé (*we had watched*)
tu avais regardé (*you had watched*)	vous aviez regardé (*you had watched*)
il avait regardé (*he had watched*)	ils avaient regardé (*they had watched*)

Aller (*to go*)	
je suis allé(e) (*I had gone*)	nous étions allé(e)s (*we had gone*)
tu es allé(e) (*you had gone*)	vous étiez allé(e)(s) (*you had gone*)
il est allé (*he had gone*)	ils sont allés (*they had gone*)

Not all instances of the word *had* in English are translated using the pluperfect. The expression **venir de** + *infinitive means to have just done something. Sometimes the imperfect in French is translated to mean someone or something had been doing something.*

Elle venait de tourner un film. (*She had just filmed a movie.*)

Nous attendions la sortie de son roman. (*We had been waiting for his novel to come out.*)

2. Negation follows the same rules as in the **passé composé** by placing **ne ... pas**, or another negative expression, around the auxiliary.

Je n'avais pas regardé ce film. (*I hadn't watched that film.*)

Elle n'avait jamais regardé un film d'horreur. (*She had never watched a horror film.*)

Nous n'étions pas allés au théâtre. (*We hadn't gone to the theatre.*)

With reflexive verbs, put the negation around the reflexive pronoun and the auxiliary.

Je ne m'étais pas trompé après tout. (*I hadn't made a mistake after all.*)

The pluperfect is often, though not always, used with the expression **déjà** *(already). In the negative, that expression becomes* **pas encore** *(not yet).*

Marie avait déjà allumé la télé quand sa mère a téléphoné.
(*Marie had already turned on the TV when her mother phoned.*)

Marie n'avait pas encore allumé la télé quand sa mère a téléphoné.
(*Marie had not yet turned on the TV when her mother phoned.*)

B Put the verbs in brackets into the pluperfect. Remember to make the endings agree.

1 Vous _____ (partir) avant de réaliser que vous avez oublié vos clés.
2 Les filles ont regardé tous les films que leur père _____ (acheter).
3 Nous _____ (manger) des parts de gâteau avant d'apprendre que c'était pour l'anniversaire de Marc.
4 Elle _____ (apprendre) la triste nouvelle après être rentrée.
5 Je _____ (ne pas dire) la vérité jusqu'à ce qu'il soit trop tard.
6 Tu _____ (connaître) ta femme depuis combien de temps avant de tomber amoureux?

C Read the paragraph about Sophie and her family and put the underlined verbs in the past. For verbs that are in the present, you must choose between the passé composé and the imperfect. For verbs that are already in the past, you must change them to the pluperfect.

Mes parents (1) *sont* _____ acteurs, mais ils ne (2) *deviennent* _____ jamais célèbres. Je (3) *vais* _____ souvent avec eux au théâtre pour les répétitions et les spectacles et je (4) *suis* _____ toujours entourée de comédiens. J'y (5) *vais* _____ pour la magie des histoires qu'on (6) *met* _____ sur scène et surtout pour le sentiment de pouvoir vivre dans un monde ailleurs. Quand (7) *j'ai* _____ 12 ans, nous (8) *déménageons* _____ pour nous installer à Hollywood où mes parents (9) *ont* _____ toujours *voulu* _____ tenter leur chance sur le grand écran. Ils (10) *ont pensé* _____ qu'ils (11) *peuvent* _____ mieux y gagner leur vie. Moi, je (12) n'*ai* _____ pas *été* _____ contente de quitter mes amis et nous (13) *sommes partis* _____ très vite, mais je (14) *comprends* _____ vite l'attrait du monde du cinéma.

The past conditional

passé du conditionnel	conditionnel
Tu aurais voulu aller	*Tu voudrais aller*

The past conditional, or **passé du conditionnel**, is used to express what would, could or should have happened, but didn't.

D Look at these instances of the past conditional. Say what tense the underlined auxiliary verbs (être or avoir) are in and give the infinitive of the main verb.

1 J'*aurais* téléphoné, mais j'avais oublié mon téléphone. _____
2 Qu'est-ce qu'elle *aurait* dit s'il lui avait demandé sa main de l'épouser? _____
3 Elle y *serait* allée, mais le film avait déjà commencé. _____

How to form the past conditional

1   To form the past conditional, take the conditional of the auxiliary, **être** or **avoir**, and use the past participle of the main verb.

Regarder (*to watch*)	
j'aurais regardé (*I would have watched*)	nous aurions regardé (*we would have watched*)
tu aurais regardé (*you would have watched*)	vous auriez regardé (*you would have watched*)
il aurait regardé (*he would have watched*)	ils auraient regardé (*they would have watched*)

Aller (*to go*)	
je serais allé(e) (*I would have gone*)	nous serions allé(e)s (*we would have gone*)
tu serais allé(e) (*you would have gone*)	vous seriez allé(e)(s) (*you would have gone*)
il serait allé (*he would have gone*)	ils seraient allés (*they would have gone*)

*Remember to follow the rules for agreement for verbs conjugated in the past with **avoir** with direct objects that precede the past participle and for all verbs conjugated with **être**.*

2   Verbs in the past conditional are also negated in the same way as with the **passé composé** by placing **ne … pas**, or another negative expression, around the auxiliary.

Vous n'auriez pas dû venir. *(You shouldn't have come.)*

Elle n'aurait jamais fini à temps. *(She would never have finished on time.)*

E   **Put the verbs in brackets into the past conditional. Remember to make agreement.**

1   On _____ (vouloir) voir ce film, mais la salle était pleine.
2   Marie et moi, nous _____ (aller) au théâtre ce soir, mais elle était malade.
3   Vous _____ (se dépêcher) mais vous aviez entendu dire que votre acteur préféré n'allait pas venir.
4   Tu _____ (ne pas regarder) les infos si tu avais su qu'on n'allait parler que des élections.
5   Anne-Sophie _____ (prendre) des billets si elle avait su que tu voulais voir ce film.
6   J'_____ (apprécier) le concert beaucoup plus si le son n'était pas si fort.

Both the conditional and the past conditional are used in news reports to describe something that is unsure or that is hearsay.

Des émeutes auraient eu lieu hier pour protester la sortie de son film.
(Riots allegedly broke out yesterday to protest about his film.)

3 When making hypothetical statements about what could have happened in the past if something else had happened, you use the past conditional + **si** + the pluperfect.

Paul aurait pu venir si elle l'avait invité. *(Paul could have come if she had invited him.)*

Note that the order of the clauses can be switched around. **si** + pluperfect + past conditional.

Si elle avait invité Paul, il aurait pu venir. *(If she had invited Paul, he could have come.)*

F **Put the verbs in brackets into either the pluperfect or the past conditional as needed.**

   1 Si nous ne nous étions pas disputés, nous _____ (pouvoir) voir la fin de l'émission.

   2 Elle ne serait pas venue si elle _____ (savoir) ce qui l'attendait.

   3 Si tu _____ (ne pas être) en colère, tu aurais compris son histoire.

   4 S'ils _____ (écouter) la radio, ils auraient su ce qui se passait.

   5 Si j'_____ (partir) deux minutes plus tôt, je ne vous aurais pas vus.

   6 Vous n'auriez pas connu votre copine si vous _____ (ne pas assister) au concert ce soir-là.

Meaning and Usage

The future perfect

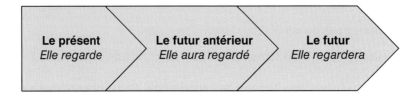

Le présent	Le futur antérieur	Le futur
Elle regarde	*Elle aura regardé*	*Elle regardera*

1 The future perfect, or **futur antérieur**, is used to describe an event, action or situation that will be completed before something else in the future or to describe an event, action or situation that will have been completed at some point in the future.

 G **Look at these instances of the future perfect. Say what tense the auxiliary verbs (être or avoir) are in and give the infinitive of the main verb.**

   1 Elle aura fini de chanter avant 20h. *(She will have finished singing before 8 o'clock.)*

   _____

   2 Nous l'aurons vu. *(We will have seen it.)* _____

   3 Tu ne seras pas encore parti. *(You will not have left yet.)* _____

How to form the future perfect

1 The future perfect is formed by conjugating the auxiliary, **être** or **avoir**, in the future tense and adding the past participle.

Regarder (*to watch*)	
j'aurai regardé (*I will have watched*)	nous aurons regardé (*we will have watched*)
tu auras regardé (*you will have watched*)	vous aurez regardé (*you will have watched*)
il aura regardé (*he will have watched*)	ils auront regardé (*they will have watched*)

Aller (*to go*)	
je serai allé(e) (*I will have gone*)	nous serons allé(e)s (*we will have gone*)
tu seras allé(e) (*you will have gone*)	vous serez allé(e)(s) (*you will have gone*)
il sera allé (*he will have gone*)	ils seront allés (*they will have gone*)

2   With conjunctions like **aussitôt que**, **après que**, **dès que**, **lorsque** and **quand**, French uses the future perfect whereas in English, you would use the present tense when the main clause is in the future.

Nous lui en parlerons aussitôt qu'il sera revenu. (*We will speak to him about it as soon as he returns.*)

3   Verbs in the future perfect are negated in the same way as in the **passé composé** by placing **ne … pas**, or another negative expression, around the auxiliary.

Elle n'aura pas fini de voir la fin de la série avant de vous voir, donc ne lui parle pas du dénouement. (*She will not have finished watching the end of the series before she sees you, so don't talk to her about the ending.*)

Vous ne serez pas partis avant notre retour. (*You will not have left before our return.*)

 The future perfect can be used alone to express an explanation or probability.

Elle n'est pas venue. Elle aura manqué son train. (*She didn't come. She must have/probably missed her train.*)

H   Put the verbs in brackets in the future perfect. Make agreement where needed.

1   D'ici la fin de la semaine, elle _____ (apprendre) son rôle.

2   Nous _____ (ne pas finir) la vaisselle avant le début de l'émission.

3   Vous _____ (voir) un film différent tous les jours avant la fin de la semaine.

4   Avant la fin du mois, j'_____ (payer) toutes les factures.

5   Demain à cette heure, elles _____ (partir) en vacances.

6   Tu _____ (ne pas finir) de regarder ce film avant minuit.

I   Put the verbs in brackets into the future or the future perfect to complete the conversation.

- Si tu veux nous faire plaisir, tu **(1)** _____ (venir) au cinéma voir le nouveau film de Romain Duris avec nous.

- Bien sûr, mais je travaille beaucoup en ce moment. Dès que je **(2)** _____ (avoir) le temps, nous pourrons y aller.

- J'espère qu'il **(3)** _____ (être) bon.

- Moi aussi!

- Si ça te dit, on **(4)** _____ (inviter) Sophie aussi.

- Je ne sais pas si elle **(5)** _____ (finir) ses examens avant la fin du mois. J'aimerais y aller avant, pas toi?

- Oui, tu as raison.

- Bon alors, tu me diras quand tu **(6)** _____ (trouver) le temps et on y ira.

- Je te le **(7)** _____ (dire).

Vocabulary

J Find the odd one out.

1 un feuilleton | un jeu télévisé | un film | une série
2 les informations | le journal | l'actualité | une bande-dessinée
3 un film d'amour | une comédie | un film fantastique | un drame
4 un journal | un magazine | un roman | un film d'horreur
5 un film policier | un dessin animé | un film d'aventures | un film de guerre
6 un western | la maquilleuse | l'ingénieur du son | l'écrivain

 Reading

K Read the first part of the article about French public subsidies for the film industry and efforts to promote French culture. Indicate if the following statements are V (vrai/true) or F (faux/false). If they are false, correct them.

1 Il n'y a que la France qui finance le cinéma.   V/F
2 En France, les contributions obligatoires proviennent des bénéfices dans le secteur du cinéma.   V/F

---

  www.lesnouvellesdujour.fr

Pourquoi financer le cinéma français?

Beaucoup de pays aident le secteur cinématographique, que ce soit pour des raisons économiques ou culturelles. La France n'échappe pas à la règle. En Allemagne, ce sont les différentes régions qui soutiennent le cinéma financièrement et au Danemark, le cinéma profite simplement d'aides directes financées par le budget de l'état. Par contre, le cinéma français est financé de façon interne, c'est-à-dire qu'il est question de contributions obligatoires de la part de toute l'industrie qui en profite: salles de cinéma, chaînes de télévision, producteurs de vidéo.

L Now, read the rest of the article and answer the questions that follow.

Fondé en 1946, Le Centre national de la cinématographie et de l'image animée (CNC) a pour but de régler la production et la diffusion du cinéma, de le soutenir et de le promouvoir. Que ce soit des programmes nationaux de sensibilisation en milieu scolaire, la diffusion de films peu connus ou bien l'organisation des festivals de cinéma comme celui de Cannes, le CNC vise à faire du secteur cinéma « un véritable pôle de développement économique et culturel » (CNC). Comme nous l'avons déjà dit, le budget du CNC ne provient pas des impôts mais prélève plutôt des taxes privées de l'ordre de 11% sur les entrées de cinéma, de 5,5% sur les diffusions télévisées et de 2% pour l'édition et l'importation des vidéos en DVD. Dernièrement, on a rajouté une taxe sur les fournisseurs d'internet, ce qui traduit la montée dans la diffusion des films en ligne.

Par ailleurs, pour faire financer son film en France, on doit satisfaire certains critères pour avoir jusqu'à 50% de financement sur le coût de sa production et jusqu'à 20% de crédit d'impôt sur le chiffre d'affaires. Par exemple, ce film doit être tourné en France en langue française. Certains genres de films ne peuvent pas toucher ces crédits d'impôt; est exclu tout film pornographique, publicitaire ou incitant à la violence. En moyenne, les aides du CNC couvrent 15% du budget d'un film.

Ce système n'est pas sans critiques. Certains pensent que le CNC tient trop de pouvoir sur la production cinématographique en France puisque c'est lui qui choisit les films qui profitent de ces crédits. On pense aussi que les grandes stars sont trop bien payées et que c'est un système inégalitaire. De plus, il n'y a que les films français qui reçoivent ces aides bien que ce soit des recettes de tous les films en salle de cinéma qui sont taxées. En outre, les taxes sur la télévision et les vidéos de tous les films, français et étrangers confondus, seraient contribuables.

C'est pour cette raison que l'Union Européenne lutte contre le financement national du secteur. Rares sont les films qui font fureur, donc les films à succès subventionnent les films à petit rendement. Finalement, si la télévision est légalement obligée de contribuer au financement du cinéma, sa réussite dépend de la bonne santé de celle-ci.

1 Qu'est-ce que le CNC? Que fait-il?

_____

2 Quelles sortes de films sont exclues du financement public?

_____

3 Quelles sont les critiques du système de financement public du cinéma en France?

_____

M Match the words from the article with their synonyms.

1 la circulation   a une star
2 le prix   b la réussite
3 l'assistance financière   c la diffusion
4 connaître un immense succès   d le coût
5 une vedette   e faire fureur
6 le succès   f les aides

N Define the following in English.

1 un crédit d'impôt _____
2 une taxe privée _____
3 le chiffre d'affaires _____
4 les entrées de cinéma _____
5 subventionner _____
6 le financement _____

✏️ Writing

O What kinds of films and TV shows do you like? Write a blog post about your film and TV preferences and describe your favourite film or TV show. Try to use a variety of verb tenses. (80–100 words)

_____

_____

_____

_____

_____

_____

_____

_____

_____

_____

_____

Try searching for French films, television channels and other media such as newspapers and radio online. Watching films and news programmes or listening to news and radio programmes in French is a great way to improve your comprehension and increase your vocabulary.

Self-check

Tick the box that matches your level of confidence.

1 = very confident   2 = need more practice   3 = not confident

Cochez la case qui correspond à votre niveau d'aisance.

1 = très sûr(e) de vous   2 = j'ai besoin de plus de pratique   3 = pas sûr(e) du tout

	1	2	3
Can use the pluperfect.			
Can use the past conditional.			
Can use the future perfect.			
Can understand detailed texts about the world of media (CEFR B2).			
Can write a clear and detailed text about the realm of media (CEFR B2).			

Sur les grands boulevards de Paris

On the grand boulevards of Paris

In this unit, you will learn how to:

✓ Recognize, form and understand the **passé simple**.

✓ Recognize, form and understand the past anterior.

✓ Use vocabulary related to architecture and cities.

CEFR: Can understand specialized historical texts (B2); Can narrate detailed information in the past about a town or city's development (B2).

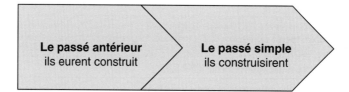

| Le passé antérieur | Le passé simple |
| ils eurent construit | ils construisirent |

Meaning and usage

The passé simple

1 The **passé simple**, or simple past, is used in French when describing things that happened in the past in formal, historical or literary texts. It is used in the same way as the **passé composé**, which is a less formal equivalent. It is virtually never used when speaking.

 A Read the following sentences and try to guess the infinitive of the underlined verb.

1 Vous <u>aidâtes</u> les pauvres. _____

2 Elle <u>partit</u> sur-le-champ. _____

3 Les Allemands <u>perdirent</u> la Seconde Guerre Mondiale. _____

2 Verbs in the **passé simple** are usually translated in English in the past, so the sentences in A are as follows in English:

1 *You helped the poor.*

2 *She left at once.*

3 *The Germans lost World War II.*

How to form the passé simple

1   For regular verbs in the **passé simple**, the stem is formed by removing the infinitive ending, -**er**, -**ir**, -**re**. It is a one-word tense with no auxiliary, hence the term *simple past*. Endings for -**er** verbs are different than for -**ir** and -**re** verbs. **Aller** is conjugated as a regular -**er** verb.

Subject pronoun	Trouver	Finir	Perdre
je	trouv-ai	fin-is	perd-is
tu	trouv-as	fin-is	perd-is
il/elle/on	trouv-a	fin-it	perd-it
nous	trouv-âmes	fin-îmes	perd-îmes
vous	trouv-âtes	fin-îtes	perd-îtes
ils/elles	trouv-èrent	fin-irent	perd-irent

2   Verbs like **manger** and **lancer** with spelling changes in the present have the same changes in the **passé simple**.

Subject pronoun	Manger	Lancer
je	mangeai	lançai
tu	mangeas	lanças
il/elle/on	mangea	lança
nous	mangeâmes	lançâmes
vous	mangeâtes	lançâtes
ils/elles	mangèrent	lancèrent

3   Irregular -**ir** verbs like **dormir** and **partir** are formed like **finir**: **je dormis, je partis**. Irregular -**re** verbs like **battre** and **suivre** are formed like **perdre**: **je battis, je suivis**.

4   Some irregular verbs in the **passé simple** have a stem that closely resembles the past participle of that verb. Their endings are -**s**, -**s**, -**t**, -**âmes**, -**âtes**, -**rent**.

Verb	Participle	je/tu	il/elle/on	nous	vous	ils/elles
avoir	eu	eus	eut	eûmes	eûtes	eurent
boire	bu	bus	but	bûmes	bûtes	burent
connaître	connu	connus	connut	connûmes	connûtes	connurent
courir	couru	courus	courut	courûmes	courûtes	coururent
croire	cru	crus	crut	crûmes	crûtes	crurent
devoir	du	dus	dut	dûmes	dûtes	durent
lire	lu	lus	lut	lûmes	lûtes	lurent
paraître	paru	parus	parut	parûmes	parûtes	parurent
plaire	plu	plus	plut	plûmes	plûtes	plurent

Verb	Participle	je/tu	il/elle/on	nous	vous	ils/elles
pouvoir	pu	pus	put	pûmes	pûtes	purent
recevoir	reçu	reçus	reçut	reçûmes	reçûtes	reçurent
savoir	su	sus	sut	sûmes	sûtes	surent
vivre	vécu	vécus	vécut	vécûmes	vécûtes	vécurent
vouloir	voulu	voulus	voulut	voulûmes	voulûtes	voulurent

5   Some verbs have an irregular stem, not related to their past participle. They also use the endings **-s**, **-s**, **-t**, **-âmes**, **-âtes**, **-rent**.

Verb	Participle	je/tu	il/elle/on	nous	vous	ils/elles
conduire	conduit	conduisis	conduisit	conduisîmes	conduisîtes	conduisirent
craindre	craint	craignis	craignit	craignîmes	craignîtes	craignirent
écrire	écrit	écrivis	écrivit	écrivîmes	écrivîtes	écrivirent
être	été	fus	fut	fûmes	fûtes	furent
faire	fait	fis	fit	fîmes	fîtes	firent
joindre	joint	joignis	joignit	joignîmes	joignîtes	joignirent
mourir	mort	mourus	mourut	mourûmes	mourûtes	moururent
naître	né	naquis	naquit	naquîmes	naquîtes	naquirent
peindre	peint	peignis	peignit	peignîmes	peignîtes	peignirent
rompre	rompu	rompis	rompit	rompîmes	rompîtes	rompirent
tenir	tenu	tins	tint	tînmes	tîntes	tinrent
traduire	traduit	traduisis	traduisit	traduisîmes	traduisîtes	traduisirent
vaincre	vaincu	vainquis	vainquit	vainquîmes	vainquîtes	vainquirent
venir	venu	vins	vint	vînmes	vîntes	vinrent
voir	vu	vis	vit	vîmes	vîntes	virent

The forms of **être** *and* **faire** *are very similar in the* **passé simple** *with only a difference of one vowel,* **-i** *or* **-u**. *Make sure to note their differences.*

B   **Transform the following sentences from the passé simple to the passé composé.**

1   Elle parla. _____

2   Tu pris. _____

3   Nous choisîmes. _____

4   J'encourageai. _____

5   Elles allèrent. _____

6   Il choisit. _____

7   Vous rentrâtes. _____

8   Ils gagnèrent. _____

C Transform the following sentences from the **passé composé** to the **passé simple**.

1 Nous avons gagné. _____

2 Elle a fait. _____

3 Vous avez donné. _____

4 Il a remplacé. _____

5 Elles ont essayé. _____

6 Tu as vu. _____

7 Ils ont peint. _____

8 J'ai réfléchi. _____

Meaning and usage

The past anterior

1 The past anterior, or **passé antérieur**, is also a literary or historical tense. It is used when speaking of past events that occurred prior to the past event or action that is being narrated usually in conjunction with the **passé simple**. As the **passé composé** is roughly equivalent to the **passé simple**, the past anterior is roughly equivalent to the pluperfect.

D Read the following sentences and indicate what tense the auxiliary, **avoir** or **être**, is in. Then give the infinitive of the main verb.

1 Elle eut commandé. _____

2 Tu eus fait. _____

3 Ils furent morts. _____

2 In conversation, it would be more common to use the pluperfect. So the examples in D, in spoken speech, would be as follows:

1 *She had commanded.*

2 *You had done.*

3 *They had died.*

How to form the past anterior

1 The past anterior is a compound tense, meaning it uses the auxiliary, **être** or **avoir**, in the **passé simple** along with the past participle of the main verb. With verbs using **être**, apply the rules of gender and number agreement.

Manger	
j'eus mangé	nous eûmes mangé
tu eus mangé	vous eûtes mangé
il/elle/on eut mangé	ils/elles eurent mangé

Entrer	
je fus entré(e)	nous fûmes entré(e)s
tu fus entré(e)	vous fûtes entré(e)s
il/elle/on fut entré(e)	ils/elles furent entré(e)s

2 The past anterior occurs most often in subordinate clauses where the main verb is in the **passé simple**. The English equivalent is usually *had* + past participle.

Elle tomba malade aussitôt que nous eûmes fini le voyage.
(She became ill as soon as we had finished the trip.)

Dès qu'il fut arrivé à Paris, il commença à parler français.
(As soon as he had arrived in Paris, he started speaking French.)

E Rewrite the following sentences using the **pluperfect** in the place of the **past anterior**.

1 Il eut fait. _____

2 Nous fûmes rentrés. _____

3 Tu eus nagé. _____

4 Elles furent parties. _____

5 Vous eûtes déménagé. _____

6 J'eus obéi. _____

F Read the following fable by Jean de la Fontaine and underline the verbs in the **passé simple** and the **past anterior**. Then give the infinitive.

Le Renard et la Cigogne

Compère le Renard se mit un jour en frais,

Et retint à dîner commère la Cigogne.

Le régal fut petit et sans beaucoup d'apprêts:

Le Galant, pour toute besogne

Avait un brouet clair (il vivait chichement).

Ce brouet fut par lui servi sur une assiette.

La Cigogne au long bec n'en put attraper miette;

Et le drôle eut lapé le tout en un moment.

Pour se venger de cette tromperie,

À quelque temps de là, la Cigogne le prie.

"Volontiers", lui dit-il, "car avec mes amis

Je ne fais point cérémonie".

À l'heure dite, il courut au logis

De la Cigogne son hôtesse;

Loua très fort la politesse,

Trouva le dîner cuit à point.

Bon appétit surtout; Renards n'en manquent point.

Il se réjouissait à l'odeur de la viande

Mise en menus morceaux, et qu'il croyait friande.

On servit, pour l'embarrasser

En un vase à long col, et d'étroite embouchure.

Le bec de la Cigogne y pouvait bien passer,

Mais le museau du Sire était d'autre mesure.

Il lui fallut à jeun retourner au logis,

Honteux comme un Renard qu'une poule aurait pris,

Serrant la queue, et portant bas l'oreille.

Trompeurs, c'est pour vous que j'écris,

Attendez-vous à la pareille.

 This and many other of Aesop's fables were rewritten in French and adapted for courtly society in the second half of the 17th century in France by Jean de la Fontaine. French people memorize them in grammar school and frequently reference them. Try looking up some others and reading them to improve your vocabulary, reading comprehension and ability to recognize the **passé simple**.

Vocabulary

G   **Find the odd one out.**

1   un toit | une façade | un trottoir | un balcon
2   le pont | l'immeuble | le monument | le parc
3   percer | raser | paver | construire
4   zinc | pierre | acier | plomb
5   théâtre | bal | spectacle | cabaret

H   Match the French with the English.

1	un réseau	a	the lighting
2	la banlieue	b	the outskirts
3	la chaussée	c	a theatre
4	la périphérie	d	a fancy townhouse
5	le percement faire	e	to develop, to change for the better
6	aménager	f	strolling
7	une muraille	g	the road surface
8	un fossé	h	a triumphal arch
9	un hôtel particulier	i	a show
10	un théâtre	j	a pit or ditch
11	un arc de triomphe	k	drilling, making an opening
12	un spectacle	l	a high wall
13	des flâneries	m	the suburbs
14	l'éclairage	n	a network

📖 Reading

I   Read the first paragraph of an article on urban planning in Paris in the 19th century. Then answer the questions.

1   Qui a fait construire les grands boulevards? _____

2   Pourquoi est-ce qu'on a commencé à y aller? _____

Sur les grands boulevards de Paris

Le désir d'aménager la ville de Paris et de la rendre plus habitable ne date pas d'hier. Effectivement, c'est en 1668 que Louis XIV décida de faire raser les murailles et de faire combler les fossés des anciennes fortifications qui furent construits par Charles V et Louis XIII. Les grands boulevards de Paris qui les remplacèrent forment un arc sur la rive droite qui s'étend de la Place de la Bastille à la Place de la Madeleine. La noblesse y construisit de magnifiques hôtels particuliers peu après. Certaines portes (La porte Saint Denis, la porte Saint Martin) furent remplacées par des arcs de triomphe qui marquèrent les récentes victoires militaires du « roi soleil ». Ce « Nouveau Cours » devint une des plus belles promenades de toute la ville. Des théâtres, des spectacles, des bals et des cabarets s'installèrent dans la partie est et l'esprit boulevardier naquit. C'est en 1778 que la chaussée fut pavée et l'éclairage au gaz apparut en 1817. Encore aujourd'hui, ces avenues continuent de constituer un lieu privilégié de flâneries.

J   Now read the rest of the article and answer the questions.

C'est Napoléon III, au dix-neuvième siècle qui eut une volonté de modernisation, que la ville de Paris connut une véritable transformation. Le percement de nouveaux boulevards, la réglementation des façades, des réseaux d'adduction et d'évacuation des eaux, l'emplacement de parcs et de monuments publics, tout contribua à assainir l'espace urbain, à faciliter la circulation, à améliorer la vie des habitants et à augmenter le prestige de la ville. Les immeubles alignés selon les règlements haussmanniens avec leurs façades en pierre, leurs nombreux balcons, leurs toits en zinc devinrent symboles d'une ville moderne et vivable.

Les Franciliens contemporains critiquèrent la destruction des vieux quartiers ainsi que les dépenses considérables de cet aménagement urbain. De surcroît, les classes aisées s'y installèrent tandis que les moins fortunés furent repoussés vers la périphérie de la ville, voire en banlieue, ce qui contribua aux disparités sociales. Mais tout comme pour la construction de Versailles, ces attitudes ne purent rien changer au résultat et passèrent vite au second plan. Les parisiens de nos jours voient cet héritage sous un œil favorable et apprécient l'effort commencé sous Louis XIV et continué pendant le Second Empire. Les lieux publics, les espaces verts, les grands boulevards, tout contribue à l'image actuelle d'un Paris ouvert, convivial, élégant.

1   Qui a décidé d'effectuer des travaux de modernisation de Paris au dix-neuvième siècle?

_____

2   Quel est le résultat de ces travaux? _____

3   Qui a critiqué les travaux? Pourquoi? _____

4   Qu'en pensent les parisiens maintenant? _____

K   Match the synonyms.

1   les promenades   a   les avenues
2   les Parisiens   b   habitable
3   les parcs   c   les flâneries
4   les boulevards   d   les Franciliens
5   vivable   e   l'aménagement
6   la transformation   f   les espaces verts

L   Find the verbs in the text which are in the passé simple and give the infinitives.

Reading novels or historical non-fiction in French can help familiarize you with these tenses and their forms, especially the irregulars. When you are reading in French, try to identify the verb in the passé simple and imagine what the passé composé would be in that instance.

Writing

M Write a blog post to describe the origins of your town or city and any recent efforts to modernize it. (80–100 words)

_____

_____

_____

_____

_____

_____

_____

_____

_____

_____

_____

_____

_____

_____

Self-check

Tick the box that matches your level of confidence.

1 = very confident   2 = need more practice   3 = not confident

Cochez la case qui correspond à votre niveau d'aisance.

1 = très sûr(e) de vous   2 = j'ai besoin de plus de pratique   3 = pas sûr(e) du tout

	1	2	3
Recognize, form and understand the **passé simple**.			
Recognize, form and understand the past anterior.			
Use vocabulary related to architecture and cities.			
Can understand specialized historical texts (CEFR B2).			
Can narrate detailed information in the past about a town or city's development (CEFR B2).			

Unit 1

A

The feminine nouns end in -**e,** whereas the masculine nouns end in a consonant

1 la, feminine **2** le, masculine **3** la, feminine **4** le, masculine

B

1 le **2** la **3** le **4** la **5** la **6** le **7** le **8** le **9** la **10** la **11** le **12** le

C

Plural	Singular
les bénéfices	le bénéfice
les transports	le transport
les musées	le musée
les traditions	la tradition
les habitudes	l'habitude (f.)
les habitants	l'habitant (m.)
les diplômés	le diplômé
les non-diplômés	le non diplômé
les immigrés	l'immigré (m.)
les descendants	le descendant
les congés	le congé
les allocations	l'allocation (f.)

D

1 les tantes **2** les filles **3** les maris **4** les foyers **5** les chevaux **6** les sœurs **7** les enfants **8** les détails **9** les pneus **10** les familles **11** les bijoux **12** les couples

E

1 feminine singular **2** feminine singular **3** masculine singular **4** masculine singular **5** feminine singular **6** masculine plural **7** masculine singular **8** feminine singular

F

1 la 2 le 3 la 4 le 5 les 6 la

G

1 un 2 des 3 un 4 un 5 un 6 des

H

1 de 2 de 3 du 4 de l' 5 du 6 des

I

1 b, iii 2 a, ii 3 c, i

J

1 la 2 une 3 le 4 la 5 un 6 une 7 un 8 du 9 de la 10 un/du 11 une/de la 12 le 13 du 14 du 15 le 16 les

K

1j 2l 3a 4c 5d 6m 7g 8i 9k 10n 11e 12f 13h 14b

L

1 Pour le mariage de Claire et de Marc. 2 Au mois de mai, à Bordeaux.

M

1 Non, certains (il y en a certains qui) viennent de New York et du Sénégal. 2 Parce que les billets d'avion sont chers (ne sont pas donnés). 3 Tout le monde arrive la veille du mariage. 4 Non, ils vont se marier à la mairie.

N

Answers will vary.

Unit 2

A

Elles is used in three sentences to mean *they*, Anne-Sophie and her friends. **Il** *(he)* is used twice to refer to Gaston. **Les** is used once to mean *to them*.

B

1 You could use *one* to translate **on** here, or use *you*, meaning *everyone*.

2 In this sentence **on** would best be translated as *we*.

C

1b 2a 3c 4b 5d

D

1 m' **2** t'/vous **3** nous **4** vous/te **5** le/la **6** les

E

1 Nous les regardons.

2 Micheline l'adore.

3 Ils les ont faites.

4 Elle aime la faire.

5 Vous l'avez fait.

6 Je l'adore.

F

1b 2a 3c 4d

G

1 leur **2** lui **3** vous **4** m' **5** te **6** lui

H

1 I **2** One **3** You **4** They **5** me **6** le **7** it/her **8** us **9** them **10** lui **11** to you

I

1 Je vous/t'achète des patins (à glace).

2 Ce casque est à moi.

3 Elle? Je pense qu'elle l'a fait(e).

4 Il va lui-même.

5 Attention! Il y a une voiture devant toi/vous.

6 Nous regardons un film chez elle ce soir.

J

2 J'y mets les fleurs.

3 Ils y assisteront.

4 Nous y pensons souvent.

5 Tu y réponds.

6 Elle y va pour acheter le journal.

7 Vous n'y allez pas souvent?

K

1 J'en reviens.

2 Ils en ont trop.

3 Tu en as besoin.

4 En France, on en mange beaucoup.

5 Tu t'en souviens?

6 Nous n'en avons pas deux.

L

1a **2**b **3**c **4**a **5**c **6**a

M

1f **2**c **3**a **4**j **5**h **6**e **7**b **8**i **9**g **10**d

N

1 passer un coup de fil

2 lire

3 sortir au restaurant

4 jouer sur l'ordinateur

O

1 V 2 F – Elle est certifiée. 3 F – Elle va souvent au Mexique.

P

1 Pour éviter les crampes, et il faut manger des bananes.

2 Nager contre le courant parce que cela fatigue.

3 Il ne faut rien toucher pour ne pas détruire l'environnement.

Q

1 J'aime la tranquillité qui m'entoure. **J'** *(I)* is a subject pronoun, **m'** *(me)* is the direct object pronoun. 2 J'y retourne souvent. **J'** *(I)* subject pronoun, **y** *(there)* pronoun replacing au Mexique. 3 Typiquement, on en boit et on en mange avant … **On** *(we)* subject pronoun, **en** *(some)* object pronoun replacing water and food. 4 Je vous conseille d'être bien reposé …. **Je** *(I)* subject pronoun, vous *(you)*. 5 … il est important d'attirer l'attention des moniteurs et de leur indiquer ce qui ne va pas … **Il** *(it)* subject pronoun, **leur** *(to them)* indirect object pronoun replacing aux moniteurs. 6 Il est important d'observer mais de ne pas toucher toutes les merveilles qu'on peut observer sous l'océan, de quoi les préserver … **Il** and **on** *(it and we)* subject pronouns, **les** *(them)* direct object pronoun replacing les merveilles.

R

Answers will vary.

Unit 3

A

Adjectives in English come before the noun and don't change. French adjectives usually come after the noun and change depending on the number and gender of the noun.

B

une fille intelligente (feminine singular); des garçons intelligents (masculine plural); des réponses intelligentes (feminine plural)

C

Possible answers: **1** blond et paresseux **2** méchant, bête, moche/laid et malhonnête

D

1 Ils ont un bel appartement qui donne sur la rue.

2 Pierre a mis longtemps avant de s'acheter un nouveau téléphone portable.

3 Elle m'a beaucoup parlé de son fol amour, mais je n'ai jamais fait la connaissance de son amant.

4 Nous avons un vieil ami que nous connaissons depuis vingt ans.

5 Stéphanie aurait envie de trouver un nouvel emploi plus intéressant que ce qu'elle fait maintenant.

6 Elle aime beaucoup son vieil ordinateur portable, mais il ne fonctionne plus.

E

1 charmante

2 blanche

3 polie

4 drôle

5 heureuse

6 fraîche

F

1 Elle n'est pas très gentille.

2 Sa femme n'est pas très belle, mais elle n'est pas laide non plus.

3 Le joli garçon n'est pas très intellectuel, il est plutôt rêveur.

4 Nous avons une chienne blanche et noire.

5 L'homme avec qui vous avez parlé était agressif et n'a pas été très aimable.

6 Il était grand, brun, travailleur et un peu fou.

G

1b 2c 3a

H

1 The only painting 2 A unique painting 3 She is an only child.

I

2 Ils n'aiment pas beaucoup les vieux trains lents.

3 Pourquoi ne veulent-ils pas aller à cette fête somptueuse et élégante?

4 Elle cherche une nouvelle colocataire propre.

5 Tu n'as pas vu une petite femme blonde dans le coin?

6 La ville a beaucoup d'anciens immeubles impressionnants.

7 Nous avons une nouvelle voiture bleue.

8 Est-ce que vous voulez acheter un nouvel ordinateur portable?

J

1 Les fromages français peuvent être forts.

2 Au printemps, les feuilles sur les arbres sont vert clair.

3 Julien et Martine sont super occupés, ils n'ont pas beaucoup de temps libre.

4 Je ne vais pas m'acheter cette robe noire, elle est trop longue.

5 Juliette et Karine sont assez paresseuses. Elles sont tout le temps fatiguées.

6 Nous ne savons pas encore si nous allons acheter une voiture neuve, celles que nous avons vues sont trop chères.

K

Answers will vary. Possible answers, depending on choices and your gender:

Je suis ...	Mes amis sont ...
If you are male: curieux, responsable, travailleur, malheureux, content, roux, grand, petit, généreux, sympathique, chauve, barbu, mince, gros, fort, rond, franc, rouspéteur, débrouillard, maladroit, décontracté, doux, bronzé. If you are female: curieuse, responsable, travailleuse, malheureuse, contente, rousse, grande, petite, généreuse, sympathique, chauve, barbue, mince, grosse, forte, ronde, franche, rouspéteuse, débrouillarde, maladroite, décontractée, douce, bronzée.	curieux, responsables, travailleurs, malheureux, contents, roux, grands, petits, généreux, sympathiques, chauves, barbus, minces, gros, forts, ronds, francs, rouspéteurs, débrouillards, maladroits, décontractés, doux, bronzés.

L

1k 2d 3l 4b 5i 6g 7h 8a 9j 10e 11f 12c

M

Adjectives: premier, pleins d'énergie, impulsifs, fiers, courageuse, indépendante.

Aries are impulsive, brave, proud, independent and full of energy.

N

1 Taureau

2 Sagittaire

3 Verseau

4 Balance

5 Gémeaux

O

1 premier; 2 sociables, charmantes, agréables, romantiques; 3 orgueilleux, ambitieux, généreux, chaleureux, nerveux, audacieux, astucieux, affectueux; 4 profonds, durables; 5 orgueilleux, fier; 6 leur, son, sa, ses

P

premier	first	dynamique	dynamic
pleins (plein)	full	agressif	aggressive
impulsifs (impulsif)	impulsive	généreux	generous
fiers (fier)	proud	chaleureux	warm
courageuse (courageux)	brave	raisonnables (raisonnable)	reasonable
indépendante (indépendant)	independent	prudents (prudent)	careful, cautious
réservée (réservé)	reserved	réfléchi	thoughtful
timide	shy	pragmatique	pragmatic
calme	calm	perfectionniste	perfectionist
fidèle	loyal	nerveux	nervous
conservateur	conservative	sociables (sociable)	friendly
traditionnaliste	traditional	charmantes (charmant)	charming
volage	fickle	agréables (agréable)	nice
instable	unstable	romantiques (romantique)	romantic
grande (grand)	tall, large	remarquable	remarkable
parfait	perfect	passionnés (passionné)	passionate
lunaire	lunar	sensuels (sensuel)	sensual
aimante (aimant)	loving	méfiante (méfiant)	distrustful
sensible	sensitive	jaloux	jealous
affable	affable	rebuté	put off
communicatif	communicative	impatients (impatient)	impatient
sentimental	sentimental	audacieux	daring
séduisant	seductive	optimistes (optimiste)	optimistic
attentionné	considerate	aventurier	adventuresome
profonds (profond)	profound	quotidiens (quotidien)	daily, day-to-day
durables (durable)	lasting	responsable	responsible
gouverné	governed	ambitieux	ambitious
orgueilleux	proud	conformiste	conformist
ambitieux	ambitious	aigu	sharp

hors norme	exceptional	affectueux	affectionate
astucieux	astute	rêveur	pensive, musing, day-dreaming
nouvelles (nouveau)	new		
exceptionnelle (exceptionel)	exceptional	poétique	poetic
froide (froid)	cold	convivial	congenial, friendly
versatile	versatile		

Q

Answers will vary.

Unit 4

A

1c 2b 3a

B

1 normalement

2 parfois

3 sous

4 dans

5 Après

6 dehors

7 bien

8 Enfin

C

For masculine adjectives ending in **-ant** and **-ent**, drop the **-nt** and add **-mment**.

D

1 sérieusement

2 éventuellement

3 apparemment

4 patiemment

5 heureusement

6 méchamment

7 aisément

8 sincèrement

9 attentivement

10 évidemment

E

1 Philippe et Marie s'installent facilement dans leur site de camping.

2 Ils partent hâtivement pour faire une randonnée.

3 Ils regardent attentivement la carte.

4 Marie trouve aisément la piste.

5 Ils veulent monter rapidement au sommet pour profiter de la vue avant le coucher du soleil.

6 Tous les deux respirent profondément l'air frais de la montagne.

7 Malheureusement, en descendant de la montagne, Philippe se tord la cheville.

8 Philippe ne peut plus faire de la marche, il a trop mal le lendemain. Or Le lendemain, Philippe ne peut plus faire de la marche, il a trop mal.

F

1 plus de + noun + que is used 2 moins de + noun + que is used 3 autant de +noun + que is used

G

1 autant que

2 plus souvent que

3 plus d'

4 moins d'

5 aussi bien que

6 plus vite que

7 moins que

8 aussi bien qu'

H

1 better film / masculine singular, comparative

2 better films / masculine plural, comparative

3 the best film / masculine singular, superlative

4 the best films / masculine plural, superlative

5 a better hike / feminine singular, comparative

6 better hikes / feminine plural, comparative

7 the best hike / feminine singular, superlative

8 the best hikes / feminine plural, superlative

I

2 Tu appelles tes parents le plus souvent.

3 Pauline est la moins belle.

4 Marc et Simon voient les arbres les plus vieux.

5 Nous regardons le paysage le plus magnifique.

6 C'est Jean-Paul qui arrive le plus souvent en retard.

7 C'est Pascale qui aime le moins faire du camping.

8 Voici l'endroit le moins apprécié du monde.

J

1c 2b 3c 4a 5d 6b

K

1e 2k 3h 4c 5l 6m 7d 8j 9a 10g 11n 12b 13i 14f

L

1 A l'est du Québec dans la péninsule de Gaspésie sur la Baie de Percé.

2 Les personnes qui aiment la nature parce que c'est au bord de l'eau, il y a beaucoup de lacs et de rivières et il y a des parcs et des réserves avec des montagnes.

M

1 des randonnées, aller à la plage, faire de la plongée sous-marine, faire du parapente, faire de la pêche, magasiner, déguster la cuisine locale, aller à l'île Bonaventure, se balader, faire du vélo, faire du canoë, faire du kayak

2 des canoës et des kayaks

3 une buanderie, un bloc sanitaire avec de l'eau chaude, un gazébo, une salle de jeux pour enfants, des emplacements avec l'électricité et l'eau

N

notamment, tranquillement, également, récemment, toujours

O

Comparative: Les emplacements à deux services (électricité et eau) pour les roulottes se trouvent plus près du cœur du camping que ceux sans service pour les tentes qui sont plus près de l'eau.

Superlative: Les parcs et réserves avec les plus hauts sommets du Québec font la joie des visiteurs. / Un site propre et reposant vous assure le meilleur séjour possible!

P

Answers will vary.

Unit 5

A

1 Combien 2 Où 3 Pourquoi 4 Comment 5 Quand 6 Combien de

B

1 Elle ne se sert pas d'un logiciel, elle fait le codage elle-même.

2 C'est une petite entreprise, donc elle a plus de liberté et elle peut être plus créative.

C

1 quel 2 quelle 3 quels 4 quelles

D

1 quel 2 quels 3 quelles 4 quel

E

Answers will vary.

F

1 que 2 qui 3 qui 4 que 5 quoi/qui 6 que

G

1 Lequel 2 Lesquels 3 lesquelles 4 Lesquels 5 Laquelle

H

1 Qu'est-ce que tu écris?/Que'est-ce que vous écrivez?

2 Qu'est-ce que tu vas lui donner? Qu'est-ce que vous allez lui donner?

3 Quel réseau social préfères-tu?/Quel réseau social préférez-vous?

4 J'ai lu tous ses articles en ligne, desquels parles-tu? J'ai lu tous ses articles en ligne, desquels parlez-vous?

I

1 Ces 2 cet 3 Ce 4 Ces 5 Ces 6 Ce 7 Cette 8 Ces

J

1 celle 2 Celle 3 ceux 4 celui 5 Celle 6 celles

K

1 Having said that, I think I prefer to listen to the radio on the Internet, it's easier.

2 It's wonderful to like one's old phone, but did you think about this, new mobile phones are better.

3 Someone left this in your postbox it must be for you.

4 What did you tell him for him to believe that?

5 I don't believe that about him, he's not capable of it.

6 Who believes that nowadays.

L

1i 2c 3f 4a 5j 6b 7h 8e 9d 10g

M

1 un clavier

2 le mot de passe

3 une souris

4 l'Internet

5 des écouteurs

6 un texto

N

1 Aimer quelque chose (le like), se faire des amis, partager des photos, envoyer des messages instantanés, répondre aux courriels, se parler par Skype et partager des documents.

2 Se protéger du piratage et parfois de son employeur.

O

1 Pour mettre en place un système de communication entre les employés et aussi avec les clients. Une entreprise doit se méfier de la sécurité et doit aussi soigner son image publique.

2 La difficulté de distinguer entre la vie professionnelle et la vie privée et le besoin de se surveiller pour éviter de poster quelque chose que l'employeur pourrait voir.

3 Tout le monde doit prendre en considération les risques et les bénéfices parce que tout le monde est concerné.

P

quels (interrogative pronoun), ceux-ci (demonstrative pronoun), ceux-là (demonstrative pronoun), qui (interrogative pronoun)

Q

Answers will vary.

Unit 6

A

1 avant = before, d' = of **2** sans = without **3** à = at **4** par = by **5** à moins de = unless **6** à la suite d' = in the wake of, following

B

1 Pierre part demain matin à dix heures.

2 Cette voiture rouge est à nous.

3 Nous prenons une croisière qui commence à Barcelone.

4 Ils sont allés au théâtre hier soir.

5 Tu es allé(e) aux toilettes dans ce bar?

6 Jean a oublié son sac à dos.

7 Elle va à l'école primaire cette année.

8 Il cherche une voiture à 1000€.

C

1 La gare est à deux kilomètres d'ici.

2 C'est la valise de Jennifer.

3 Le train de Paris est arrivé en retard.

4 Ils étaient tous dans la salle de conférence quand le patron est arrivé.

5 Il y a une meilleure façon d'aller à Lyon.

6 Tu peux/Vous pouvez réciter ce poème de mémoire?

7 Ce sont les amis du voisin.

8 C'est l'eau du chat.

D

1 dans 2 en 3 dans 4 en 5 en 6 dans

E

1 sur 2 sur 3 sous 4 sous 5 sur 6 sous

F

1 en 2 au 3 à 4 des 5 aux 6 au 7 en 8 de

G

1i 2g 3h 4a 5d 6j 7b 8c 9e 10f

H

1c 2b 3a 4c 5c 6a

I

1 à la gare

2 à l'aéroport

3 au guichet

4 Le contrôleur

5 la visite guidée

6 la place centrale

7 les congés payés

8 un visa

J

1j 2l 3k 4b 5i 6c 7d 8e 9f 10g 11a 12h

K

Non, elle avait peur au début, mais elle a évité les endroits sans trop de monde et elle a pris un guide qui l'a accompagnée partout.

L

1 Elle est partie en vacances au Maroc.

2 Elle a visité la ville et la Médina.

3 Elle a mangé dans un restaurant qui s'appelle La Table du Palais. Elle y a mangé un tagine au poulet et aux olives vertes.

4 Après Marrakech, elle est allée à Agadir pour se détendre dans une station balnéaire.

5 Oui, mais on venait trop souvent nettoyer la chambre.

6 Oui, à cause du climat et du soleil ainsi que l'accueil chaleureux des Marocains.

M

au Maroc (in Morocco)

la ville de Marrakech (the city of Marrakesh)

au sud du pays (in the south of the country)

peur de sortir (fear of going out)

sans trop de monde (not too crowded, lit. without a lot of people)

trop d'argent (too much money)

en plein milieu de la Médina (right in the middle of the Medina)

dans un vieux restaurant (in an old restaurant)

au poulet et aux olives vertes (with chicken and green olives)

du Palais (of the Palace)

dans un vieux palais (in an old palace)

à Marrakech (in Marrakesh)

pour descendre (to go down)

au sud (in the south)

au bord de la mer (on the seaside)

dans un spa (at a spa)

à mon arrivée (on/upon my arrival)

à la station balnéaire (at the spa)

à Agadir (in Agadir)

contente de (happy to)

dans ce paradis (in this paradise)

loin de (far from)

de la ville (of the city)

à l'écoute des clients (listening to the clients)

je n'ai manqué de rien (I wanted for nothing)

cinq fois par jour (five times a day)

à l'heure à laquelle (at the hour at which)

du climat (of the climate)

des marocains (of the Moroccans)

contribué à (contributed to)

au fond de mon être (the core of my being)

la raison pour laquelle (the reason why)

on part en voyage (one travels)

N

Answers will vary.

Unit 7

A

The first one is the direct object, the second one is the subject of the sentence.

B

1 relative pronoun: qui **2** relative pronoun: qui **3** relative pronoun: que **4** no relative pronoun: ne... que is a negative **5** relative pronoun: qui **6** relative pronoun: qu'

C

1 que **2** qui **3** qui **4** qui **5** qui **6** que **7** que

D

2 C'est un gâteau en forme de bûche que nous mangeons pour le réveillon de Noël.

3 J'ai commandé un café que j'ai bu.

4 J'ai parlé avec des amis qui avaient envie de sortir prendre un pot.

5 Elle a aimé ce vin qui date de l'année 2010.

6 Tu n'as pas aimé la quiche que tu as commandée?

E

qui, qu', que, à qui, ce qui, sur lesquelles

F

1b 2c 3b 4c 5a 6b

G

1 avec qui 2 ce que 3 pour lesquels 4 ce qu' 5 Ce dont 6 à qui

H

1 I would like to reserve a table for four people for Saturday night, inside if possible.

2 Have you decided? Would you like to order?

3 What do you recommend?

4 Can I serve you something to drink?

5 And to start, what would you like as your first course?

6 I would like the steak cooked medium, please.

7 The bill (the check), please.

8 Is the service (the tip) included?

I

Answers will vary.

J

1c 2i 3e 4a 5h 6d 7j 8b 9g 10f

K

1F 2F

L

1 Pour se retrouver en famille ou avec des amis pour prendre un verre et manger quelque chose avant de se mettre à table. C'est un moment agréable et un signe du savoir-vivre français.

2 Le champagne, le pastis, les vins de noix ou de fruits, le martini, la bière, le soda et le whisky. For the remaining questions, answers will vary.

3 C'est de la nourriture qui est facile à manger et il n'y a pas de vaisselle à faire après.

M

Answers will vary.

Unit 8

A

1 je parle 2 je marche 3 je voyage

B

In the **je**, **tu**, **il/elle/on**, **ils/elles** forms, the **y** may change to an **i** or remain unchanged. The **nous** and **vous** forms are the same in either case.

C

In the **je**, **tu**, **il/elle/on**, **ils/elles** forms, the **y** changes to an **i**. The **nous** and **vous** forms are like the infinitive.

D

The **je**, **tu**, **il/elle/on**, **ils/elles** forms have a double **ll**. The **je**, **tu**, **il/elle/on**, **ils/elles** forms add an accent. These forms are only one syllable.

E

1 préfère 2 préfères 3 préfère 4 préférons 5 préférez 6 préfèrent

F

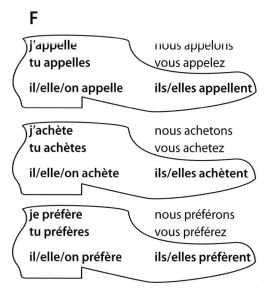

j'appelle — nous appelons
tu appelles — vous appelez
il/elle/on appelle — ils/elles appellent

j'achète — nous achetons
tu achètes — vous achetez
il/elle/on achète — ils/elles achètent

je préfère — nous préférons
tu préfères — vous préférez
il/elle/on préfère — ils/elles préfèrent

G

1 agace **2** vouvoies **3** déménageons **4** dirigent **5** envoyez **6** ennuie **7** essaie/essaye **8** espère

H

1 sommes **2** font **3** vais **4** vient **5** allez **6** a **7** sais **8** allez **9** est **10** connaît

I

The use of **ne** and **pas** around the conjugated verb makes the sentence negative.

J

1 jamais **2** guère **3** pas **4** plus **5** rien **6** personne **7** rien **8** nulle part

K

Sample answers:

1 Ce n'est pas possible.

2 Les patrons ne pensent jamais aux conditions de travail des ouvriers.

3 Je ne peux pas du tout faire des heures supplémentaires.

4 Je ne fais rien.

5 On ne doit absolument pas être poli avec tout le monde.

6 Il ne faut plus dire la vérité.

L

1d **2**f **3**b **4**g **5**h **6**c **7**a **8**e

M

1 la formation **2** travailler **3** la retraite **4** le retraité

N

1 Elle travaille pour une compagnie indépendante de production de films.

2 Oui, elle aime son travail parce qu'il n'y a pas de routine et elle aime le cinéma.

O

1 F She manages the people who mind the stars.

2 F Her job is difficult and interesting.

3 F She is updating her CV because she is looking for a new job.

4 V

5 V

6 F She hasn't been able to save a lot of money.

P

1 travailler **2** aimer **3** organiser **4** rencontrer **5** s'occuper de **6** gagner **7** finir par **8** économiser

Q

1 gérer **2** envoyer **3** voyager **4** espérer

R

Answers will vary.

Unit 9

A

When we say **il pleut**, we don't mean that any specific person or thing is raining. It is an impersonal subject and is translated as *it*.

B

1f or e **2**a **3**a or d **4**f or e **5**c, e or f **6**b

C

Answers may vary.

1 Il faut

2 Il suffit

3 Il importe

4 Il paraît

5 Il arrive

6 Il convient

7 Il vaut mieux

8 il s'agit

9 Il y a

10 Il se trouve

D

Both personal and impersonal: suffir, importer, paraître, arriver, convenir, avoir, se trouver
Only impersonal: falloir, valoir, s'agir (de)

E

1 veux **2** peux **3** voulez **4** dois **5** devons **6** pouvons **7** voulez **8** peuvent **9** doivent **10** devons or pouvons

F

1 She doesn't want to go out. The weather is too bad.

2 We will go out for a walk this afternoon.

3 Jeanne can't swim. She never learned how.

4 You want to go to the beach in this rain? You're crazy.

5 Souleymane wanted to join us, but he missed his train.

6 You must have loved it/him/her very much.

7 Who was supposed to come and help you?

8 He owes him how much? £100? Isn't that a lot?

G

1 le vent

2 l'arc-en-ciel

3 le froid

4 les averses

H

The weather is normal for the season.

I

1 De la Franche-Comté au Nord-Pas-de-Calais ainsi que sur les Midi-Pyrénées et l'Aquitaine. Parce qu'il y a neigé récemment.

2 Sur la côte est (de la Bretagne jusqu'en Aquitaine) à cause des intempéries.

3 Il fait beau maintenant sur la côte est (de la Bretagne jusqu'en Aquitaine).

4 Il fait le plus froid à Lille et le moins froid à Ajaccio.

5 Le matin, il fera gris partout sauf sur la Méditerranée avec du soleil plus tard dans la journée partout sauf dans le nord.

J

Il va geler, geler

Il règne maintenant le calme, régner

Il fait beau mais froid, faire

Il fait du soleil, faire

Elles peuvent, pouvoir

Il fera deux degrés, faire

On doit, devoir

K

Beau Temps	Mauvais Temps
Un temps paisible	Le ciel sera couvert
Il fait beau	du brouillard
Il fait du soleil	le verglas
Un temps relativement calme	la neige
Un temps ensoleillé	des inondations
	les intempéries
	les perturbations
	froid
	quelques précipitations
	un temps gris
	des brouillards
	les grisailles

L

Answers will vary.

Unit 10

A

1 Intention

2 **Penser que** can be followed by present or future

3 *If* clause followed by future

4 Prediction, probability

5 Expression of time uses future both before and after the verb

6 Command or order

B

1 Nous allons faire les courses. Nous ferons les courses.

2 Tu ne vas pas vouloir aller au supermarché. Tu ne voudras pas aller au supermarché.

3 Vous allez choisir vos vêtements la veille au soir. Vous choisirez vos vêtements la veille au soir.

4 Ils vont multiplier leurs efforts. Ils multiplieront leurs efforts.

5 Je vais aller chez l'épicier acheter des fruits. J'irai chez l'épicier acheter des fruits.

6 Elle va passer à la caisse pour régler ses achats. Elle passera à la caisse pour régler ses achats.

7 Vous allez payer par chèque ou en liquide? Vous payerez par chèque ou en liquide?

8 Nous allons acheter une voiture neuve. Nous achèterons une voiture neuve.

C

1 courir, mourir, devoir, recevoir, pleuvoir

2 avoir, aller, envoyer, être, faire, falloir, pouvoir, savoir, tenir, venir, voir, vouloir

D

1 J'irai à la gym demain matin.

2 Mes amis et moi, nous sortirons seulement le vendredi soir.

3 Tu ne mangeras pas trop.

4 Elle arrêtera de boire des boissons sucrées.

5 Il appellera sa mère le dimanche.

6 Je quitterai le travail à une heure raisonnable.

7 Il dépensera moins en vêtements.

8 Elles se lèveront plus tôt.

E

1 ferez 2 aurai 3 irons, serons 4 viendrez 5 sera 6 verrai, rappellerai

F

1e 2f 3b 4c 5a 6d

G

1 l'opticien

2 le kiosque à journaux

3 la banque

4 l'horloger

5 la librairie

6 la bijouterie

7 la pharmacie

8 l'épicerie

H

Le shopping sera différent, peut-être pas plus facile.

I

1 Le shopping sera plus rapide et plus simple.

2 Les clients recherchent avant tout la rapidité dans les achats.

3 Les magasins ne fermeront pas leurs portes parce que les clients veulent pouvoir acheter ce qu'ils désirent à toute heure.

4 La fraude à distance, l'usurpation d'identité et le manque de confidentialité sont les risques des nouvelles technologies.

J

1g 2e 3f 4a 5c 6b 7d

K

1 sécurité 2 connecté 3 vigilant(e) 4 le client, le consommateur

L

Answers will vary.

Unit 11

A

Unlike other verb forms, there is no subject pronoun with imperatives. The **-s** is missing from the first example.

B

1 Lavez, the second person plural (**vous**) form is used when talking to more than one person or someone with whom you are being formal.

2 Lavons, the first person plural (**nous**) form is used when you are including yourself and one or more other people.

3 Lave, the second person singular (**tu**) form is used when addressing one person with whom you are familiar; the **-s** is dropped with **-er** verbs.

C

1 Sors la poubelle.

2 Sortez la poubelle.

3 Sortons la poubelle.

4 Mets la table.

5 Mettez la table.

6 Mettons la table.

D

2 Changeons les draps.

3 Repassez les chemises.

4 Passe l'aspirateur.

5 Nettoyons la salle de bains.

6 Ayez une chambre propre.

7 Finis la lessive.

8 Tondez le gazon.

9 Recyclons les canettes.

10 Sois pratique.

E

1 Occupez-vous des courses. Occupe-toi des courses.

2 Débrouillez-vous pour faire un gâteau. Débrouille-toi pour faire un gâteau.

3 Arrêtez de vous disputer. Arrête de te disputer.

4 Dépêchez-vous. Dépêche-toi.

5 Habillez-vous. Habille-toi.

6 Amusez-vous à la fête. Amuse-toi à la fête.

F

2 Non, ne le fais pas avec une recette, fais-le sans recette.

3 Non, ne les coupe pas en julienne, coupe-les en dés.

4 Non, n'en mettons pas, mettons du sel.

5 Non, ne repasse pas les serviettes, utilise des serviettes en papier.

6 Non, ne la mettons pas, mangeons dans le salon.

G

1V 2F 3V 4F 5F 6V

H

Answers will vary.

I

Example sentences:

1 Faisons le ménage ensemble ce matin.

2 Range ta chambre avant d'aller au lit.

3 Pliez le linge qui est dans le sèche-linge.

4 Essuyez la vaisselle avant de la ranger.

5 Occupons-nous des tâches ménagères.

6 Balaie or balaye la cuisine s'il te plait.

J

It is a yogurt maker (une yaourtière).

K

1 Du yaourt et du lait

2 8 à 10 heures

3 Il faut le débrancher.

4 Il ne faut pas le plonger dans de l'eau.

5 Du lait en poudre

6 Parce que le yaourt ne prendra pas.

L

1 nettoyer 2 utiliser 3 brancher 4 ranger 5 garder 6 verser 7 ajouter 8 éviter

M

Answers will vary.

Unit 12

A

aimer – to like or love

adorer – to adore

aller – to go

détester – to hate or detest

désirer – to want or desire

devoir – to have to (should in the conditional)

espérer – to hope

pouvoir – to be able to, can (could in the conditional)

préférer – to prefer

savoir – to know

sembler – to seem

sentir – to feel

sortir – to go out

vouloir – to want

B

1 Putting the cart before the horse. (Literally, putting the plough before the oxen.)

2 Giving a little to get a lot. (Literally, one has to know when to give an egg in order to get back an ox.)

3 Giving is giving, taking back is stealing.

4 Do well and leave the talking to others.

5 The straw that broke the camel's back. (Literally, the drop of water that caused the vase to overflow.)

6 Robbing Peter to pay Paul. (Literally, undressing Paul to clothe Jacques.)

7 Still water runs deep. (Literally, be wary of still water.)

8 I have other fish to fry. (Literally, I have other cats to whip.)

C

1 aime sentir

2 adorent partir

3 vais faire

4 déteste faire

5 désirons nous voir

6 dois rappeler

7 espérons avoir

8 sort voir

D

1 She likes to feel the wind on her skin.

2 They love to go away at the weekend/on the weekend.

3 I am going to go hiking Saturday morning.

4 Jean hates to do his homework.

5 We want to see each other more often.

6 I have to call back later, someone is at the door.

7 We hope to have the pleasure of seeing you again.

8 He is going out to see a concert this evening.

E

1 de **2** ø **3** à **4** de **5** à … de **6** de **7** à **8** d'

F

1 Il est essentiel de boire au moins un verre de vin rouge par jour.

2 Vous nous défendez de sortir?

3 Il ne faut pas trop manger.

4 Nous sommes tristes de le voir partir.

5 Il est nécessaire d'accepter ses défauts/Il vous est nécessaire d'accepter vos défauts.

6 Elle te demande d'y aller avec eux.

G

Ne personne *(nobody)* and **ne que** *(only)* don't go before the infinitive, they go around it like in simple negation of conjugated verbs.

H

1 Nous choisissons de ne pas sauter nos séances de gym.

2 Elle veut arrêter de ne rien manger le matin.

3 On m'a conseillé de ne plus fumer.

4 Tu t'habitues à ne voir personne tous les jours.

5 Il décide de ne pas être si perfectionniste.

6 Vous vous efforcer de ne plus boire des bières tous les soirs.

7 Claire promet de ne jamais nourrir ses émotions hostiles.

8 Nous cessons de ne faire attention qu'à nos défauts.

I

2 Elle est déçue de ne pas avoir pris la bonne décision.

3 Nous sommes quand même heureux d'avoir acheté notre propre maison.

4 Paul n'est pas content de ne pas être arrivé à vaincre ses émotions.

5 Elles sont désolées de ne pas être venues hier, elles ont eu un empêchement.

6 Ce n'était pas une bonne idée de faire une fête surprise pour l'anniversaire de Robert. Il n'était pas du tout content.

7 Il est au désespoir d'avoir été licencié hier.

J

1 l'amour 2 le bonheur 3 la surprise 4 la haine 5 la peur 6 la colère 7 la tristesse 8 le désir

K

1 aimer 2 être heureux 3 surprendre 4 haïr 5 craindre, avoir peur
6 se fâcher 7 s'attrister, se désoler 8 désirer

L

1 la réussite professionnelle, l'achat d'une voiture de luxe, la somme d'argent qu'on aura épargnée avant de pouvoir prendre sa retraite.

2 Parce que c'est une façon de vivre, non pas un but auquel on peut arriver.

M

1 la famille, la santé, l'amour, les amis, les loisirs et la vie professionnelle

2 son attitude

3 apprécier les petits détails de la vie, prendre son temps pour se faire plaisir, pour faire de nouvelles découvertes, se fixer des objectifs, se réjouir à l'avance, s'entourer de personnes positives

N

Infinitives: pouvoir, prendre, se sentir, accepter, aimer, vivre, atteindre, contribuer, prendre, se rendre, se demander, changer, apprécier, prendre, se faire, faire, faire, être, se fixer, se réjouir, être, savoir, s'entourer, partager, profiter

Past infinitives: avoir atteint, avoir réussi

O

Answers will vary.

Unit 13

A

1 no **2** yes **3** no **4** yes **5** yes **6** no

B

C'était trop beau!

C

Even though **sortir** is an irregular verb in the present, it follows the pattern of regular verbs in the imperfect.

D

The **je/tu/il/elle/on/ils/elles** forms keep the **ç**, but the **nous** and **vous** forms do not.

je commençais

tu commençais

il/elle/on commençait

nous commencions

vous commenciez

ils/elles commençaient

E

1 habitions 2 était, avait 3 alliez 4 adoraient 5 taquinais, était 6 devais, t'ennuyais

F

1 Vous attendiez quelqu'un.

2 Est-ce que tu me posais une question?

3 Pourquoi est-ce qu'elle était là?

4 Nous venions pour vous demander quelque chose.

5 Je ne savais pas quoi lui dire.

6 Vous aviez besoin de quelque chose?

G

1 Son fils était toujours difficile.

2 Quand nous étions jeunes, nous allions régulièrement à l'école à pied.

3 Tu jouais souvent dehors avec tes amis.

4 Nous allions au parc toutes les semaines.

5 D'habitude, vous étiez bavards et aimables.

6 Je lisais le journal tous les matins pendant que je déjeunais.

H

1V 2F 3V

I

1 Il était bon élève et il avait de bonnes notes.

2 Il jouait au foot.

3 Elle était égoïste, mal polie et capricieuse.

4 Parce que sa sœur n'avait pas droit à sa glace, elle ne se comportait pas bien.v

J

In **Et, si nous allions à la plage?** the imperfect tense can be used to make a suggestion, it always follows **si** in this case.

K

1 Je passais beaucoup de temps avec eux.

2 Je les adorais.

3 Mes parents m'aidaient avec mes devoirs.

4 Tout le monde disait qu'elle était un petit diable.

5 Elle faisait tout le temps des caprices.

6 Je me comportais toujours bien.

L

Answers will vary.

Unit 14

A

1 avons 2 a 3 ont 4 Avez 5 ai 6 as

B

1 choisir 2 habiter 3 louer 4 vendre 5 emménager 6 réussir

C

-**er** verbs take -**é**, -**ir** verbs take -**i** and -**re** verbs take -**u**

D

1 vidé 2 fini 3 vendu 4 bâti 5 restauré 6 attendu

E

1 admis **2** émis **3** omis **4** permis **5** promis **6** remis

F

1 as entendu

2 ont grandi

3 avons interdit

4 avez perdu

5 a rénové

6 ai découvert

7 as eu

8 avez compris

9 ont poussé

10 avons rendu

G

1 e

2 es

3 s

4 ø

5 e

6 ø

H

1 sommes

2 es

3 suis

4 est

5 êtes

6 sont

I

When it is formed with **être,** the past participle agrees in gender and number with the subject of the sentence, so they add nothing in the masculine singular, **-e** in the feminine singular, **-s** in the masculine plural and **-es** in the feminine plural.

J

1 Il est parti après nous.

2 Nous sommes rentré(e)s hier matin.

3 Vous êtes montés dans votre chambre.

4 Tu es né(e) au mois de mars.

5 Je suis tombé(e) par terre.

6 Elles sont allées cet après-midi.

7 Ils sont descendus au sous-sol.

8 Elle est sortie vers quatre heures.

K

1 Je n'ai jamais habité une maison de campagne.

2 Nous n'avons pas encore loué un appartement à Paris.

3 Vous n'y êtes jamais allés?

4 Ils n'ont aimé que ce matelas.

5 Elle n'a parlé à personne.

6 Il n'a rien dit.

L

1 Est-ce que tu as vu la piscine? As-tu vu la piscine? Est-ce que vous avez vu la piscine? Avez-vous vu la piscine?

2 Est-ce que Théo a habité ce quartier? Théo a-t-il habité ce quartier?

3 Est-ce qu'elle est passée vous voir? Est-elle passée vous voir?

4 Est-ce que vous avez reçu une offre d'achat? Avez-vous reçu une offre d'achat?

5 Est-ce que vous êtes rentrés dans la maison? Êtes-vous rentrés dans la maison?

6 Est-ce tu l'as appelée hier? L'as-tu appelée hier? Est-ce que vous l'avez appelée hier? L'avez-vous appelée hier?

M

1 was – imperfect, knocked – passé composé

2 left – passé composé, was raining – imperfect

3 was – imperfect, lived – imperfect

N

2 Elle a fermé les boîtes en carton pendant que son mari promenait le chien.

3 Elle a nettoyé la cuisine pendant que son mari faisait les courses.

4 Elle a couvert les meubles avec des draps pendant que sa fille regardait la télé.

5 Elle est montée au grenier pour le vider pendant que son mari faisait la cuisine.

6 Elle est sortie chercher les clés de la nouvelle maison pendant que sa mère tricotait.

7 Elle a téléphoné au fournisseur d'Internet pour changer l'adresse pendant que son fils bricolait au sous-sol.

8 Elle a confirmé l'arrivée des déménageurs le lendemain pendant que son père lisait le journal.

O

1 était

2 voulaient

3 cherchaient

4 habitaient

5 a rencontré

6 a expliqué

7 avaient

8 ont vu

9 est tombée

10 a dit

P

1k 2f 3i 4l 5a 6n 7d 8c 9m 10e 11h 12j 13g 14b

Q

Answers will vary. Possible answers include: une maison, une maison de campagne, un appartement, un loft, un château, un logement

R

Elle est allée à Grenoble, en France. Pour faire des études.

S

1 Elle a trouvé son appartement dans les annonces immobilieres en ligne.

2 Non, elle n'a pas acheté de meubles. Jean-Baptiste a laissé ses meubles quand il est parti.

3 Oui, elle a beaucoup aimé son appartement, il était petit mais bien décoré.

4 Elle a réarrangé les meubles et elle a repeint la chambre.

5 Elle a laissé des photos de la Guadeloupe dans des cadres dans le salon comme cadeau pour remercier Jean-Baptiste.

T

Answers will vary.

Unit 15

A

1 would recycle **2** would take **3** would reduce

B

2 present, future. If you recycle, you will reduce greenhouse gases.

3 present, infinitive, imperative. If you want to reduce greenhouse gases, recycle!

4 imperfect, conditional. If you recycled, you would reduce greenhouse gases.

C

1d **2**b **3**d **4**c **5**c **6**a

D

1 Je réduirais

2 Nous réussirions

3 Il prendrait

4 Tu finirais

5 Elle économiserait

6 Vous croiriez

7 Ils planteraient

8 Nous rendrions

E

1 lanceraient 2 nagerais 3 préféreriez 4 mangerions 5 répéterait 6 avancerais

F

1 nettoieraient 2 achèterions 3 appellerais 4 lèverait 5 jetteriez 6 essaierions/essayerions

G

1 Vous pourriez

2 Il aurait

3 Nous courrions

4 Tu enverrais

5 Elle serait

6 Ils iraient

H

2 prendre 3 pourrait 4 aimerait 5 ferait 6 mettre 7 pourrions 8 apprendraient

I

Bonne	Mauvaise
le covoiturage	les sacs en plastique
une voiture électrique	les déchets nocifs
les panneaux solaires	une empreinte carbone
une ferme bio	
les transports en commun	

J

1 les ressources 2 l'environnement 3 l'hybride 4 la pollution

K

1 des sacs en plastique 2 ferme bio, poulaillers 3 des panneaux solaires 4 planter 5 en voie de disparition

L

1f 2h 3d 4c 5g 6e 7a 8b

M

Elle voudrait adopter des poules. L'avantage serait que les poules mangeraient ses ordures ménagères.

N

1 Elle leur demanderait de l'aider à construire un poulailler.

2 Elle aimerait faire un petit jardin potager.

3 Elle les vendrait au marché.

4 Elle pourrait installer des panneaux solaires.

O

aimerais, voudrais, pourraient, m'aideraient, aiderais, devrais, voudrais, demanderais, voudrais, coûterait, resterait, pourrais, planterais, cultiverais, cuisinerais, aimerais, aurais, pourrais, installerais, pourriez

P

Answers will vary.

Unit 16

A

1 Tu <u>te</u> lèves à 6 heures du matin? C'est tôt!

2 Ils <u>se</u> changent en rentrant du boulot.

3 Nous <u>nous</u> promenons dans le parc.

4 Je <u>me</u> réveille de bonne heure pour aller à la pêche.

5 Vous <u>vous</u> couchez après avoir regardé un film.

6 Elle <u>s'</u>habille dans des vêtements chic pour aller au bureau.

The pronouns change with the subject of the sentence. **Se** changes to **me**, **te**, **nous** or **vous** with **je**, **tu**, **nous** or **vous**. They don't change with **il/elle/on** or **ils/elles**.

B

1 We're getting the suitcase ready.

2 We're getting (ourselves) ready.

3 They are watching the show.

4 They are looking into each other's eyes.

C

1 to go

2 to amuse, to entertain

3 to perceive, to see

4 to call

5 to ask

6 to send in haste

7 to marry (when one person marries two other people)

8 to spend (time), to hand

9 to smell

10 (no other meaning)

11 to deceive or to cheat (on someone)

12 to find

D

1 elle se lave

2 nous nous aimons

3 ils se disputent

4 je m'asseois / je m'assied (either conjugation is correct)

5 vous vous écrivez

6 nous nous couchons

7 tu te trompes

8 elles se téléphonent

E

1a 2b 3c 4c 5a 6b

F

1 réveillez-vous **2** levez-vous **3** lave-toi **4** habille-toi **5** brossez-vous **6** dépêchez-vous

G

1 Te trompes-tu souvent?

2 S'aiment-ils?

3 Vous amusez-vous?

4 Te maquilles-tu?

5 Allons-nous nous habituer à ce genre de vie?

6 Se parleront-elles?

H

1 Thomas et Juliette sont très athlétiques, ils ne se fatiguent pas facilement.

2 Je ne me souviens pas très bien de mon enfance.

3 Nous nous sommes promenés toute la journée.

4 Vous n'allez pas vous disputer encore une fois.

5 Dépêche-toi, nous sommes en retard!

6 Tu te débrouilles très bien.

I

1 third person feminine singular

2 first person plural

3 third person plural

4 second person singular, feminine (the only indicator that it is feminine is the **e** on the past participle)

J

1 ø 2 ø 3 e 4 ø 5 ø 6 e

K

1e 2f 3g 4a 5h 6d 7b 8c

L

1 Ils se sont rencontrés quand ils étaient étudiants à l'université.

2 Martin étudiait la sociologie et Anne étudiait la science politique. Elle est devenue avocate et il a travaillé dans le marketing.

M

1 Martin est déprimé parce qu'il est au chômage.

2 Martin se lève encore de bonne heure, il se brosse les dents, il prend une douche, il s'habille. La plupart du temps, il prend le petit déjeuner avec sa femme.

3 Martin et sa femme se font plaisir en faisant de bonnes choses à manger le soir.

4 Elle lui a dit de se prendre en main et de se trouver un boulot parce qu'il s'ennuie et il est temps.

N

se lever (reflexive)

se coucher (reflexive)

se promener (reflexive)

se connaître (reciprocal)

s'établir (reflexive)

se faire embaucher (reflexive)

se retrouver (neither)

s'arrêter (reflexive)

se forcer (reflexive)

se lever (reflexive)

se brosser les dents (reflexive)

s'habiller (reflexive)

se parler (reciprocal)

s'occuper (reflexive)

se faire plaisir (reflexive)

se disputer (reciprocal)

se réveiller (reflexive)

se regarder (reciprocal)

se prendre en main (reflexive)

se trouver (reflexive)

s'ennuyer (neither)

se marier (reciprocal)

se disputer (reciprocal)

O

Answers will vary.

Unit 17

A

1 a fact

2 an obligation/same form of **aller** as in 3 (subjunctive)

3 an uncertainty/same form of **aller** as in 2 (subjunctive)

B

1 tombe 2 sache 3 aille 4 puisse 5 fassiez 6 ait 7 prenne 8 attrappe 9 veuilles 10 reçoivent

C

Answers will vary.

D

1 Elle ne croit pas que ce soit important.

2 Vous ne pensez pas que les vaccins doivent être obligatoires.

3 Tu ne trouves pas qu'il ait l'air blême.

4 Il n'est pas vrai que nous devions faire moins de sport.

5 Nous ne sommes pas sûrs que Claire soit malade.

6 Elles ne disent pas que ce soit bon.

E

1 dises

2 a

3 veut

4 soit

5 commande (indicative)

6 soient

7 ait

8 arrive (subjunctive)

F

1 arrivent

2 ailles

3 maigrisse

4 dois

5 fasse

6 vienne

7 a

8 puisse

G

1 rhume 2 fièvre 3 mal à la gorge 4 toux 5 comprimés 6 reposer 7 médicament 8 digestion 9 consultation

H

1 un thermomètre **2** la radiographie **3** une piqûre
4 attraper la grippe **5** un pansement **6** le cancer

I

1V **2**F **3**F

J

1 Elle a plus de temps à passer avec les patients et moins de stress. Les gens sont là pour la prévention et leur bien-être et pas pour les traumatismes.

2 La thalassothérapie a beaucoup de bienfaits physiques et psychologiques.

3 Elle veut dire que c'est important de se soigner, de faire attention à sa santé, c'est à dire bien se nourrir, bouger, ne pas se croire seul au monde et s'intéresser aux autres.

K

1c **2**f **3**e **4**a **5**d **6**b

L

Answers will vary.

Unit 18

A

1 Paul conduit le camion.

2 Les voyageurs prennent le train.

3 Tout le monde respecte Michelle.

4 Un camion a renversé la moto sur l'autoroute.

B

1 Son roman a été lu par des millions de personnes.

2 Le trophée a été remporté par celui qui a couru le plus vite.

3 Sa mobylette a été volée.

4 Les pompiers ont été avertis par le propriétaire que sa maison avait pris feu.

5 Il est aimé de tout le monde.

6 Puisque tu as fui la scène de l'accident, tu seras recherché par la police.

7 La circulation est affectée par l'accident sur la route.

8 Espérons que la loi sur les pistes cyclables sera votée.

C

1 On évite les accidents en faisant attention à la route.

2 On attend l'arrivée de l'avion.

3 On déposera les bagages à la gare.

4 On n'a pas mis le clignotant.

5 On a crevé le pneu.

6 On n'a pas respecté le code de la route.

7 Un auto-stoppeur a arrêté une voiture.

8 La police recherche des témoins de l'accident.

D

1 Le capitaine a dit, « Il faut mettre les gilets de sauvetage ».

2 Elle a dit, « Je n'aime pas du tout conduire ».

3 Vous déclarez, « Nous serons prêts à partir dans dix minutes ».

E

Il dit que ce n'est pas trop loin, heureusement.

Il dit qu'il fait d'habitude la navette à vélo pour se rendre au boulot.

Il dit que le trajet lui prend d'habitude près d'une demi-heure.

Il dit que, dans la ville de Lyon et en région lyonnaise, on a aménagé l'espace urbain pour mieux l'adapter aux piétons et aux cyclistes.

Il dit qu'il y a un réseau important de pistes cyclables et qu'il se sent en sécurité quand il prend son vélo. Il dit que les jours où il fait trop mauvais, il prend les transports en commun.

Il dit que si elle est disponible, sa femme le dépose à la station de métro.

Il dit qu'ils ont de la chance d'habiter si près.

Il dit que c'est pratique, propre et rarement bondé.

F

Jeanne lui a dit de relâcher le frein à main.

Jeanne lui a dit de poser son pied sur la pédale du frein.

Jeanne lui a dit de mettre la clé de contact et de la tourner.

Jeanne lui a dit d'enclencher le levier de vitesse.

Jeanne lui a dit de lever son pied du frein et d'appuyer sur la pédale d'accélérateur.

G

1 Elle affirme que toutes les voitures doivent passer une inspection annuelle.

2 Nous avons dit que nous nous méfions des systèmes de géolocalisation.

3 Le policier lui demande de lui donner ses papiers d'identité.

4 Nous l'avons cautionné de faire attention quand il fait nuit parce qu'il y a des cerfs dans le coin.

5 Le conducteur de la voiture a assuré qu'il ne roulait pas à 160 kilomètres à l'heure.

6 Il a crié de venir au secours.

7 Vous avez dit que vous prendrez un café quand vous serez arrivé.

8 Tu as répondu que tu avais réussi à faire un créneau.

H

2 Iris me demande si je peux l'aider. Elle dit qu'elle a eu un pneu crevé.

3 Iris me demande si je sais mettre une roue de secours. Elle dit qu'elle en a une.

4 Elle me demande si je saurais la retrouver. Elle dit qu'elle est sur le périphérique juste après la porte d'Orléans.

5 Iris me demande si tu me laisseras prendre ta voiture pour aller l'aider. Elle dit qu'elle serait très reconnaissante.

I

1 un train de banlieue **2** obtenir son permis **3** faire du covoiturage **4** défaut de ceinture
5 les transports en commun **6** faire la navette

J

Transport aérien	Transport terrestre	Transport maritime
un hélicoptère	un taxi	une péniche
une montgolfière	une camionnette	un paquebot
un avion	un camion	une barque
	une moto	un bateau
	une voiture	un kayak
	un tramway	un canoë
	un bus	
	un autocar	
	le métro	

K

Answers will vary.

L

1 la conduite agressive **2** la rage au volant

M

1 Prendre son temps, pardonner et oublier autant que possible, minimiser les gestes et les cris, ne pas utiliser le klaxon trop facilement, être poli et patient.

2 Eviter de provoquer un conducteur agressif, rester calme, rester dans la voiture, noter la description du conducteur et de sa voiture.

3 Respecter le code de la route et les autres conducteurs.

N

Answers will vary.

Unit 19

A

The auxiliary verbs are in the imperfect.

1 manger 2 apprendre 3 sortir

B

1 étiez parti(e)s 2 avait achetés 3 avions mangé 4 avait appris 5 n'avais pas dit 6 avais connu

C

1 étaient 2 n'étaient jamais devenus 3 allais 4 étais 5 allais 6 mettait 7 avais 8 avons déménagé 9 avaient toujours voulu 10 avaient pensé 11 pouvaient 12 n'avais pas été 13 étions partis 14 ai vite compris

D

The auxiliary verbs are in the conditional.

1 téléphoner 2 dire 3 aller

E

1 aurait voulu 2 serions allé(e)s 3 vous seriez dépêché(e)(s) 4 n'aurais pas regardé 5 aurait pris 6 aurais apprécié

F

1 aurions pu 2 avait su 3 n'avais pas été 4 avaient écouté 5 étais parti(e) 6 n'aviez pas assisté

G

The auxiliary verbs are in the future indicative.

1 finir 2 voir 3 partir

H

1 aura appris 2 n'aurons pas fini 3 aurez vu 4 aurai payé 5 seront parties 6 n'auras pas fini

I

1 viendras 2 aurai 3 sera 4 invitera 5 aura fini 6 auras trouvé 7 dirai

J

1 un film

2 une bande-dessinée

3 un drame

4 un film d'horreur

5 un dessin animé

6 un western

K

1F, Beaucoup de pays financent le cinéma

2V

L

1 C'est le Centre national du cinéma et de l'image animée en France. Il est chargé de régler la production et la diffusion du cinéma, de le soutenir et de le promouvoir.

2 Les films pornographiques, publicitaires ou incitant à la violence sont exclus.

3 Que le CNC a trop de pouvoir, que les acteurs célèbres sont trop bien payés et que le système est inégalitaire, la télévision doit contribuer au cinéma, donc il faut que celle-ci ait du succès pour subventionner l'autre.

M

1c 2d 3f 4e 5a 6b

N

1 a tax credit

2 a private tax

3 sales

4 movie ticket sales

5 to subsidize

6 financing

O

Answers will vary.

Unit 20

A

1 aider

2 partir

3 perdre

B

1 Elle a parlé.

2 Tu as pris.

3 Nous avons choisi.

4 J'ai encouragé.

5 Elles sont allées.

6 Il a choisi.

7 Vous êtes rentré(e)(s).

8 Ils ont gagné.

C

1 Nous gagnâmes.

2 Elle fit.

3 Vous donnâtes.

4 Il remplaça.

5 Elles essayèrent.

6 Tu vis.

7 Ils peignirent.

8 Je réfléchis.

D

They are in the **passé simple**.

1 commander

2 faire

3 mourir

E

1 Il avait fait.

2 Nous étions rentrés.

3 Tu avais nagé.

4 Elles étaient parties.

5 Vous aviez déménagé(e)(s).

6 J'avais obéi.

F

se mit	se mettre
retint	retenir
fut	être
fut servi	servir
put	pouvoir
eut lapé	laper
prie	prier
dit	dire
courut	courir
loua	louer
trouva	trouver
servit	servir
fallut	falloir

G

1 un trottoir

2 le parc

3 raser

4 pierre

5 bal

H

1n **2**m **3**g **4**b **5**k **6**e **7**l **8**j **9**d **10**c **11**h **12**i **13**f **14**a

I

1 Louis XIV.

2 Pour les promenades, pour voir les spectacles et pour aller au théâtre, aux bals et aux cabarets.

J

1 Napoléon III.

2 L'espace urbain est plus sain, il est plus facile de circuler, la vie des habitants est améliorée, le prestige de la ville a augmenté.

3 Les Parisiens de l'époque, à cause du prix et des disparités sociales.

4 Ils pensent que c'est bien.

K

1c **2**d **3**f **4**a **5**b **6**e

L

décida	décider
furent	être
remplacèrent	remplacer
construisit	construire
furent	être
marquèrent	marquer

devint	devenir
s'installèrent	s'installer
naquit	naître
fut	être
apparut	apparaître
eut	avoir
connut	connaître
contribua	contribuer
devinrent	devenir
critiquèrent	critiquer
s'installèrent	s'installer
furent	être
contribua	contribuer
purent	pouvoir
passèrent	passer

M

Answers will vary.

Adjectives are used to provide more information about nouns. Most adjectives follow the noun, others go before the noun. **Un hôtel élégant** *(An elegant hotel)*, **une voiture neuve** *(a new car)*.

Adverbs usually provide more information about verbs. **Il attend patiemment.** *(He waits patiently.)* They can also be used to modify adjectives or even other adverbs. **Il a très bien réussi.** *(He succeeded very well.)*, **Il ne boit pas trop souvent.** *(He doesn't drink too often.)* In English, adverbs often end in *-ly*, the French equivalent is **-ment**.

Article: there are three types of articles: definite, indefinite and partitive. In English, the definite article is *the*. **Le, l', la, les** in French. **Le nain** *(the dwarf)*, **l'adolescent** *(the adolescent)*, **la dame** *(the lady)*, **les éléphants** *(the elephants)*.

Clause: a clause is a group of words containing a subject and a verb. A clause that stands on its own is a complete sentence, known as an independent clause. A clause that is dependent on another clause is known as a subordinate clause.
Je lui parlerai quand nous le verrons. *(I will speak to him* (independent clause), *when we see him* (subordinate clause).)

Comparative: to make comparisons in English, we add *-er* to or use *more, less* or *as* with an adjective. In French you use **plus**, **moins** or **aussi**.
Elle est plus intelligente que lui. *(She is smarter than him.)*
Cette orange est moins amère que l'autre. *(This orange is less bitter than the other one.)*

Conditional: the conditional is one of four moods in French. The indicative, the imperative and the subjunctive are the others. The conditional is used to express what might happen or what could happen. It is also used as a form of politeness.
Elle pourrait venir si elle en avait envie. *(She could come if she wanted to.)*
Tu pourrais fermer la porte s'il te plaît? *(Could you shut the door please?)*

Conjugation in French is when the verb endings change or an auxiliary (**avoir** or **être**) is used to express person, number, voice, tense, mood, etc. **Je suis** *(I am)*, **tu es** *(you are)*, etc.

Conjunctions like **et** *(and)*, **mais** *(but)* and **parce que** *(because)* connect two or more words or clauses.
Victor et Charles sont de bons amis, mais parfois ils se disputent à cause de la politique. *(Victor and Charles are good friends, but sometimes they argue because of politics.)*

Demonstratives like **ce, c', cette** *(this, that)* and **ces** *(these)* serve to designate someone or something in context.
Ce livre est intéressant. *(This book is interesting.)*
Cette voiture est à moi. *(That car is mine.)*

Gender: in French, gender is used to designate not only male and female persons or animals. Gender is also used to designate objects and beings of indeterminate sex. In English, *table* is considered neuter, but in French it is feminine and *day* is masculine. **La table** *(the table)*, **le jour** *(the day)*.

Imperative: The imperative is a mood used to express warnings, orders or directions.

Fais attention! *(Watch out!)*
Venez ici! *(Come here!)*
Prenons le métro. *(Let's take the underground.)*

Indicative: the indicative is one of four moods. The others are the conditional, the imperative and the subjunctive. The indicative is used to make assertions in a variety of tenses in the past, present and future.
Elle est montée *(She went up)*
Nous avons *(We have)*
Tu iras *(You will go)*

Infinitive: the infinitive is the basic form of the verb. It is the form you will find in a dictionary. In French, infinitives end in **-er**, **-ir** and **-re**. Unlike in English, they can be used as nouns or as gerunds, the *-ing* form in English.
Être ou ne pas être, voilà la question. *(To be or not to be, that is the question.)*
Finir à temps, c'est important. *(Finishing on time is important.)*

Irregular verb: some verbs do not follow the set pattern of verb conjugation. These are called irregular verbs. They are usually the most common verbs in French like **être** *(to be)*, **aller** *(to go)*, **avoir** *(to have)*, **faire** *(to do* or *to make)*, **vouloir** *(to want)*. Their forms are listed in the table at the end of the course.

Nouns designate a person, place or thing. In French, they usually need an article:
la fille *(the girl)*, **le chien** *(the dog)*, **les animaux** *(the animals)*, **une fille** *(a girl)*, **un chien** *(a dog)*, **des animaux** *(some animals/animals)*.

Object: the object of a sentence can be direct, indirect (**à** + a person) or used with a preposition.
Il regarde _la télévision_. *(He is watching _television_.)*
Tu donnes un cadeau _à ton mari_. *(You give a gift _to your husband_.)*
Nous marchons _avec elle_. *(We walk _with her_.)*

Past participle: a past participle is derived from the infinitive of a verb and is used with an auxiliary, **être** *(to be)* or **avoir** *(to have)*, in compound tenses.
Elle a mangé une pomme. *(She ate an apple.)*
Nous n'avions pas fini de travailler. *(We hadn't finished working.)*
Tu ne seras pas arrivé avant son départ. *(You will not have arrived before he leaves.)*

Plural: in French, these are usually expressed in writing with either an **-s** or **-x** ending to indicate plurality of things or people. **Les amis** *(the friends)*, **les chevaux** *(the horses)*.

Possessives are adjectives or pronouns used to express ownership or custody. Words like **mon** *(my)* or **notre** *(our)* are possessives, as are **le mien** *(mine)* or **le nôtre** *(ours)*.

Prepositions like **à** *(at)*, **de** *(from* or *of)*, **pour** *(for, in order to)*, **dans** *(in)*, **chez** *(at someone's house)* are words that link one part of a sentence to another.
Allons à la piscine. *(Let's go to the pool.)*
Agnès part dans trois minutes. *(Agnès is leaving in three minutes.)*

Pronominal verbs need a reflexive or reciprocal pronoun because the subject performing the action is also the person or people receiving the action.
Je me lave. *(I am washing myself.)*
Nous nous regardons. *(We are looking at each other.)*

Pronouns generally take the place of a noun and are often used to avoid repeating a noun that has already been mentioned, as in the case of the subject pronoun **ils** *(they)* here:
Marie et Yann sont mariés depuis trois ans et ils n'ont pas d'enfants. *(Marie and Yann have been married for three years and they don't have children.)*

Subject: the term *subject* expresses a relationship between a noun or a pronoun and a verb. The subject of a sentence typically performs the action of a verb.
Jean-Marc lit. *(Jean-Marc is reading.)*
Tu fais le ménage. *(You do housework.)*

Subjunctive: the subjunctive is a mood that is rarely used in English, but you can find it in sentences like *It is essential that you be there.* French uses the subjunctive more frequently than in English.

Superlative: a superlative is a form of an adjective which is used to say something is *the most, the best* or *the worst.*
C'est toi le meilleur! *(You are the best!)*
C'est le livre le moins intéressant. *(It's the least interesting book.)*

Tense: most languages use changes in the verb to indicate an aspect of time. These changes are referred to as tense and the tenses may be in the past, the present or the future.
Nous sommes sortis. *(We went out.)*
Elle est chez lui. *(She is at his house.)*
Tu partiras demain. *(You will leave tomorrow.)*

Verbs express actions (**jouer**, *to play*), states of being (**exister**, *to exist*) or sensations (**sentir**, *to feel*). Verbs usually have a subject and may be defined by their role in a sentence.
Elle travaille. *(She works.)*
Nous aimons la plage. *(We like the beach.)*

FRENCH–ENGLISH GLOSSARY

This glossary contains only those words which you may need for quick reference to help you with a grammar or reading exercise, but remember to use your dictionary to look up and write down the words you need to know and learn.

A

à l'heure	on time
à moins que	unless
accélérateur (m)	accelerator
achat (m)	purchase
actualité (f)	current event
agacer	to annoy/irritate
agitation (f)	commotion/unrest
agréable	pleasant/enjoyable
ail (m)	garlic
ailleurs	elsewhere
ajout (m)	addition
alentour (m)	surrounding
allocation familiale (f)	benefit/allowance for families
améliorer	to improve
anchois (f)	anchovy
annonce immobilière (f)	property advert
appareil (m)	appliance
arc-en-ciel (m)	rainbow
atteindre	to reach
attrait (m)	attraction
au bout du compte	in the end/ultimately
auparavant	formerly
auto-stoppeur (m)	hitchhiker
autoroute (f)	motorway
avoir une peur bleue	to be scared to death

B

baisser	to lower
banlieue (f)	suburb
banque de donnée (f)	database
bavard	chatty
bénévolat (m)	voluntary/charity work
béquille (f)	crutch
besoin (m)	need
bien que/qu'	although
bise (f)	kiss
blague (f)	joke
blême	pale
boîte (f)	box/company/club
bondé	packed
bord (m)	edge
brouillard (m)	fog
bruyant	noisy

C

campagne (f)	campaign, countryside
canette (f)	can
cantine (f)	cafeteria
câpre (f)	caper
capricieux(se)	capricious
centrale nucléaire (f)	nuclear powerplant
cerf (m)	deer (male)
certes	of course

chaleur (f)	heat	départ (m)	departure
charmant	charming	dépister	to track down
chômage (m)	unemployment	déranger	to bother
clé de contact (f)	ignition key	dessin animé (m)	cartoon
clignotant (m)	turn signal	déverser	to pour/dump
code de la route (m)	highway code	devoirs de vacances (m)	holiday homework
colis (m)	package		
colocataire (f/m)	housemate	direction (f)	management
colonie de vacances (f)	summer camp	diriger	to manage
compromettant	compromising	disponible	available
conciliant	conciliatory	dommage	shame
concilier	to reconcile	dossier (m)	file
conducteur (m)	driver	drap (m)	sheet
congé maternité et paternité (m)	maternity and paternity leave		

E

conseil (m)	advice	éclater	to burst
conseiller	to advise	effectivement	indeed
consigne (f)	instruction	effectuer	to make
conte (de fée) (m)	(fairy) tale	égoïste	selfish
corail (m)	coral	élevé	high
cour d'appel (f)	Court of Appeal	emballer	to pack
course (f)	errand	embouteillage (m)	traffic jam
créneau (m)	parallel parking	embrasser	to kiss
croissant	growing	émission (f)	TV show
		empêchement (m)	hold up
		emplacement (m)	place

D

débrouillard	resourceful	empreinte carbone (f)	carbon footprint
déchet (m)	rubbish		
découverte (f)	discovery	en ligne	online
déçu	disappointed	en plein milieu	in the middle
démarche (f)	approach	encadrer	to frame
déménageur (m)	mover	endroit (m)	place

énième	umpteenth	grivois	bawdy
ennuyer	to bore	grossesse (f)	pregnancy
entreprise (f)	business		
épargner	to save	**H**	
épice (f)	spice	habitant (m)	inhabitant/resident
époque (f)	era	hauteur (f)	height
ère (f)	era	Hollandais	Dutch person
état (m)	state	homard (m)	lobster
étranger	foreign/abroad	hôte (m)	host
être d'accord	to agree		
éviter	to avoid	**I**	
exaspéré	exasperated	imprimante (f)	printer
exigeant	demanding	inévitablement	inevitably
		infirmière (f)	nurse
F		ingénieur (m)	engineer
façonner	to shape	inoubliable	unforgettable
facture (f)	bill	inquiétude (f)	worry
faire des économies	to save (money)	intempéries (f/p)	bad weather
faire la navette	to commute	interminable	never-ending
faire la queue	to wait in line		
falloir	to have to/must	**L**	
faute (f)	mistake	levier de vitesse (m)	gear stick
fournisseur d'Internet (m)	Internet provider	licencié	laid off/fired
		licenciement (m)	layoff/firing
		location (f)	rental
foyer (m)	household	loger	to stay/to reside
frein (m)	break	louer	to rent
frein à main (m)	handbrake	lune de miel (f)	honeymoon
G		**M**	
gérer	to manage	magie (f)	magic
grand écran (m)	big screen	mairie (f)	town hall
grandes vacances (f/p)	summer holidays	maîtresse (f)	schoolteacher
grève (f)	strike	manque de (m)	lack of

mélange (m)	mix	piratage (m)	pirating/ hacking
météo(rologie) (f)	weather forecast	piste cyclable (f)	bicycle lane
meublé	furnished	plâtre (m)	cast
mijotant	simmering	pleinement	fully
moindre	lesser	plusieurs	several
moitié (f)	half	pneu (m)	tyre
		poste (m)	job

N

niveau (m)	level
nouvelle (f)	news item

O

ordonnance (f)	prescription
orthographe (f)	spelling
ouvrier (m)	labourer

P

paisible	peaceful
palais (m)	palace
panier (m)	basket
par ailleurs	otherwise
par contre	on the other hand
paradis (m)	heaven
paresseux	lazy
parfois	sometimes
partager	to share
patron (m)	boss
périmé	expired
périphérique (m)	ring road
permettre	to allow
perte (f)	loss
piéton (f)	pedestrian
piqûre (f)	injection

pratique	useful
prendre feu	to catch on fire
prendre un pot	to grab a drink
privé	private
propre	clean/own
protéger	to protect
(PV) procès verbal (m)	ticket

Q

quant (à)	as for
quitter	to leave

R

rapport (m)	report
ravi	delighted
rayon (m)	aisle
réchauffement climatique (m)	global warming
redoubler	to double
redouter	to fear/dread
réduire	to reduce
réglementation (f)	regulation
régner	to reign
répetition (f)	rehearsal
reposant	relaxing
réseau (m)	network

retrouver	to find/recover	situé	located
réunion (f)	meeting	soin (m)	care
réussite (f)	success	soja (m)	soy
rondelle (f)	slice	somme (f)	sum
roue de secours (f)	spare tyre	souci (m)	worry
rouler	to drive	sous peu	shortly
rouspéter	to gripe	souvent	often
		sucré	sugary

S

s'entourer	to surround oneself with		

T

salarié (m)	salaried employee	tabac (m)	tobacconist's
santé (f)	health	tableau (m)	painting/picture
sauf	except	témoin (m)	witness
sauter	to skip	tout de suite	right away
se dégager	to clear	transport en commun (m)	public transportation
se disputer	to argue		
se méfier	to be suspicious		

U

se mettre à table	to sit down to eat	urgences (f/p)	A&E, the ER

V

se protéger	to protect oneself	vaincre	to beat/defeat
se réjouir	to be glad/rejoice	veille (f)	eve
se rendre heureux	to make oneself happy	venir en aide à	to come to somebody's help/ rescue
se retrouver	to meet up/get together		
se réunir	to get together	vente au détail (f)	retail
séjour (m)	a stay	véritable	true
selon	according to	vers	around
sentiment (m)	feeling	vider	to empty
sinon	if not/otherwise	voire	even

The following list includes only some of the most common irregular verbs. Verbs with an asterisk*
are stem- or radical-changing verbs. They are presented in only some of the tenses and moods.

acheter*

present and past participle: **achetant, acheté**

pres. ind.: **j'achète, tu achètes, il achète, nous achetons, vous achetez, ils achètent**

imperative: **achète, achetons, achetez**

imperfect: **j'achetais, tu achetais, il achetait, nous achetions, vous achetiez, ils achetaient**

pres. subj.: **j'achète, tu achètes, il achète, nous achetions, vous achetiez, ils achètent**

future/conditional stem: **achèter-**

aller

present and past participle: **allant, allé**

pres. ind.: **je vais, tu vas, il va, nous allons, vous allez, ils vont**

imperative: **va, allons, allez**

imperfect: **j'allais, tu allais, il allait, nous allions, vous alliez, ils allaient**

pres. subj.: **j'aille, tu ailles, il aille, nous allions, vous alliez, ils aillent**

future/conditional stem: **ir-**

appeler*

present and past participle: **appelant, appelé**

pres. ind.: **j'appelle, tu appelles, il appelle, nous appelons, vous appelez, ils appellent**

imperative: **appelle, appelons, appelez**

imperfect: **j'appelais, tu appelais, il appelait, nous appelions, vous appeliez, ils appelaient**

pres. subj.: **j'appelle, tu appelles, il appelle, nous appelions, vous appeliez, ils appellent**

future/conditional stem: **appeller-**

avoir

present and past participle: **ayant, eu**

pres. ind.: **j'ai, tu as, il a, nous avons, vous avez, ils ont**

imperative: **aie, ayons, ayez**

imperfect: **j'avais, tu avais, il avait, nous avions, vous aviez, ils avaient**

pres. subj.: **j'aie, tu aies, il ait, nous ayons, vous ayez, ils aient**

future/conditional stem: **aur-**

boire

present and past participle: **buvant, bu**

pres. ind.: **je bois, tu bois, il boit, nous buvons, vous buvez, ils boivent**

imperative: **bois, buvons, buvez**

imperfect: **je buvais, tu buvais, il buvait, nous buvions, vous buviez, ils buvaient**

pres. subj.: **je boive, tu boives, il boive, nous buvions, vous buviez, ils boivent**

future/conditional stem: **boir-**

commencer*

present and past participle: **commençant, commencé**

pres. ind.: **je commence, tu commences, il commence, nous commençons, vous commencez, ils commencent**

imperative: **commence, commençons, commencez**

imperfect: **je commençais, tu commençais, il commençait, nous commencions, vous commenciez, ils commençaient**

pres. subj.: **je commence, tu commences, il commence, nous commencions, vous commenciez, ils commencent**

future/conditional stem: **commencer-**

croire

present and past participle: **croyant, cru**

pres. ind.: **je crois, tu crois, il croit, nous croyons, vous croyez, ils croient**

imperative: **crois, croyons, croyez**

imperfect: **je croyais, tu croyais, il croyait, nous croyions, vous croyiez, ils croyaient**

pres. subj.: **je croie, tu croies, il croie, nous croyions, vous croyiez, ils croient**

future/conditional stem: **croir-**

devoir

present and past participle: **devant, dû**

pres. ind.: **je dois, tu dois, il doit, nous devons, vous devez, ils doivent**

imperfect: **je devais, tu devais, il devait, nous devions, vous deviez, ils devaient**

pres. subj.: **je doive, tu doives, il doive, nous devions, vous deviez, ils doivent**

future/conditional stem: **devr-**

espérer*

present and past participle: **espérant, espéré**

pres. ind.: **j'espère, tu espères, il espère, nous espérons, vous espérez, ils espèrent**

imperative: **espère, espérons, espérez**

imperfect: **j'espérais, tu espérais, il espérait, nous espérions, vous espériez, ils espéraient**

pres. subj.: **j'espère, tu espères, il espère, nous espérions, vous espériez, ils espèrent**

future/conditional stem: **espérer-**

être

present and past participle: **étant, été**

pres. ind.: **je suis, tu es, il est, nous sommes, vous êtes, ils sont**

imperative: **sois, soyons, soyez**

imperfect: **j'étais, tu étais, il était, nous étions, vous étiez, ils étaient**

pres. subj.: **je sois, tu sois, il soit, nous soyons, vous soyez, ils soient**

future/conditional stem: **ser-**

faire

present and past participle: **faisant, fait**

pres. ind.: **je fais, tu fais, il fait, nous faisons, vous faites, ils font**

imperative: **fais, faisons, faites**

imperfect: **je faisais, tu faisais, il faisait, nous faisions, vous faisiez, ils faisaient**

pres. subj.: **je fasse, tu fasses, il fasse, nous fassions, vous fassiez, ils fassent**

future/conditional stem: **fer-**

mettre

present and past participle: **mettant, mis**

pres. ind.: **je mets, tu mets, il met, nous mettons, vous mettez, ils mettent**

imperative: **mets, mettons, mettez**

imperfect: **je mettais, tu mettais, il mettait, nous mettions, vous mettiez, ils mettaient**

pres. subj.: **je mette, tu mettes, il mette, nous mettions, vous mettiez, ils mettent**

future/conditional stem: **mettr-**

partir

present and past participle: **partant, parti**

pres. ind.: **je pars, tu pars, il part, nous partons, vous partez, ils partent** imperative: **pars, partons, partez**

imperfect: **je partais, tu partais, il partait, nous partions, vous partiez, ils partaient**

pres. subj.: **je parte, tu partes, il parte, nous partions, vous partiez, ils partent**

future/conditional stem: **partir-**

payer*

present and past participle: **payant, payé**

pres. ind.: **je paye/paie, tu payes/paies, il paye/paie, nous payons, vous payez, ils payent/paient**

imperative: **paye/paie, payons, payez**

imperfect: **je payais, tu payais, il payait, nous payions, vous payiez, ils payaient**

pres. subj.: **je paye/paie, tu payes/paies, il paye/paie, nous payions, vous payiez, ils payent/paient**

future/conditional stem: **paier-** or **payer-**

pouvoir

present and past participle: **pouvant, pu**

pres. ind.: **je peux, tu peux, il peut, nous pouvons, vous pouvez, ils peuvent**

imperfect: **je pouvais, tu pouvais, il pouvait, nous pouvions, vous pouviez, ils pouvaient**

pres. subj.: **je puisse, tu puisses, il puisse, nous puissions, vous puissiez, ils puissent**

future/conditional stem: **pourr-**

prendre

present and past participle: **prenant, pris**

pres. ind.: **je prends, tu prends, il prend, nous prenons, vous prenez, ils prennent**

imperative: **prends, prenons, prenez**

imperfect: **je prenais, tu prenais, il prenait, nous prenions, vous preniez, ils prenaient**

pres. subj.: **je prenne, tu prennes, il prenne, nous prenions, vous preniez, ils prennent**

future/conditional stem: **prendr-**

savoir

present and past participle: **sachant, su**

pres. ind.: **je sais, tu sais, il sait, nous savons, vous savez, ils savent**

imperative: **sache, sachons, sachez**

imperfect: **je savais, tu savais, il savait, nous savions, vous saviez, ils savaient** pres. subj.: **je sache, tu saches, il sache, nous sachions, vous sachiez, ils sachent**

future/conditional stem: **saur-**

sortir

present and past participle: **sortant, sorti**

pres. ind.: **je sors, tu sors, il sort, nous sortons, vous sortez, ils sortent**

imperative: **sors, sortons, sortez**

imperfect: **je sortais, tu sortais, il sortait, nous sortions, vous sortiez, ils sortaient**

pres. subj.: **je sorte, tu sortes, il sorte, nous sortions, vous sortiez, ils sortent**

future/conditional stem: **sortir-**

venir

present and past participle: **venant, venu**

pres. ind.: **je viens, tu viens, il vient, nous venons, vous venez, ils viennent**

imperative: **viens, venons, venez**

imperfect: **je venais, tu venais, il venait, nous venions, vous veniez, ils venaient**

pres. subj.: **je vienne, tu viennes, il vienne, nous venions, vous veniez, ils viennent**

future/conditional stem: **viendr-**

vouloir

present and past participle: **voulant, voulu**

pres. ind.: **je veux, tu veux, il veut, nous voulons, vous voulez, ils veulent**

imperative: **veuille, voulons, veuillez**

imperfect: **je voulais, tu voulais, il voulait, nous voulions, vous vouliez, ils voulaient**

pres. subj.: **je veuille, tu veuilles, il veuille, nous voulions, vous vouliez, ils veuillent**

future/conditional stem: **voudr-**

voyager*

present and past participle: **voyageant, voyagé**

pres. ind.: **je voyage, tu voyages, il voyage, nous voyageons, vous voyagez, ils voyagent**

imperative: **voyage, voyageons, voyagez**

imperfect: **je voyageais, tu voyageais, il voyageait, nous voyagions, vous voyagiez, ils voyageaient**

pres. subj.: **je voyage, tu voyages, il voyage, nous voyagions, vous voyagiez, ils voyagent**

future/conditional stem: **voyager-**

COMPARING CEFR AND ACTFL LANGUAGE PROFICIENCY STANDARDS

The two major frameworks for teaching, learning and assessing foreign language proficiency are the Common European Framework of Reference for language (CEFR) used with the European Language Portfolio (ELP) and the American Council on the Teaching Foreign Languages (ACTFL) proficiency guidelines. Both are used for testing and certification as well as in textbooks, language teacher training, curriculum development and development of assessment standards. While little empirical research is available to compare the two systems, an approximate correspondence can be established. Note that the ACTFL system divides the skills into receptive (reading and listening) and productive (speaking and writing), with the expectation of different proficiency levels in those skills. This table shows a comparison of the CEFR global descriptors and ACTFL proficiency levels. For both systems, language proficiency is emphasized over mastery of textbook grammar and spelling.

CEFR	ACTFL	
	RECEPTIVE	PRODUCTIVE
C2 Can understand with ease virtually everything heard or read. Can summarize information from different spoken and written sources, reconstructing arguments and accounts in a coherent presentation. Can express him/herself spontaneously, very fluently and precisely, differentiating finer shades of meaning even in more complex situations.	Distinguished	Superior
C1 Can understand a wide range of demanding, longer texts, and recognize implicit meaning. Can express him/herself fluently and spontaneously without much obvious searching for expressions. Can use language flexibly and effectively for social, academic and professional purposes. Can produce clear, well-structured, detailed text on complex subjects, showing controlled use of organizational patterns, connectors and cohesive devices.	Advanced High/Superior	Advanced High
B2 Can understand the main ideas of complex text on both concrete and abstract topics, including technical discussions in his/her field of specialization. Can interact with a degree of fluency and spontaneity that makes regular interaction with native speakers quite possible without strain for either party. Can produce clear, detailed text on a wide range of subjects and explain a viewpoint on a topical issue giving the advantages and disadvantages of various options.	Advanced Mid	Advanced Low/Advanced Mid
B1 Can understand the main points of clear standard input on familiar matters regularly encountered in work, school, leisure, etc. Can deal with most situations likely to arise whilst travelling in an area where the language is spoken. Can produce simple connected text on topics which are familiar or of personal interest. Can describe experiences and events, dreams, hopes and ambitions and briefly give reasons and explanations for opinions and plans.	Intermediate High/Advanced Low	Intermediate Mid/Intermediate High

A2	Intermediate Mid	Intermediate Low
Can understand sentences and frequently used expressions related to areas of most immediate relevance (e.g. very basic personal and family information, shopping, local geography, employment). Can communicate in simple and routine tasks requiring a simple and direct exchange of information on familiar and routine matters. Can describe in simple terms aspects of his/her background, immediate environment and matters in areas of immediate need.		
A1	Novice High/Intermediate Low	Novice High
Can understand and use familiar everyday expressions and very basic phrases aimed at the satisfaction of needs of a concrete type. Can introduce him/herself and others and can ask and answer questions about personal details such as where he/she lives, people he/she knows and things he/she has. Can interact in a simple way provided the other person talks slowly and clearly and is prepared to help.		
Ø	Novice Low/Novice Mid	Novice Low/Novice Mid

This chart represents an approximate comparison between the CEFR and ACTFL language proficiency levels. For more information, see the following resources:

American Council on the Teaching of Foreign Languages. Assigning CEFR ratings to ACTFL assessment. 2016. Available at https://www.actfl.org/sites/default/files/reports/Assigning_CEFR_Ratings_To_ACTFL_Assessments.pdf

American Council on the Teaching of Foreign Languages. ACTFL proficiency guidelines 2012. 2012. Available at http://actflproficiencyguidelines2012.org/

American Council on the Teaching of Foreign Languages. ACTFL performance descriptors for language learners. 2012.

American Council on the Teaching of Foreign Languages. NCSSFL-ACTFL Can-Do statements: Progress Indicators for Language Learners. 2013.

American Council on the Teaching of Foreign Languages. NCSSFL-ACTF Global Can-Do Benchmarks. 2013. http://www.actfl.org/global_statements

Council of Europe. Common European Framework of Reference for Languages: Learning, Teaching, Assessment. Cambridge, UK: Press Syndicate of the University of Cambridge, 2001.

Council of Europe. The European Language Portfolio. http://www.coe.int/en/web/portfolio

Council of Europe. Language Policy homepage. http://www.coe.int/t/dg4/linguistic/